The Plant Doctor and her own rose guinea pigs. (Photo: Eleanor B. McClure.)

Plant Doctoring
Is Fun

by CYNTHIA WESTCOTT

D. VAN NOSTRAND COMPANY, INC.

PRINCETON, NEW JERSEY
Toronto · London · New York

D. VAN NOSTRAND COMPANY, INC.

120 Alexander St., Princeton, New Jersey
257 Fourth Avenue, New York 10, New York
25 Hollinger Rd., Toronto 16, Canada

All correspondence should be addressed to the
principal office of the company at Princeton, N. J.

PRINTED IN THE UNITED STATES OF AMERICA

To My Brother

FRANK TOURTELLOT WESTCOTT

FOREWORD

IN February, 1953, Wellesley College invited four
alumnae of diverse occupations to speak briefly
about their work at Alumnae Council. My talk, "Plant Doctoring
Is Fun," came at the very end, after the delegates had had two full
days of serious discussion. They found the trials and tribulations of
the plant doctor hilarious and suggested they might go into a book.
It could not be started immediately; I had to complete one new
book and rewrite an old one for a new edition. I finally got around
to writing it this past year, the first part during winter travels in
the South, the latter part at home.

Unfortunately, I'm no Betty MacDonald. I can't duplicate *The
Egg and I*. The trials that seemed so funny rattled off in twelve
minutes seem a bit grim spread out on these pages. The publishers
have suggested that perhaps the title should be changed, that some
of the rain and travel trouble might be deleted. I have cut out a few
references to rain, but have kept the rest. After all, weather is the
most important thing in the world to a plant doctor. It decides
whether or not you earn a living this day, or week, or month. It also

determines the amount and kind of disease in different localities or in different seasons. I am a far better plant pathologist because I have been lucky enough to meet so much "unusual" weather in my wanderings.

As for trouble, it was all part of the fun, part of learning about my country. I may have been uncomfortable but never unhappy. I have been amused by my predicaments but seldom discouraged.

The title stays. Fun it has been ever since Freshman Botany at Wellesley. I may be a trifle queer to enjoy learning how to recognize diseases and pests and to like teaching others about them. Perhaps not everyone can understand my savage delight in outwitting these pests, in keeping a garden ornamental when all about are ravaged. For me, it has been supremely satisfying.

The plant doctor owes much to many individuals—gardeners and scientists; to many groups—garden clubs and universities, amateur and professional societies. Some have been mentioned by name but there are many, many more. To all who have provided encouragement, information, or physical help, to all who have harbored me in travels, who have shown me gardens despite rain and ice and snow, and to the editors who have commissioned the articles and books which have kept the plant doctor going, my grateful thanks.

Glen Ridge, New Jersey   CYNTHIA WESTCOTT
January, 1957

CONTENTS

1. GROWING UP   1
   Childhood   3
   Wellesley   10
   A Taste of Teaching   13

2. GRADUATE YEARS   16
   Learning Again   16
   Habitations   19
   The Academic Side   25
   European Sojourn   30
   The Depression   39
   Personal Research   40
   Rutgers   43

3. THE BIG CHANCE   51
   Getting Started   53
   Plant Doctor Diary   58
   Side Lines   67
   Back to Work   70
   More Side Lines   74
   Writing Again   78

4. WANDERING   81
   The Southeast   81
   Home Again   97
   The Southwest   103

5. PLANT DOCTOR DAYS   127
   1939   129
   1940   131
   1941   132
   Wartime   134

6. ONCE IN A LIFETIME   140
   Alabama Bound   143
   Interlude at Home   155
   South Again   156
   Thrill of a Lifetime   162
   Spreading the Gospel   164

7. FOR FINGERTIP REFERENCE   171
   A Book on Bugs   172
   A Book on Diseases   174
   Revising   184
   Compromises Don't Always Pay   189

8. THE LIMELIGHT   190
   Doctor, Save My Roses   191
   A Profile   193
   Profile Aftermath   196

9. BLOSSOMS AND BLIGHTS   202
   Quarantine Hearing   202
   Camellia Flower Blight   204

10. ROSES   211
    A Little Rose Book   213
    A Rose Society   219
    Rose Day   228
    Slowing Down   230

11. THE PLANT DOCTOR GOES AROUND IN CIRCLES   234
    Doctoring   236
    Consulting   242
    Testing   244
    Lecturing   245
    Writing   250
    Belonging   252
    Housekeeping   254
    Satisfactions   255

   APPENDIX. Slapdash Cookery   257

   INDEX   275

CHAPTER 1

GROWING UP

PLANT DOCTORING is FUN. It is also desperately hard work. It is very definitely precarious with most of the rewards pretty intangible. There is no regular monthly pay check from an institution, no pension on retirement, no provision at all for old age, for Social Security does not yet recognize my particular brand of self-employment. Yet on the few occasions that I have been offered a regular job I have not even hesitated before saying "No." To me, independence is the greatest joy of all and most of the time the uncertainty of my life is part of the fun.

Two questions particularly have plagued me through the quarter of a century that I have been a practicing plant physician. The first is inevitable. "How did you happen to be a plant doctor; did you plan it from childhood?" Except for tiresome repetition it should not bother me. But it always comes just before a lecture, perhaps in an interview with a newspaper reporter thrust upon me without warning, or from a guest at a luncheon, or from the program chairman about five minutes before the meeting is due to start. There seldom is time to explain properly and if there is time to go into details the recital uses up a lot of energy required for the lecture.

The second question comes in a letter. Sometimes it is from a girl just finishing college or horticultural school and she asks if I will give her a job. More often it is from an older woman who has read the newspaper interview, thinks how wonderful it would be to play around with flowers, and so asks me how to get started. She hasn't any training but she loves to putter in her own garden and it seems to be a perfect solution for a widow who has to earn a living or for a retired schoolteacher. A good many years ago, after there was a brief paragraph about my work in *Reader's Digest,* someone wrote a story about a middle-aged woman who, after her children were grown, took up plant doctoring as a glamorous and lucrative occupation. The story was sent to me for criticism and I think I killed it; at least I did not see it in print. It would be cruel to hold out such an alluring picture even though I still maintain that plant doctoring is fun—for me.

Other questions have come in by the hundreds, of course. "What is the matter with the enclosed leaf?" "Why did my roses die?" "Where can I buy lime-sulfur?" "What's one spray good for everything in the garden?" I have answered them as best I could, every Sunday, year in and year out. Church has become a selfish pleasure. When I go, many inquiries have to be left unanswered, for there is never time during the week to handle any more than the regular business mail in addition to spraying fifty or more gardens, giving a lecture, meeting a deadline with an article, taking care of my own house and garden, getting myself fed at highly irregular hours.

To help answer the flood of questions I have written books, technical books which, because our pests and chemicals are constantly changing, have to be rewritten at too frequent intervals, with revision far harder than doing the original. I have spent the past two winters redoing the *Gardener's Bug Book* and am committed to the *Plant Disease Handbook* for the next two or three. In between, I am declaring a moratorium on technical writing and doing this personal, autobiographical affair to answer those two recurring questions:

"How did you happen to be a plant doctor?" and "Tell me what to do to be a plant doctor?"

CHILDHOOD

Becoming a plant doctor was pure happenstance. I certainly did not plan it and I am not sure how much influence my childhood interests had on it. I'm a New Englander, born and brought up in North Attleboro, a small town in Massachusetts, rather proud of the fact that on my mother's side I trace back to Roger Williams and that my paternal forebear was Stukely Westcott who went with Roger Williams to settle Rhode Island. My father used to say that having ancestors who were kicked out of Massachusetts was no cause for pride.

I can't remember any early interest in insects but Frank, my brother, and I had somewhat more than the usual assortment of animals. I used to dress up the kittens and rabbits in doll clothes and take them out to ride in the doll carriage. We even had a couple of sheep, acquired solely because, when mother and father were going away for a day or two, I howled and demanded the sheep for consolation. I can't imagine why I wanted them and think I must have been both unpleasant and unreasonable.

We also had a horse, for a brief time two, to go with the carriages that filled our barn after grandfather Westcott died. He had had a factory in Hopedale, making spindles for the Draper Mills, and there must have been a rig for every occasion. At any rate, we inherited a "surrey with the fringe on top," which we called a canopy top; a closed station wagon which took us to dancing school; a smart high buggy; a wide low buggy; and a democrat wagon, about like a pick-up truck.

Our horses had no real personality for me, though I remember one that had to be sold after it developed a habit of kicking through the dashboard every time it got displeased with life. My pride and joy was a Shetland pony, Brownie, and my first horticultural endeavors were strictly for the purpose of raising money to buy her. I grew radishes to sell to the neighbors and picked blackberries to sell to the fruit man. We had the most luscious blackberries I have ever tasted and they grew in an unpruned tangle of brambles. I often think present imperviousness to rose thorns must go back to early days when I was scratched from head to foot by blackberries.

Frank and I put all birthday and Christmas money in the pony fund and soon Brownie arrived in a crate. She was a shaggy youngster, about the size of a St. Bernard dog. Our neighbor went around saying "Westcott wanted a horse and he wanted one bad so he bought all the horse he had money for." By the time we earned money for a bridle and saddle Brownie was big enough to take a child on her back. When we had earned a basket cart, she was strong enough to pull it with mother and us inside, Dad going along on a bicycle. That being the only training she ever had, she was pretty lazy when we were out by ourselves; she always wanted something to race.

Possessing Brownie made us fairly popular and there was always a gang around after school. Boys, even with the best of intentions, are not too kind to ponies and Brownie learned to defend herself with her heels. She looked on all men and boys, except Frank and Dad, as her natural enemies. Sometimes she got out of the pen when we were at school and mother would call up the office for one of Dad's surveyors. He never got anywhere; he was too scared of the heels. Then Frank would come home, still a very little boy, and tell Brownie to behave and she would. She loved to go swimming in a pond and refused to go through a puddle. All my spills in riding came when Brownie stopped dead at a puddle and I kept on going.

My adult choice of an outdoor life must, I think, go back to childhood. Father was a civil engineer, by way of Brown and M.I.T., but he almost always had a town job too. In my early days he had charge of the roads which also included snowplows for the sidewalks. In New Jersey I have to shovel my own walks when it snows. Up in New England the walks were cleared before daylight. When Dad left at 4 a.m. mother would start frying doughnuts and have coffee ready for the men when they came around.

Summers were wonderful. Often we would go along with Dad in the canopy top when he went to inspect the township roads, buying deviled ham, cheese, crackers, and bananas at a country store and eating our lunch beside a trout stream and the first mayflowers (arbutus) or in a pine woods full of pink lady-slippers.

We also had two farms to enjoy. The one about a mile from home was my uncle's. Mother was the oldest of nine children. After helping to bring up the others she went to Bryant and Stratton Business College in Providence and, beginning at sixteen, taught there for nine years. After she married and settled in North Attleboro her youngest brother and my grandmother bought a farm in the same town. We were always driving up to the farm with Brownie and eventually mother had a one-room cabin, with an enormous stone fireplace, built there. It enabled her to get away sometimes from the noisy gangs in our back yard. My own one-room shack on Long Island (which I can reach only two or three times a year) is the same sort of blessed hideaway.

Every Christmas was spent at Uncle Fred's with all the aunts and uncles and cousins and mountains of food. There was turkey, of course, for dinner, with all the winter vegetables, mince and squash pies, and then supper featuring ribbon cake, walnut cake, chocolate cake and many other varieties. Thanksgiving Day, in the few years before the Westcott grandparents died, was in Hopedale in a rather formal town house. Here after dinner I would sit on a scratchy horsehair chair in the seldom-used parlor and gaze at all the curios on the whatnot and admire the big golden cathedral which was a clock.

Although grandfather lived in Hopedale he retained the family farm on Chopmist Ridge, Scituate, Rhode Island. On his death father and Uncle Will bought out the other four heirs, so now Frank and I had three hundred acres to roam in. The farm was thirty miles

from home. To reach it, we took a train to Providence, then had **a**
long streetcar ride to the village of Scituate. There we hired a rig
at the livery stable and drove for another hour. In winter, we had
hot soapstones to keep from freezing. All in all, it was quite a jaunt
for a winter weekend and one that we did not repeat too often. In
summer, our family had use of the farm for half the time; Uncle
Will had the other half.

Part of the house was occupied by the farmer and his two sisters.
Mr. Davis was blind but it was scarcely a handicap to him. He
walked a mile to church every Sunday; he milked the cows; he hoed
the vegetables. The very few things that required sight were done by
a tenant farmer who lived on the next place with a whole raft of
children.

I loved every square inch of Chopmist Ridge and particularly the
walled-in burying ground. I'd lie for hours listening to the wind
sighing through the pine trees. Early acquaintance with death was
very peaceful. People lived out their long, full lives and were ready
for the end. Great-aunt Jane lived in Providence and when she died
the funeral took all day for we went by horse and carriage all the
twenty miles to Scituate. But no one was very sad and it was a fine
chance for the little cousins to get acquainted and for the grownups
to exchange family news. And there was, after she was laid to rest
under the pines, the traditional big meal in the farmhouse.

Some summers on the farm we ate with the Davises. Breakfast was
promptly at 6:30. Usually we had Rhode Island johnnycake, which
was more like corn pone than corn bread—a mixture of white corn-
meal, salt, and boiling water baked on a griddle. I did not like it
much as a child and I'd give anything to have some right now. We
also often had for breakfast creamed dried beef and hard-boiled
eggs and boiled potatoes. Dinner was at noon, meat and potatoes
again, fresh corn and other vegetables from the place. Supper was
at 5:30, crackers and milk, which I never learned to like, and big
bowls of blueberries picked during the day, or fresh apple sauce,

and great slabs of Miss Eurania's fruit cake. I loved supper because of the cake.

Some summers we cooked for ourselves, swinging pots from the crane in the ancient fireplace or using the summer kitchen outside. In those days when a "girl" fresh from Ireland or up from the South could be employed for only three dollars a week we sometimes had a maid who went to the farm with us. I loved southern Addie and she loved the farm, even to driving the hay cart, until the day when she saw a black snake. Thereafter she stayed near the house. We were so far from civilization that any team, coming along after the milk had been collected in the morning, meant company. Addie could hear company coming farther than anybody and we used to boast that by the time they had arrived at the picket fence around the yard she had already wrung the neck of a chicken and plucked it and had ice cream started.

I shudder when I think of the way we carelessly left our ice-cream dishes, willow pattern ware or the even older pale blue, sitting around on top of stone walls. There are a few unbroken pieces now in my possession but not many.

Although Frank has shown no horticultural inclinations in adult years (he builds bridges for a vocation and plays tournament bridge for avocation), he did plant a thriving peach orchard at the farm, which was more than I did. I contented myself with enjoying the lily-of-the-valley and tiger lilies in the front yard, fenced in to keep out chickens, ducks, turkeys, etc., with making a small fern garden over the wall, and just wandering around. I picked lots of checker-berries (a turnpike now goes through that part of the farm) and ate swamp cheeses (which I know now are the young stage of leaf galls on wild azaleas) and brought home flowers from the soap bush to use when washing up in the tin basin before dinner.

One of my jobs was to hunt turkey nests. Once a hound dog was trailing along when I discovered one and before I could report the nest he ruined most of the eggs. I was heartsick.

I had an early introduction to lime-sulfur, which I still swear by as a dormant spray. We used it for dipping goats in the spring. One of our less than successful ventures was the purchase of a herd of forty-two goats from the Lowney Chocolate factory near home. I don't remember how they got transported to the farm—whether someone had to drive them that thirty miles or if they had a ride. They were supposed to clear up the weeds and make pasture land but some found sheep laurel and died. There was one mean old billy goat that eventually died of old age and orneriness. His horns were quite marvelous and Dad had his head stuffed. The goat odor lingered and mother wouldn't allow it in the house; it adorned the wall of the barn in North Attleboro for many years.

Some summers Brownie was driven through to the farm but she refused to be treated as an animal; she was a member of the family. No matter what field she was pastured in, or how high the fence, she was out of it and by the kitchen door by morning.

Vacations are more vivid in my memory than the rest of the year. School was not difficult but I always ended up in bed with a spell of tonsilitis for the last week or two. Quite often it lasted over my birthday, June 29th, and the planned party had to be given up. Mrs. Ballou, our next-door neighbor, always brought me roses—great fragrant bunches of hybrid perpetuals—and perhaps this started my lifelong adoration of the Rose. We had a few ourselves. One must have been *Rosa primula,* with prickery stems and creamy single flowers always opening for Memorial Day. I have never known the identity of the other bush, which is still living, covered with double, rose-crimson flowers in June and some through the summer; it has had no spraying or feeding for fifty years.

I went to the Universalist Sunday School and continued to exchange Christmas greetings with my teacher all down the years. I like the beauty and simplicity of the Universalist creed and it imposed no conflict between the scientist I was to become and religion. But in Sunday School I heard so much about parables that I was rather astonished, when I took Biblical History in college, to learn that so much of the Bible was literally true.

High school classmates considered me something of a grind and I was twitted for dropping Domestic Science because I only got a B in it instead of an A. I did no dating until senior year. Then, during the course of the class play where I was appropriately cast as an old maid, I acquired a steady boy friend to everyone's surprise. The play was to raise money to go to Washington during spring vacation. As we were the last class in our school to be allowed this pleasure, some of the other students, including my brother, went along, paying their own way.

The Westcott family gave the chaperones gray hairs. The girls were quartered six to a room and after a day of walking we immediately took off our shoes and flopped down on the beds. My bare foot encountered a razor-sharp corn knife someone had carelessly left on a bed under some newspapers. Luckily the cut just missed an artery but it was quite a mess and after the stitches were taken I was not allowed to let that foot touch the ground. I could not seem to manage the makeshift crutches. When we got to New York the program called for a visit to the Hippodrome and they did not want to leave me behind. I remember being carried down the aisle in the arms of a big policeman but not much else about the performance.

I could not go home by boat so they sent me and the boy friend and a chaperone by train—my first experience with a parlor car, as well as a deck of playing cards which my boy friend purchased on the train to make me forget the foot.

Meanwhile brother Frank was seeing New York by subway, having figured out just how many hours and miles he could go for a nickel. Came time to herd the students to the boat, no Frank. One chaperone stayed at the hotel to wait for him; the rest went on. Finally my kid brother nonchalantly walked in, assured the chaperone there was plenty of time to reach the boat by subway if not by cab, and proved his point. I don't wonder they gave up high school trips to Washington. But it was a good memory and we all did shake hands with President Wilson, see the White House, the Mint, and Congress and all the things I have never done since on numerous visits to the Capitol.

I had to keep off the foot for about six weeks and remained too dumb to use crutches without falling down or wrenching my armpits. So mother got a wheelchair and the boy friend squired me around. I apparently reveled in this attention instead of being ashamed of my ineptness. I did walk down the aisle for graduation and gave the valedictory address. That June, 1916, I thought I knew a lot and had answers to most everything. Every year since I have known less and less.

WELLESLEY

I always knew I was going to Wellesley and was registered there years in advance. Aunt Mima offered financial assistance if I would go to Mount Holyoke, her alma mater, but I brushed aside any help this might have been to my parents. As a matter of fact, the education of two children did mean the loss of the farm, for being an absentee farmer was too expensive a luxury with tuition fees as well. Giving up the farm and Brownie, who was sent to a cousin, meant the end of childhood, the end of having everything we really wanted and the beginning of having to choose that which was most important.

Our school did not rank high enough to get in without College Board examinations. I passed but did not distinguish myself. Two years later Frank came along and made the same good grades on College Boards that he got in high school.

I went to college intending to major in German and Latin. Two sciences were required and Phila Helt, Wellesley 1913, who taught English at North Attleboro High, told me to be sure and choose botany as the first science. I did, and was lost!

Freshman Botany, under Dr. Margaret Ferguson's inspired guidance, was no dry laboratory and library affair. In autumn we planted bulbs under the trees in the orchard; in winter we learned to identify bare trees by their outlines against the sky; in spring we sketched a pear bud as it unfolded and was pollinated. We each had a tiny garden with a wide variety of plants and we had to identify all the weeds we pulled up as well as every seedling.

That freshman course was the best "come-on" I have ever known. We rapidly progressed to sterner things, with the work in Botany 13 senior year on a graduate level. In between, I had some taxonomy of lower plants, mosses and fungi, and bacteriology. Taxonomy of higher plants was scheduled for the final year but I never got to take the course. Miss Ferguson informed me I was taking plant physiology instead. This was the first year such a course had been given at Wellesley and the first time our brilliant new professor had taught an undergraduate class. So I took the physiology and to this day have never learned the right names of higher plants, which most people consider the main part of botany.

It was a good course! We had little or no equipment and learned to improvise—to carry out complex experiments with crude apparatus. Nowadays when an assistant tells me something can't be done (and they always do when things don't work the easy way) I think back to Dr. Howard Pulling's course and suggest that we try a little harder. Much of the time our professor talked way above our heads. He assured us he did not care so long as we saw there was a place to swim up to. We swam, and sometimes we did get our heads above water for a little while. I guess it was good for me. I have continued to get in over my depth and while I have always dreaded starting new ventures, learning new ways, I am compelled to plunge in.

Wellesley years were happy years. It was wartime but beyond knitting for soldiers I had little personal contact with it. Freshman year I ended up in the infirmary with tonsilitis just as I had ended up school terms but this time it went on to quinsy. I knitted to pass the time and when the head nurse objected to my doing it on Sunday I protested that knitting was perfectly all right on Sunday so long as it was for soldiers.

Those were days of many restrictions, of being in the dormitory by 9:45 at night, no smoking. It was also the era of blue serge bloomers and middy blouses for gym. I was always rotten at sports. The first year they made me take archery and I was terrible. The next year I was allowed to play tennis and was slightly better. I could swim a little and often took out a sponson canoe (the kind almost impossible to tip over) to study or eat a picnic supper on the lake. Graduation night it was tradition to show one's emancipation from the 9:45 p.m. curfew by staying out in a sponson all night.

Interest in Latin petered out at the end of freshman year and I stayed only two years with German. I had a smattering of zoology and chemistry but English finally ranked next to botany. Gladys Bagg, now Gladys Tabor, who writes that charming Diary of Domesticity in the *Ladies Home Journal* and so many novels and books on dogs, was in my class. I never could write fiction; my dialogue is utterly unreal. Sometimes my descriptive pieces passed muster. I was complimented for a vivid theme on pain, inspired by the foot episode, and also for one on the sounds of a cold morning, with noises of the radiator and wheels in the snow outside. I certainly never expected to make any money out of writing, and English composition was mostly a prelude to some literature courses—a delightful one on Chaucer under Martha Hale Shackford and one on 19th century poets under Margaret Sherwood.

Long before graduation I knew that I wanted to go on and do advanced work in botany. Cornell University was first choice because Miss Ferguson had gotten her degree there. I knew also that I could no longer sponge on my parents and must have an assistantship. Looking back, I think I might have done more in the line of self-help as an undergraduate. I did do some summer work. One year I worked in a local jewelry factory, nine-hour days, six days a week, for the enormous sum of sixteen and two-thirds cents an hour. Then at the end of the summer I blew it all in on a trip to Maine to visit a classmate and to New York for the wedding of my Wellesley senior. I was chagrined about the latter trip. Mother did not trust me to traverse New York City alone and sent Frank, three years younger, along as a guide. That inclination to spend all I earn and more wandering around the country is still with me. It is part of the fun of plant doctoring.

A TASTE OF TEACHING

Cornell has very few assistantships for women, and when Miss Ferguson told me in June there was no chance of getting one for the next year I signed up to teach science and mathematics at North-boro High School. I had had no physics and spent that whole fiendishly hot summer in Cambridge at Harvard Summer School. We had two lectures and an hour-long quiz every morning and laboratory all afternoon. We wrote up experiments and studied for the next day's quiz all night. I can't say I learned much, if any, physics, for my mind does not work when there is no time for things to sink in between doses; but I passed the course. I did learn something about insects. In that airless rooming house I made my first—and last—acquaintance with the bugs that inhabit beds.

Less than a week after signing up to teach school, and before taking that torturing summer course, I had a letter from the Plant Pathology Department at Cornell asking if I would be interested in a graduate assistantship. The school contract said I could be released on a month's notice so I filled out the papers and was overjoyed to learn the job was mine. When I tendered my resignation to the school superintendent he refused to accept it. He said I couldn't resign before even starting. Probably a legal issue could have been made of it but I did not want to begin a career by breaking faith, so I decided to stick. Cornell heartily disapproved of this and said it was very unlikely I would have another chance.

Although hired to teach science, on arriving at Northboro I

learned that teaching penmanship to the eighth grade had been added
to high school classes. I was appalled! Mother had taught penmanship for those nine years at business college and wrote a beautiful
hand but no one had ever been able to read my writing. Protests
got nowhere. I was told: "Make the pupils do as you say, not as
you do." I ask you, how can anyone teach penmanship without
setting a good example? I couldn't, and discipline became an immediate problem.

I had had the required course in education at Wellesley but no
practice teaching. I couldn't make those wild eighth grade kids
behave, nor those in Study Hall while I was teaching algebra in
the other half of the room. Never having had any thrill out of
algebra myself I could not do much about imparting it to a class
when most of my attention was occupied with trying to keep another group of youngsters from throwing spitballs, chewing gum
and talking. I was rooming with a Wellesley classmate who taught
English and languages to the same group. Dot had no disciplinary
problems whatever; she never raised her voice; she never expected
to be disobeyed and she never was.

It was much better with the real science classes. I was so interested
that the students had to be, and discipline was something we did
not even think about. Coming from four years of mostly laboratory
work I was shocked to learn that the school did not possess a microscope and that those country children did not know the names of
the commonest trees, shrubs and flowers all around them. Heretofore biology had been taught from books. We remedied that by
raising money. The pupils sold candy and we put on various enter-
tainments until we could buy a microscope and present it to the
school.

The boys brought frogs and I pickled them and then we learned
how they are made. They also brought live snakes and snakes are
my one horror. The little laboratory room was down in the basement with a stairway leading outdoors. I passed some sort of test
the day a lad appeared at the top of the stairs with a big snake by

the tail and I remained outwardly calm and collected at the foot of the stairs. There was no more trouble trying to see how I'd react.

We took all sorts of field trips, to dairies, museums, most everything. Once we went to Wellesley and my very wonderful chemistry professor performed various experiments for the class that I could not do at school and endeared herself to all of us by brewing hot chocolate in Ehrlenmeyer flasks and serving it in beakers. We did have a few chemicals in our laboratory but the wooden cabinet I attempted to keep locked was pretty flimsy. There were numerous unscheduled experiments when my back was turned. Luckily, the only casualty that year was a girl getting her hair singed; it could have been far, far worse.

Among other things Dot and I took turns chaperoning a dancing school and sleigh rides. Dances are easy; sleigh and hay rides get you worried.

The girls wanted to be Girl Scouts and there was no organized troop or leader. I did not know enough to refuse even though I had never been a Scout myself. I made periodic trips into Boston for instructions and kept one step ahead of the troop in passing tests and earning badges. Somewhere among my possessions I have a Girl Scout Thanks badge, also a uniform that would get only half around me now.

With all this kaleidoscopic public life there was still a personal side. Dot and I shared a large, comfortable room in a sort of old-folks home. It was a high class boarding house and nursing home that took in a few poor school teachers at half price and one personable young man. The old folks had a marvelous time vicariously. They loved to have Dot sing after dinner, to my faltering accompaniment. They raised eyebrows when the young man and I went for walks in the moonlight but warmed to Dot's engagement to a native. She stayed on to teach another year. I was not invited to return, doubtless both because of my poor discipline and too revolutionary teaching ideas, wanting to work with real material rather than with books.

CHAPTER 2

GRADUATE YEARS

I HAD THOROUGHLY enjoyed the year at Northboro
but never intended to go back, even if they had
wanted me. I was merely fulfilling that contract; my heart was still
at Cornell. I wrote to see if there was any chance whatever of an
assistantship. Just one! If Dick White (Dr. R. P. White, now
executive vice president of the American Association of Nurserymen) took a job offered him at Rutgers I could come in at the bottom
in the Department of Plant Pathology. He decided in August and
I reported for duty on September 1, 1921. After I got there the Botany
Department said they had been going to offer me work when they
learned I was already tied up with plant pathology. So it was pure
chance that put me in the field of plant diseases rather than physiology or taxonomy.

LEARNING AGAIN

I was terribly green on arrival. When asked about my interest
in mycology I did not even know what the word meant, though

the course I had had at Wellesley on lower plants was really mycology in part.

My office mate invited me out for the first Sunday. I thought it would be the usual sort of date and was somewhat taken aback when it turned into a collecting expedition, with all conversation centered on diseases noted along the way. I soon learned that that was normal, in fact, inevitable, for a plant pathologist and I have never since been able to go anywhere, on foot, by car, train, or plane, without noticing, consciously or unconsciously, disease symptoms en route.

I was the only girl in a department of about forty men, and I was in charge of the materials room, the one job allotted to a woman. Up to my advent the turnover had been pretty rapid and so far as I know I am still the only one they were not able to marry off. My predecessors had been Wellesley, which was why I had been chosen, and my immediate predecessor had just married the new head of the department, Dr. Louis M. Massey, who headed up my graduate committee.

Cornell was, and is, famous for its method of teaching plant pathology. The system was developed by Professor H. H. Whetzel, affectionately called Prof by staff and students alike ever since 1907, when he started the first department of plant pathology in an American university. His was a laboratory and conference method of teaching, with the weekly lecture more for inspiration than for imparting specific information. Each student, with the aid of an instructor, chose fifteen diseases for study, representing all types. He had his own microscope and would come to the materials room window to check out a tray for each disease. I had previously prepared it with mimeographed sheets on the life history of the organism, symptoms and control of the disease, and references for further study; slides; specimens, dried or preserved in alcohol or formalin; sometimes fresh material. When the student had learned all he could, he signed up for a conference with an instructor who asked questions designed to show whether the man had done some real thinking on the implications of the disease or merely learned

answers by rote. If the conference was successful, the student returned his tray and checked out materials for another disease. He
could work at his own speed. Men who had field assistantships and
had to leave in April worked extra hard during the winter.

Although I had no inkling then of later work, nothing could
have been better training for future plant doctoring. I prepared
microscopic slides as I had been trained to do at Wellesley in Botany
13. I dried and pressed diseased leaves and put them into packets.
Other specimens went into bottles or crocks. The smell of a sick
head of cabbage in a crock of formalin is still with me. Instead of
learning fifteen diseases, as the students did, I learned several times
that number very intimately indeed.

I also, that first year, helped teach the three-month Short Course
which took in people of various backgrounds and educational foundation. Many were veterans of World War I. I learned to take care
of one man with epileptic seizures but had more difficulty with
his neighbor who fainted at the sight.

Twenty hours of work a week was required for an assistantship
and I usually put in a lot more. The rest of the time went for course
work for a Ph.D. Cornell said not to bother with a master's degree
for there were few problems in plant pathology that could be solved
in such a short time.

I learned, only too well, what mycology was. We studied fungi
under the microscope every night and all day on Sunday. We went
on marvelous collecting trips. In those days the country around
Cornell had not been slicked up for tourists. When we wanted to
cross a gorge we did it by crawling over on a fallen tree. When we
wanted to swim in the icy pool at the base of Taughannock Falls
we dressed behind some bushes. Sometimes we went on overnight
camping and collecting trips.

All the graduate students were living on next to nothing and
enjoying life in the process. My salary for the first two years was
$750 a year. Wives of the married assistants worked as stenographers
to help their men through school. When everyone was poor no one

minded. Our good times were mostly picnics, either a few of us around a campfire or the whole department, which ran to about a hundred with wives and children. Even on our budgets we could have real steak in those days, not hamburgers. Someone taught me to cook bacon, apples, and sugar down to a mouth-watering marmalade to go with the steak. Once learned, I had to keep performing at every picnic.

When we had a department supper indoors the men usually cooked chicken and rice in the autoclaves or pressure cookers. I still depend on chicken and rice for a big party. We had tea every afternoon (one of Prof's ideas for getting more work out of people), and although I got it ready the men always cleaned up.

HABITATIONS

The first year I had a third-floor room with a wonderful private family who did not object to my having a Sterno and getting some meals. I suspect it was a fire hazard and I know it encouraged mice. Mother was visiting me once when I was in bed with a cold and I watched her eyes follow the mice around the room but she did not move because she thought I was asleep. That was sheer heroism on her part; she did not have my immunity to such things. Up in Bailey Hall (our department was in the basement of the big auditorium) we had rats. Mostly they waited until night to come and play around the materials room but not always. Sometimes during afternoon seminars we could hear them running back and forth. I killed some in traps, poisoned a few. Then a friend said that if you belled a rat it would keep the others away. He provided a trap for catching one alive and we got a great granddaddy of a rat. But before my friend could get on the scene the other men had that rat outside on the snow with a ring of dogs around it. So I never did find out how you can bell a rat without getting chewed up in the process.

Sometimes Mrs. White, my good landlady, invited me to dinner.

She could stretch food money a long way with most satisfying results. A treasured recipe is her feather-light chocolate cake which takes only one egg for both cake and frosting. Other meals were eaten at "Domecon," the home economics cafeteria. Thirty cents was about the limit for lunch and I remember a pea, cheese, and pickle salad repeatedly on the menu that provided sustenance if not enjoyment.

Despite walking at least four miles a day up and down those steep Ithaca hills and a meager food allowance, I gained twenty pounds the first six weeks I was at Cornell. Why, I'll never know. Up to that time I had been too thin. My back had gotten such a curve I had to wear a brace most of senior year at Wellesley, and my home doctor was sure I could not finish out the year without supplementary food. He prescribed an eggnog or hot chocolate between meals, and a pound of peanuts a week, which played hob with my complexion but did not add much weight. Then the change to upper New York State and the start of a continual, and always losing, fight to keep the pounds down.

For a while I was a guinea pig for a girl doing graduate work in nutrition. I had to lose ten pounds within a certain time while another girl had to gain ten. She did not make it. I lost my quota right on schedule and I had all the basic foods you are supposed to have but I certainly did not gain the sense of well-being you are expected to acquire. I was completely miserable when I tried to drink milk. I thought of food instead of work. One afternoon, right after lunch, the hunger pangs were so acute that I telephoned my mentor and she came over with two slices of dry whole-wheat bread. Never had anything been so satisfying. My colleague in the test is still thin; I am still a balloon. I try to eat wisely and not too much but every time I go on a diet, limiting intake to that prescribed by nutritional standards, I am acutely unhappy, mentally and physically. I am writing these words just after a "good" meal. I had lean roast beef with no gravy, a green vegetable, cabbage salad, a corn stick instead of potatoes, black coffee, no dessert. I'm hungry, right now.

The second year at Cornell another girl and I took a three-room apartment, sharing the bath with another roomer. Mostly we had to heat water for the bath in a tea kettle on the kitchen stove. Our landlady made us scrub out the tub with a concoction of kerosene and vinegar, the thought of which makes me gag even after more than thirty years. Mildred had a car and we usually had to use the tea kettle to thaw out the radiator on winter mornings.

The next year I moved into Sigma Delta Epsilon. This graduate women's scientific fraternity (I always have to explain we are not a sorority) had been founded at Cornell just before I arrived. Some of the members lived together. The year I joined the group we rented a house from a professor on sabbatical leave. We all had kitchen privileges and sometimes we cooked meals together but no one was in charge of scrubbing. When the professor's wife returned she strongly intimated that a clean-up job was in order and I found myself scouring broiler pans and washing kitchen paint for a whole day. Meanwhile we had rented another house for the next year and having let myself be railroaded into being house manager I had to get that one cleaned up before we could move in.

About that time, June 1924, I was called home. Mother was in the hospital; she had already had a preliminary operation for cancer; major surgery was to follow. We had not dreamed she was so ill! She died following the second operation after ten days of terrific suffering. We could not have wanted her agony prolonged but she was only 55. My brother who had gone through school in record time, graduating from M.I.T. at 20, was working with a construction firm in Chicago. He gave it up to be with Dad and started his own construction business from North Attleboro.

I stayed home that summer to keep house for them both. Frank bid on a project near Providence and was pretty shocked when he was awarded the work. His low bid was far below that of established firms and he expected to lose his shirt. He worried all summer. I put up a lunch for him every day and he brought it home at night practically untouched. When it rained he would sometimes drive down in the middle of the night to make sure the work was safe. He came out on top, as he has ever since with always larger jobs, but he still worries.

In September, I returned to Cornell and the new fraternity house. Being manager, I took the small unheated cubbyhole on the top floor. By October, the house was running quite smoothly and my father and aunt drove out to visit. To show off some of the scenic beauty of the Finger Lakes region I took them through Watkins Glen, a very strenuous walk. I knew that Dad sometimes took pills for "indigestion" but had no knowledge that he had a serious heart condition. He died, suddenly, the next night on the way back to North Attleboro from Ithaca. I bitterly blamed myself and the family doctor who should have told me. Two funerals in a family in four months is a pretty numbing experience, especially with guilt feelings included. Some say that flowers should be omitted at funerals, that the money should be spent for something more lasting. I don't agree; I learned through them of the wealth and variety of father's friends. I was especially touched by tributes from the two Catholic priests at home, for our Universalist faith was far removed from theirs.

My brother was engaged and a Thanksgiving wedding had been planned. Mildred was wonderful. She canceled arrangements for a real wedding and moved up her marriage date so I would not have to stay away from work too long. Neither of us wanted Frank living alone at this time, but a girl deserves a joyous and not a sad honeymoon. I have always been grateful to my sister-in-law and to her family, for they immediately made me part of them.

I did not go home that first Christmas, finding some scientific meetings in Washington a little easier to take, but as the winter wore on I kept thinking of Dad's Model T Ford standing unused in the barn at home, for Frank was driving mother's Chevrolet. I went home at Easter to get it, disregarding the fact that I had never learned to drive. Once Dad started to teach me. I started the car, way out on a country road, but had not learned to stop it when a cow ambled

across the road. I kept pushing her along, at about 5 miles an hour, until Dad got the brake on. I don't think she was really hurt but I lost all interest in driving. Now I needed a car for work and there was no sense in the Ford being idle. A girl from California who was seeing Boston for her vacation agreed to drive back with me. She had a license but could only drive a gear-shift car. I had a learner's permit. Frank had little time to teach me all I needed to know so he decided on the hard part. We went to another country road and I practiced backing and turning around. The next day we started back to Ithaca, picking up another intrepid passenger in Springfield. By the end of the two days I was driving reasonably well.

The Ford had a starter but it was most erratic. It was not working the morning I was scheduled to take the driver's test. I coasted downhill from the fraternity house and kept my fingers crossed. By incredible luck the engine kept going until the test was over but it died while the papers were being filled out. I had to get a mechanic from a garage to start it again.

There was no garage with our house and I had a very large square of heavy canvas made up to protect the Ford from the elements. I used it as originally intended just once, but it has been indispensable in plant doctoring. All the soil from all the rose beds we have ever dug has been piled on this canvas and it has carried leaves to the compost pile every autumn since 1933.

With the Ford for transportation I became official greeter for new arrivals at the house, official guide to Watkins Glen, Enfield, Taughannock Falls, all the wondrous Finger Lakes country of hills and gorges. The old model T had some disadvantages: you had to get out to put the curtains on when it rained; you had to back up the steep Ithaca hills when the gas was low; but it got places no modern low-slung car could ever attempt. Along with the Ford I inherited a Buffalo robe, from grandfather's collection. One Cornell friend was Irene Dobroscky, later my partner in plant doctoring. She loved the outdoors even more than I and sometimes the Ford and Irene and I would go out along the Lake (Cayuga) for overnight, sleeping under the stars on the Buffalo robe, soft as any mattress.

Elizabeth Bodger was one of the new arrivals whose train I met. Of the famous Bodger Seeds family, El Monte, California, and destined to be America's foremost woman hybridist, Liz's clothes matched her colorful personality. My mousy New England taste was a bit upset by her arrival in a rather violent purple dress and hat, but that was right for Liz and she became a staunch friend and helpmate.

Our house on Dryden road had a grand group of girls and of course there were always beaus swarming around. I momentarily forgot about the latter when I bought, out of my slight salary, a fine Cape Cod hammock for the porch. I figured I could relax on it at the end of an arduous day, perhaps sleep on it when the third-floor cubbyhole got too hot. Disillusioned on being able to use it myself I tried to "rent" it out—so many hours in the hammock for so much garden work. All I ever got were promises to pay up later except from Liz who really wanted to help plan and work a garden. It was because she, whose family grew flowers by the thousands of acres, had never had a garden of her own. We grew vegetables, annuals, and roses. This was my first rose garden, my first test garden for sprays and dusts. The roses were mostly hybrid perpetuals with Mme. Caroline Testout the one standing out in memory.

Sunday mornings on Dryden road were a riot. We had a big kitchen and every girl had her shelf of eatables. The big round table was always littered with boxes of cereal and bottles of milk but on Sundays there were also waffles and a few beaus. We rented with the place an enormous old waffle iron, the kind you put on the stove. I came down early Sunday mornings and made up lots of waffle batter and started gallons of coffee. I was quite proud of my waffles and somewhat hurt when one of the boys presented me with his mother's recipe. I tried it once, then went back to my own version of Fanny Farmer.

THE ACADEMIC SIDE

Running the house and, for one year, being president of Sigma Delta Epsilon, were purely side activities. Academic work took most of the twenty-four hours a day. After two years I was promoted to rank of instructor with increased salary but I retained the same materials room job. The major course work for my degree was, of course, in plant pathology and it was strongly recommended that I take minors in physical chemistry and plant physiology. I wish now that I had dared to insist on entomology, but I meekly obeyed instructions.

The physical chemistry instructor took one look at my first paper and said that if I wanted to pass his course I would buy a typewriter. I did, and as usual I had to plunge in without time to learn how. As a result, I have never learned to type properly despite years of doing book manuscripts. I am continually expecting to have publishers refuse a manuscript until it is redone by a public stenographer, but so far they have been lenient.

There were two professors of plant physiology of equal rank and they alternated teaching graduate students. Despite double exposure I never did understand plant physiology the way I did plant diseases where I was working behind the scenes.

I had a summer cram course in organic chemistry which left as little impression as the Harvard summer course in physics. We had to pass a reading examination in French and German. A little boning up on high school French passed that hurdle and I took Professor Whetzel's course in reading scientific German, getting a good deal more out of it than from college classes in German. Prof taught by a system of "cognates," guessing at meanings of words where the roots were similar in English and German. In a few months students with no previous experience in German could pass their reading examinations.

Four years of working part time, studying part time, completed course work and I came up for preliminary oral examination. The ordeal was scheduled for 2 p.m. Thinking it would be fatal to cram too hard at the last minute I spent the morning downtown shopping for a new hat. When I arrived all keyed up for the examination I was told that one of the professors had forgotten about it and gone off for the day. The oral was postponed until 7:30 that evening. I was frightened, for I am never too bright in the evening, but I was game. I got along fairly well for the first two hours that night but then something snapped and I thought I had utterly lost my mind. It was the most terrifying experience I had ever undergone. The questions kept coming, deeper and deeper in a single subject, trying to trip me up on a single point, and I could not think at all. The torture lasted until after 11 p.m. and then they gave up.

I had failed! I, Cynthia Westcott, all-A student in high school, Phi Beta Kappa at Wellesley, could not pass a Cornell examination. Dr. Massey was kind, said there were extenuating circumstances and that he was sure I was still doctorate material (some people get "busted out" immediately), but I was bitterly disappointed in myself. I suppose it is good training to get slapped down once in a while, but the memory remains of being very close to insanity the last hour or two of that oral examination. I took it over when the required time had elapsed and have no recollection of the exam I passed—merely the searing memory of the failure.

With course work ended, Professor Whetzel offered me a full-time job as his research assistant, on funds provided by the Heckscher Research Foundation. The pay was excellent compared to the $750 a year I started on, and I loved working for Prof. He scared some people. He always expected too much, dictated too fast and often had the stenographers in tears. He never bothered me. I'd do as much as I could as fast as I could and if things piled up so much I got upset I'd open my desk drawer and do a little sneak reading in the *Saturday Evening Post*. Like my father before me, I have been a life-long addict of the *Post*. The cover alone relaxes tension!

I spoke of the rats as one of the problems of working in the basement of Bailey Hall. Now my arch enemy was dust, for the work was mostly maintaining pure cultures of the fungi Prof was studying. Huge organ pipes went along the ceiling in our office; it was never possible to clean them properly and whenever the organ was played the dust jarred off. But that, too, was good training. I learned to hold the tubes expertly enough and to work quickly enough so there was almost never contamination in making transfers. We grew the fungi on slants of potato agar and my job was mostly menial. I had to cook up potatoes, strain the broth (sometimes I took the potatoes home to eat) add the agar and dextrose, cook and stir until melted, then fill tubes and flasks, sterilize in the autoclave, remove and cool on a slanting position. Anyone who is a good laboratory technician should be a good cook. Both mean following recipes exactly and both mean a lot of time spent washing dishes.

When I was not making media and transferring cultures I was measuring spores under the microscope, as a means of identifying species in the genus Sclerotinia, and sometimes making camera lucida drawings. My first drawing cost the Heckscher Foundation a lot of money for it took a solid month to section the material, make the slides and sketches and then put them together into one big drawing of a cross section of a stem invaded by a sclerotial fungus. I must have learned a lot, though, for I have since been able to make reasonably clear diagrammatic sketches to illustrate books without any talent as an artist.

Collecting trips were part of the job and I loved these, even in early spring with snow on the ground. The genus Sclerotinia and its close relatives (which in one form or another have followed through my life) are characterized by having a resting body, called a sclerotium, made up of interwoven white fungus threads and a hard outer rind, usually black. These sclerotia may be formed inside stems, causing stem rot of many vegetables and some flowers; on stems, as in Botrytis blight of peonies; in leaves, as with some of the tree diseases; or in petals, as in azalea and camellia flower blights.

In spring, when weather conditions are right and the host plant (Prof preferred the term suscept) is in a susceptible stage, these sclerotia put out little stems which expand at the top into cup or saucer-shaped bodies called apothecia. The concave surface of each apothecium is lined with hundreds of club-shaped sacs, each containing eight spores. When there is a change in humidity, as occurs when the leaf litter or mulch is disturbed, there is a chemical change in the sacs (asci) and the spores are literally shot out in clouds, then carried by air currents to appropriate plant parts overhead or nearby. The sclerotia and apothecia are usually minute, ⅛ inch or less across, sometimes up to ½ inch, and they resemble the earth in color. They are very hard to see with the untrained eye but my eye was constantly trained for six years. Flat on my stomach, in the snow and ice and mud of early spring, I collected apothecia, took them to the laboratory and measured their ascospores. I made single-spore cultures by fastening an apothecium to the lid of a petri dish and letting it shoot its spores down onto an agar plate, then carefully cutting out, under a microscope and without contamination, a single germinating spore.

That training took me to Europe and my Wellesley training in making do with materials at hand enabled me to make single-spore cultures in a hotel room with a piece of fine wire stuck in a match and flamed over a candle.

That training is responsible, in a not too indirect way, for my writing these words, some thirty years later on a pleasant February morning, in New Orleans, for I have been lecturing here on camellia flower blight. The New Orleans I know and love from many southern visits is not the Mardi Gras and French Quarter known to tourists. It is the city of gardens. When the maid comes to clean my room I wander around a few blocks. The other day, walking toward the less desirable section I saw the most beautiful roses imaginable, a whole yard full of well-tended hybrid teas. This morning, walking into the Garden District with its fine old residences, I saw pink Cherokee roses and masses of yellow Banksia in the tree tops, hedges of old Louis Philippe, vast banks of azaleas, camellias everywhere (some of which unfortunately are blighted). I saw a garden with borders of white tulips. These are an experiment in New Orleans; tulips have to be chilled before planting because of the mild winters. I also saw, on the same brief walk, iris, calendulas, pansies, snapdragons, sweet peas, gerberas, plumbago, jessamine, lantanas, hollyhocks, violets, oxalis, sedums, kalanchoe, begonias, geraniums, and Japanese magnolias all blooming madly in midwinter.

My first extended traveling was not connected with work but purely for fun. Elizabeth Bodger had finished her two years of study for a master's, working with those huge dahlia-flowered zinnias, and had gone home to hybridize for the family firm. When I had saved enough money I spent my month's vacation on a trip to California. It was October when I stopped off in New Mexico to take the Indian Detour. I was equally entranced with the Indian pueblos, the blue, blue sky, and Santa Fe. Liz and her mother and father met me at Grand Canyon and we drove across the hot desert to California. Their big ranch house with its wide overhanging roof was built for warm weather; in common with other houses of its era it had no central heating. My abiding recollection of California, based on this trip and several subsequent visits (always in fall or winter) is of being cold. I know I wasn't always, for I can recall warm, sunny noondays, but that first time I vowed that a flannel nightgown and a hot water bottle would be the first things packed for the next trip. Of course I was coming back; I loved it, and the people were as warmhearted as their houses were chilly. We had dinner with the parents of another Cornell graduate student. They told me how they had worried about Margaret in the cold Ithaca winters. I couldn't reply; my teeth were clamped together to keep them from chattering.

While Liz worked during the day I did the usual tourist stunts of visiting the lion farm, riding an ostrich, seeing Hollywood, and all the rest. My interest in gardens must have been dormant; I can't remember special efforts to see them.

EUROPEAN SOJOURN

When Professor and Mrs. Whetzel went to Europe on sabbatical leave I trailed along as his assistant, feeling very important with a diplomatic passport. I had my regular salary but paid my own passage and other expenses. We sailed from New York, January 1930, in a snowstorm, on a small one-cabin ship of the American Merchant Line. Before we got out of New York Harbor I bent over to unpack my suitcase and learned I was the world's worst sailor. The ship was not full and the girl assigned to room with me quickly got transferred away from the unpleasantness. For two days I could not lift my head, sneaking out steamer letters from under the pillow to read without moving. Someone had given me a glamorous gardenia corsage for bon voyage. It remained on the other side of the cabin, too far away to throw out of the porthole. I have never really liked gardenias since. I recovered and enjoyed the rest of the eleven-day crossing despite rough seas. They put racks on the table for dishes and dancing was like climbing up a mountainside.

We went first to England, for a sojourn at Kew, working in the Herbarium, living nearby at The Priory. My first act was to buy a tweed dress, so scratchy I was never able to wear it later in America, and a little copper tea kettle to heat water on the gas trivet for a hot-water bottle. This time I had the flannels and the bottle with me.

There was a Canadian scientist staying at The Priory and some evenings we four played cards, taking turns sitting in front of the gas grate but keeping our coats on. I remember England as the place where you wear your winter coat in the house and change to spring weight when you go outdoors. Even in the Herbarium, where there was some central heat, they kept the thermometer at 65° F., a little cool for a hot-house foreigner. We went calling once on the Director of a laboratory. In honor of his visitors he had the gas heater lit but the window was wide open and it was snowing outside.

I was still measuring spores, working from type specimens there at Kew. If I used electric light for the microscope when there was a glimmer of sunlight outdoors I was considered grossly extravagant. Because of the fire hazard to priceless herbarium specimens we were not given tea at Kew but dismissed at 4:30 to go home for that meal. I loved the English teas—nice fattening things like thin bread and butter, scones, muffins, jam, cake—and I did not care so much for dinner. The meat was always good but the vegetable, cabbage, cauliflower, brussels sprouts or other member of the cole family, was cooked too long and the coffee with hot milk nearly undrinkable. In self-defense I learned to take it black and have ever since. Some of the desserts, such as plum or gooseberry tart, were too sour for American tastes, but I liked trifle very much and collected recipes for it.

When invited out to dinner at a private home we could choose between trifle and gelatin for dessert. Sometimes we were asked just for dessert and coffee, an easy entertainment idea I adopted when I came home, or for a sherry party. The advantage of a working trip to Europe instead of going as a tourist is that you meet people in your own field and enter their homes. When we were invited for a lunch of bread and cheese and ale it was a little hard on me. I felt about English ale, and any kind of beer, the way I did about Mexicali beer when Liz and I went over the border into Mexico to try it. Liz took one sip, made up a face, and said, "Putrid horse-flesh!" I agreed.

We did lots of regular sightseeing. We took in the Tower of London and the Crown jewels, Windsor Castle and the Queen's Doll's House, saw the changing of the guards, ate at the Cheshire Cheese, known to Dr. Johnson, and also at Simpson's Fish Ordinary, where the meal began with grace and ended with thanks. The last course was cheese, and if anyone guessed the height, girth, and weight of the big wheel correctly, champagne was on the house for all diners. I can't remember the name of the place where we went for a lunch entirely of fruit, served on a grape leaf, for a shilling.

We went to Hampton Court and, of more moment scientifically, to Darwin's home and to the lovely gardens of Wisley where I collected specimens of rose diseases. Kew was always beautiful and I often wandered around in the twilight between tea and dinner, watching the friendly little English robins, so different from our own. There was a big crane that also wandered around Kew. He seemed friendly until you tried to pet him; then he would untie your shoelaces. If you persisted in trying to scratch his head, he made you desist with a few sharp digs.

Prof's plan was to follow the spring northward so we began collecting in Holland in March. We lived in Lisse at the Witte Swan and our base of operations was the Laboratorium voor Bloembollenonderzoek (the Bulb Laboratory). The Director was (and still is) Professor Dr. E. van Slogteren, a great scientist, a fine man, a wonderful friend to me through all the years since 1930. Americans are spoiled in going abroad. The natives speak our language so well we seldom have to learn theirs. I did learn to say in Dutch, "It is a fine morning" and since nearly every morning was fine and I came in beaming each day with those words I was given credit for more linguistic ability than I possessed. I could never manage the proper G sound; it was more like H.

For the first time in my life I had a laboratory assistant to wash the glassware when I made media. They had intercom telephones, too, which we did not at Cornell (until my last year when we moved into the big new Plant Science Building). In Lisse all I had to do was go to the phone and say "Gerrit, koom" and Gerrit would koom, learn by my gestures what I wanted, and do it forthwith. There was also the luxury of coffee brought to my desk every morning, tea in the afternoon.

After I had been in Europe a few months I decided that if I were blindfolded, put aboard a plane, set down in some unknown country and given breakfast I would know where I was. In Holland we had cold bread, cold meat, eggs, cheese and jam for breakfast. In England the bread was toasted but it was put on the rack to cool while the bacon and eggs were prepared. You were not supposed to eat your marmalade with those; you had it later with more toast. In Holland you ate the sweet jam right along with the meat and eggs. Lunch there was practically the same as breakfast.

Dinner at the Witte Swan was delicious, with more varied vegetables than in England and often a trace of mace in the spinach. We had salad every night, not just on Sunday as in England, and our waiter mixed the dressing before us. First, a mashed hard-boiled egg, then the seasonings, oil and vinegar. I still do it that way when I have company. Dutch candies and pastries are marvelous. Mrs. Whetzel and I used to glue ourselves to the shop windows looking at them. Most places they look a lot better than they taste, but this was not true in Holland.

Once or twice Professor van Slogteren took us to a fine restaurant by the sea for a many-course dinner with appropriate wines. Once I went myself for a weekend at a seaside resort. One Sunday the Whetzels and I decided to walk over the dunes to the sea. Each time we neared the crest of a dune we thought surely there would be water beyond only to find more sand. When we finally reached the beach I was shuffling along in a pair of wooden shoes someone had discarded. My feet had so many blisters I couldn't keep my own shoes on.

Our little Inn was eternally being scrubbed; we climbed over pails on the staircase on our way to breakfast every morning. My bedroom was immaculate and cold. Evenings we shared a small private sitting room with a stove, but if I stayed there very long with the door closed and Prof smoking Dutch cigars I soon felt as if I were back on shipboard. All my life I have been somewhat allergic to smoke. I learned to take Prof's inevitable pipe at Cornell with some equanimity but when it came to those cigars in a small room I had to flee. The only thing left to do was go to bed.

All this time we were living in the glory of the Dutch bulb fields. We arrived as the crocuses were coming into bloom and stayed through the whole pageant, ending with Darwin tulips. They were unbelievably brilliant. There was one carpet of scarlet tulips near the laboratory so dazzling I could not look at it in the sun without hurting my eyes.

Growers producing bulbs for sale are not allowed to sell flowers, for that would mean cutting stems as well and divert some of the food being manufactured for the bulb. They do, however, carefully remove all flowers or flowerets by hand so the plant does not waste energy going to seed. The canals were always full of scows piled high with pink and blue hyacinth blooms, the air redolent with their perfume.

Our own research had little to do with the work of the Bulb Laboratory itself. That was for the study of all bulb diseases, including viruses and nutritional disorders. They taught the growers sanitation. There was continual field inspection, under an umbrella for easier detection of symptoms. Some plants were rogued (pulled up and burned); others, where there was a chance of spreading germs during the removal process, were covered with glass jars and left for disposal at the end of the season, after the healthy bulbs were dug. Under Professor van Slogteren's guidance the laboratory has kept expanding. I have not been back since 1930, but pathologists who have visited it in recent years tell me the equipment and facilities make them drool with envy. When Professor van Slogteren was over here in 1955 he showed movies of their present techniques, which include horses to provide serum for the quick detection of plant viruses.

During our stay we went to Aalsmeer, famous for its flower mart. They were having a big flower show the day of our visit and we saw Princess Juliana, now the Queen, and her grandmother as they opened the show. We also went strictly tourist and took in Volendam where I fell for Dutch costumes for myself and to send back to my two young nephews.

While based in Holland there was an interlude of collecting in France, Germany, and Switzerland. Sometimes the Whetzels and

I traveled independently, both because we wanted to see different things and because I learned so much going by myself. I found that Europeans are extraordinarily kind to a female traveling alone but pay no attention to a self-sufficient group. They were particularly pleasant before the summer influx of tourists. When the latter arrived and I saw a few of my countrywomen in action, I wondered why the Europeans did not hate us en masse.

I had a few days in Paris by myself, in a pension on the left bank, but with Dr. Dufrenoy, who had worked at Cornell, to keep an eye on me. I bought a hat, just to say it came from the Rue de la Paix, and had a couple of dresses made. They were rather flimsy and pretty well worn out by the time they got back through customs, not worth nearly the duty imposed.

Going to Dresden for Easter holidays I fell in love with the Sistine Madonna and heard Parsifal. Opera in Dresden began at 5 p.m. with an intermission for a meal of cold meat, salad, and port. I arrived late at the hotel, unpacked only enough for the opera, and left everything else locked in the suitcase. When I returned close to midnight I could not find the key and never did discover where I had lost it. The hotel was of no assistance and I had to sleep in what I was wearing. Easter in Germany was a four-day holiday with no shops open, no locksmiths available. The next morning the hotel manager got the lock broken for me but could not get it repaired. I have never again locked a suitcase. I briefly regretted this resolution recently when I flew to Texas and watched them *throw* all the luggage out of the belly of the plane. I had visions of all of my intimate apparel being strewn over the Texas landscape. Nothing happened but it gave me one more reason for preferring to travel by train or Ford.

From Dresden I took an all-day sightseeing trip through the countryside. There were no other Americans on the bus but quite a lot of Scandinavians, most of whom spoke German. I could understand some of their remarks about the "Amerikanische Dame" and at the end of the day, when I ventured a few German words, they were considerably taken aback. But they had said nothing mean, merely poked a little fun about a woman traveling alone.

I went to join the Whetzels at Heidelberg. I arrived without dinner and too late to get any at the pension. Prof and Mrs. Whetzel had gone out for the evening with some scientists. Wandering around to find food I came on a coffee house where the chief sustenance was cake with lots of whipped cream. I woke up at 5 a.m. with acute indigestion, which I had never before experienced. I did not know where Mrs. Whetzel's room was but I finally aroused a chambermaid and she got a doctor, a nice woman doctor who knew less English than I knew German. We conversed by means of my English-German dictionary and agreed on a verdict as to cause, "Es war der Kuchen." She prescribed various medications and all day long an elderly maid sat with me and ministered to me, for which not one penny was put on my bill. I surely remember Heidelberg with affection, if not with pleasure.

We collected in Switzerland, glorying in the mountains and gentians in bloom while looking for Sclerotinias. I liked the Swiss honey with rolls and coffee for breakfast as I had the chocolate and croissants in France and the substantial zweites Frühstück in Germany.

Along about Whitsuntide we closed up shop in Holland and went north to Denmark by one of those train and ferry hopscotch crossings, where you eat on the ferries at heavily laden smorgasbord tables. This trip I was not seasick and enjoyed the food.

Our new headquarters were at the laboratory at Lyngby, outside of Copenhagen, right next to King Christian's summer palace. He was always going out alone on horseback by our building and I always just missed seeing him.

The Danish language looks akin to German but it does not sound like it. I never learned to say a word. Some evenings when I was working late alone at the lab a farmer would come to the door with a specimen, wanting to know what was the matter with his crop.

I was most ashamed that I could not even say, "I don't speak Danish" in his tongue. He must surely have wondered about this tongue-tied female. When I heard Danes talking on the telephone all I could think of was a string of liquid ls; there seemed to be no pauses or inflection. Once someone stopped me on the street in Copenhagen and asked directions. I answered without thinking and later wondered how that had been possible. I decided we must both have been speaking German.

We lived with a private family and in the custom of the country. In Germany we had half roasted and half frozen under featherbeds that covered either our shoulders or our toes but not both. In Denmark we learned that bed linen was not changed daily as in hotels, or weekly as at home, but only at long intervals. There was always a square of goat cheese (the color of peanut butter) for breakfast. It had an embroidered band around it to hold on to while you sliced. For lunch we took a neat packet of Danish sandwiches to the lab with us. A sandwich is one slice of dark bread covered with smoked salmon or cheese or pickled eels, but I never would try the latter. We came back to the house for dinner which was very good.

Despite elaborate public smorgasbords, Danish home meals seemed to be quite simple: soup and a main course, or main course and dessert, seldom all three unless a real "company" dinner. When the Director asked us to family dinner I ate heartily of the soup and fish set before me. Then we adjourned to the living room for coffee. Prof, remembering dinners in Holland where fish was merely the prelude to roast and sometimes game as well, had merely toyed with the fish, keeping his appetite for what was to follow. He was a mighty hungry man before morning.

Never having learned to like buttermilk I was not much interested in the Danish dessert of buttermilk soup, but I thought their beer soup excellent even though I hated beer. It was made of black bread boiled in beer, spices and lemon added, and eaten with cream. It sounds horrible but is truly delicious. We were told of sickly English children that came to live in Denmark. The doctor ordered beer soup and it quickly brought them back to health. Rolle-pulse, veal rolled around prune or other fruit stuffing, was also very good. On my birthday Fru Bache produced a wonderful cake, baked at the time she did one for her son a few weeks earlier. It had been stored in a cold place about the way we freeze cakes today.

From Denmark we made trips to Norway and Sweden. I took another separate holiday, going by fiord and overland from Oslo to Romsdal Pass. The scenery was even grander than Switzerland. Nights were at small village hotels. One evening I walked part way up a mountain road. Two little old ladies summering at the hotel were quite shocked. "Allein?" they gasped. It was unthinkable to them that any woman would walk alone on a country road at night, even if it was practically daylight. We were not quite as far north as the midnight sun but we had to sleep with our eyes covered with black silk. When I took the train to Stockholm I looked out from my berth at midnight and saw a man reading a newspaper on a station platform.

Our Danish friends gave us a tender farewell and I treasure highly their parting gift of a Jensen silver sugar spoon. We went back to England over the North Sea. Again I was a rotten sailor. We were already docked when I regrettably bent over to fasten my suitcase.

We spent the latter part of that summer at Rothamsted Experiment Station, living at a very respectable Pub in Harpenden; the barmaid put everyone out promptly at 10 p.m. The food was reasonably good (though I never got used to breakfast toast being put on the table early to cool off) and the landlord tried so hard to please us he scoured the markets for American corn-on-the-cob. The Station provided a bountiful tea, so we all stayed on and worked hard until 7 or 7:30 p.m. Both at Kew and Rothamsted there were women in responsible positions. It seemed to me perhaps easier for a woman to get recognition in science in England than in America. At Kew Dr. Elsie Wakefield was a renowned mycologist; at Harpenden Dr. Winifred Brenchley was doing pioneer work in soil deficiencies.

The end of summer brought a lot of American colleagues over

to the Botanical Congress at Cambridge. Afterwards Anna Jenkins and I went for a weekend by the sea at Bournemouth, in one of the enormous hotels standing as a relic of Victorian days. I had worn a winter coat most of the summer but that weekend it was so hot we couldn't even walk on the beach. We lay on our beds and looked at the water through the windows.

The Whetzels and I landed back in New York on one of our nasty-hot September days. We had to stay at anchor in the harbor all night and the fan in the stateroom screeched so it was impossible to sleep with it on and it was impossible to breathe with it off. I was a little too conscientious about declaring purchases for customs for most of them were already well used. The inspector's opinion of their present valuation was a lot higher than mine and it took all the rest of my travel fund to get back into the country. My brother and sister-in-law met the boat and drove us to Montclair, New Jersey, where Frank was constructing a reservoir. I little dreamed then that I'd be living in that vicinity later.

THE DEPRESSION

The 1929 stock market crash happened just before we went to Europe but it seemed rather remote from our academic lives. Not so on our return. Real estate by then was in a terrific slump. This affected the Heckscher Foundation and meant the end of my job. There was a small grant to allow me to finish the year for Prof and complete the research for my thesis but I was in the market for work.

During the Cornell years a few other jobs had been offered but I was contentedly in a rut and uninterested. In the back of my mind was always the comforting thought that if my position folded up I could get work with the United States Department of Agriculture. I hopefully took Civil Service examinations and much, much later received my rating: "#1—Female; prospects of certification and appointment UNCERTAIN because there is little or no demand

for female eligibles." I had not known until then that we were
rated according to our sex; it was my first chance to learn first-hand
how the cards are stacked against the woman scientist. Up to now,
things had come to me and I had followed the path of least resistance.
Now I was out in the cold. I learned that there were still a very few
jobs for a woman graduate assistant but none when she had completed her work and was ready for a career. Eventually I landed
the promise of a part-time assistantship, chiefly as a bacteriologist,
at the New Jersey Experiment Station, Rutgers University. Meanwhile I had to finish my thesis, tie up the loose ends of the work for
Prof, and take a summer course in bacteriology to brush up for
the new job.

PERSONAL RESEARCH

During most of the years at Cornell I was studying rose diseases
nights and Sundays. I started in with blackspot, trying to see if there
were varietal differences as to susceptibility. I remember that the
University financed a trip to Bobbink and Atkins' nursery in New
Jersey and to the Conard-Pyle Company in Pennsylvania to collect
specimens of blackspot on many different kinds of roses but I was
not smart enough to see a thesis along this line. Problems that are
left when a disease has already been explored as to general symptoms
and life history of the pathogen are harder. Many years later, W. R.
Jenkins, on a fellowship sponsored by the American Rose Foundation, showed that there are many different strains of the blackspot
fungus.

I turned to something easier. All of a sudden, in the spring of
1926, a new disease showed up on all of the climbers in the Cornell
test and display garden. The causative fungus was in a group being
studied by a United States Department of Agriculture worker but
the disease was at Cornell and I was interested in control rather
than mycological angles, so I started in on it. Anything I learned
would be new so it was sure fire for a thesis.

We did know the name of the fungus, *Coniothyrium werns-dorffiae,* cousin of the *C. fuckelii* that causes a very common rose canker. We knew the new disease was serious in Germany, where it had been named Brandfleckenkrankheit, literally "burn-spot-sick-ness" but translated here as brand canker. There had been one report from Canada and one from Minnesota, but how it got to Cornell or why it appeared in such epiphytotic form we never knew. More than ninety per cent of the climbers were infected. There were burned black areas at the base of the canes and when these were entirely girdled they died back to the ground. The climbers had been extra well protected that year, being laid on the ground and wrapped in burlap before being mounded with soil, but it was a long time before I tumbled to the full significance of that fact.

Meanwhile I grew the fungus in culture and measured its spores, comparing them with those of other species in the genus. I learned minimum, optimum and maximum temperatures for growth in culture and on rooted cuttings inoculated in the greenhouse. I tried every sort of control measure. I went out at 6 o'clock in the morning to spray the roses in the test garden, going home to clean up and get to my regular job before 9. I dusted roses in the evening, then went swimming in the creek across the road from the garden to wash the dust out of my eyes. At that, I usually had to cry myself to sleep because of the irritation of sulfur particles on my eyeballs. The gardens were about four miles from campus, so the Ford earned its keep those years.

I learned the hard way about bordeaux mixture. Suddenly I noticed that the climbers that had been sprayed with it, at the generally recommended strength, were losing practically all their leaves. The superintendent of the garden was decidedly cool to me when that angle developed.

I also learned that bordeaux mixture ruins a sprayer. The Department had given me a good copper compressed air sprayer. I thought I had cleaned it out sufficiently in the fall but come spring it had pretty well corroded. Dr. Massey didn't like that. Such hard-won knowledge is never forgotten. All through my plant doctoring days I have been warning people about bordeaux mixture, teaching them *how* to clean their sprayers. Dr. B. O. Dodge at the New York Botanical Garden did not quite believe my bordeaux experience for they had been using it for some years in their rose garden without injury. Then, one summer, weather conditions were right (or perhaps wrong) and his spray, too, took the leaves off most of his roses. He joined my warning chorus.

I tried all kinds of winter protection for the Cornell climbers. Some were covered with boxes full of leaves, some were wrapped in waterproof coverings, some were covered with burlap, some with soil, some with burlap and soil, some left uncovered. After four years of hard work I learned that control was ridiculously easy. You simply did not coddle the roses. This was a cold temperature fungus. It was not active in the heat of summer, so spraying or dusting during the growing season had no effect. If the climbers were removed from their supports early in autumn while the canes were still flexible, held down with crossed stakes, and the grass allowed to keep growing but no other protection given, there was no spread of disease during the winter. But if there was any covering that kept the base of the canes warm and moist over winter the disease spread rapidly.

The evidence stood up conclusively even when treated statistically. I was not a statistician; my mathematics were never good enough; but by copying examples set up by a friend I worked out probable errors and other things that made the thesis sound scientific. I could not, however, couch it in sufficiently involved language. I invariably say, "You do" instead of "The facts tend to indicate that it would be advisable to. . . ." Dr. Massey despaired of me. He said, "If you could only learn to write!"

With the thesis accepted, there still remained the final oral examination. Again I failed! I am hazy on the details now. My course work was five years and a trip to Europe behind me and I suppose I was too busy to bone up sufficiently on physical chemistry. I think

I did know plant pathology. I had to report to Rutgers that I was not yet the *Dr.* Westcott they were expecting.

I hated to leave Cornell and I hated to leave my apartment. The fraternity sisters had long since given up the idea of living together and I had moved into a four-room apartment at the top of a wooden firetrap building still known as Frosh Hell from the days when it had been a rooming house. It was unfurnished and the rent was so modest I paid for painting and papering myself.

The rooms were low and the ceiling sloped to the outside. I could walk anywhere but tall friends had trouble. Whenever there was a party all the guests signed their names on the papered ceiling where their heads hit. There were many famous names on my ceiling; it became a show piece. Visiting scientists were usually entertained with a Sunday breakfast party, which began around 9 a.m. and ended when I started shooing people out about 4 p.m.

I had sent for my share of the antique furniture from the farm, which included a curly maple rope bed, desk and chairs. I put an innerspring mattress on the ropes but I left the bedroom for guests, sleeping on the back porch, no matter how far below zero the thermometer fell. I sublet the apartment furnished when I started off to New Jersey.

RUTGERS

The first year in New Jersey was not too happy. A reduction from $2000 a year for a full-time job to $900 for a part-time assistantship was quite a wrench. So was New Jersey weather. The first two weeks in September were terrifically hot and humid and, after Ithaca, I felt as if the heavens were sitting on my forehead. My third floor room was unbearable. I put a comforter on the floor in the hall at the top of the stairs to try to sleep. At the end of the second week I took bus and train to Point Pleasant on the New Jersey shore and told the cab driver to take me to an inexpensive hotel. I was lucky; it was both pleasant and respectable. But by the time I reached there the weather had changed and I could have saved my money.

I was allowed to get breakfasts and an occasional supper in my room. Dinner was at noon with Mrs. Stryker, a warmhearted Irish-woman who served a good, home-cooked meal to impoverished staff members at a more than moderate price.

The work was in the Seed Laboratory, where samples of seeds and legume inoculants being sold in New Jersey were tested. My chief duty was to test the cultures, agar or humus, of beneficial bacteria sold for the inoculation of legume seed. There are nine strains of such nitrogen-fixing bacteria, for vetch, clover, sweet pea, beans, soybeans etc., and I had to show that the strain was correct as listed on the label as well as check the bacterial count. I think I spent at least nine hours making media and washing dishes for every hour spent in actual testing. You can use up a powerful lot of test tubes and petri dishes in a few minutes in bacteriology. I tested the different strains by growing plants in the greenhouse, inoculating them, and checking on the nodules formed. Soybeans were easy; they grew quickly and the nodules were large and conspicuous. Along with washing dishes in the laboratory I was continually scrubbing out greenhouse crocks.

When legume work was slack I was set to sorting clover seed, counting the amount of dodder and other weed seed in a packet. My eyes rebelled. I have always worn glasses and had never had any eye trouble through all the years of working with a microscope all day and half the night. Now I needed new glasses but instead was given a course of exercises to "strengthen" the eyes, which rapidly made them worse. I was miserable for months while I was studying to take that Cornell oral examination over again. I passed it this time and at long last, after ten years of struggling, had my Ph.D. It was given in absentia and I have no idea now where the sheepskin is. Once achieved, it was no longer important.

Of more moment after passing the exam was finding a good eye doctor and the right glasses. Then I celebrated by dipping into savings for a wonderful vacation. I can always argue myself into believing that travel is education and therefore a justified expense.

Irene Dobroscky, with whom I had gone camping under the stars at Cornell, was coming back from the Philippines and I arranged to meet her at Yellowstone Park. Irene was an entomologist and had been at Boyce Thompson Institute working on insect transmission of virus diseases. Her field work had been in the New Jersey cranberry bogs, with headquarters at Double-Trouble Laboratory. There she had proved that the blunt-nosed leafhopper transmitted the virus of cranberry false blossom. When her urge to travel got too strong she drove across the country to California, then shipped her car to Hawaii. The Hawaiian Pineapple Canners Association then commissioned her to go to the Philippines to collect parasites for the thrips ruining Hawaiian pineapples. She was, I believe, the first woman to be sent on such a mission and she was successful. She also got a lot of practice changing tires. The natives resented Americans and were quite apt to throw tacks in her road.

Driving back with Irene was quite an experience. It was before the days of good roads and motels with private baths. We had sheets with us, cooking utensils, and a dishpan. The cabins were cheap, about a dollar a night, and they had a bed, usually a stove and wood. The shower was a long, dusty walk away. We hit a pleasant dude ranch in the Big Horn Mountains and stayed over a day to ride horseback among the sheets of blue lupine. Thirty kinds of wild flowers were blooming around the cabin door.

We detoured for a look at the majestic Tetons and then hit the hot Plains in August. Never a tree in sight, unless fenced in around a farmhouse; no place to eat lunch except inside the burning car. The tires got so hot traveling on gravel we had a blowout, and only Irene's skill and determination kept us upright. Reaching Iowa and trees again was like heaven. Everywhere we went little boys looked at the Philippine license plate on the Dodge and yelled, "How'dja get across the water?" I have had easier cross-country trips since that one but never one more interesting.

The next year at Rutgers was much better. I had an apartment downtown. It was so tiny that when the in-a-door bed was down the rest of the furniture had to be jammed against the wall. The window faced a blank wall a few feet away. It was, however, home and I could have a few friends in for meals. I had made friends on the staff and was taken to see some of the better parts of New Jersey. The first year I thought it was all like the part seen from the train windows between New Brunswick and New York.

With eyes no longer rebelling, I used the spare half time taking courses, one in statistics, which still meant little to me, and one in microbiology with Dr. Selman Waksman which meant a great deal. I can still feel the reverence with which that great man (great then but famous later as the discoverer of streptomycin) pronounced the word humus. I was also reading and abstracting everything that might be helpful in the future but I did not know where I was going and could specialize in nothing. I had only a stopgap job. Where did any future lie for me, a woman?

In February my beloved Professor Whetzel came down to work in the Herbarium at the New York Botanical Garden and invited me to join him for the day, have dinner and a talk. He was really concerned about my future, perhaps more than I was. For years he had been trying to get some of his men students to go into practical plant doctoring but no dice. It was too insecure and there were still jobs with a regular salary for *men*. Now he turned all his old arguments on me and added another. He said I was too bossy to work for others all my life; I'd be far happier being the boss myself. He was right. I decided then and there to take the plunge, to invest such old-age security as I had inherited from my parents in setting myself up professionally as a plant doctor. There remained only the question of how and where.

Almost everyone at Rutgers was interested and helpful. I tendered my resignation to take effect September 1st but with the month's vacation due me I could leave August 1st.

By this time I knew that parts of New Jersey had lovely gardens and the suburban New York area seemed a logical place to settle. I visited many real-estate offices but the men had short shrift for this crazy woman with her impractical idea. If they did tell me of a house they would rave about the two tiled baths and ignore the tiny lot. I subscribed to the *Newark Evening News* and read the For Sale ads every night. Eventually I found it: "To sell at sacrifice to settle an estate, large garden, fruit trees, grapes."

Irene, who had not yet settled in a permanent job since her Philippine jaunt, was contemplating becoming the entomological half of The Plant Doctor. We went together to look at the advertised house in Glen Ridge. It was in poor repair. The plaster was cracked, the rooms dark and gloomy; it would need a new roof before long. The coal furnace was old, there was only one bath, the barn was nearly falling down, the garden had been untended for two years and was a mass of weeds. But it was May! Wisteria was in bloom all over the porch and was climbing over the pink dogwood (it later killed it). The very large and decorative apple tree was covered with blossoms; the soil appeared fertile; there were phlox, lilies-of-the-valley, daylilies, and many other plants in between the weeds. The lot was narrow, only 54 feet wide, but it stretched back 320 feet and up a hillside (that could be a wild garden) to another street. The location seemed ideal.

I looked up some Glen Ridge residents in the Wellesley alumnae directory and went to call on a retired schoolteacher. She said Glen Ridge was a fine town to live in. It is entirely residential; so, before final papers were signed, I petitioned the Borough Council and obtained a ruling that I would be considered a professional like an M.D.

My brother came down to look the place over and procured a bank appraiser who told me the top price I could pay without making it a bad investment. He also told me that the school near by depreciated the property. I like children and couldn't see why. Later I learned that owning a horse-chestnut tree in a school district made a front lawn impossible. I bought the place, not knowing one soul in Glen Ridge except the schoolteacher I had visited.

Professor Whetzel had been enthusiastic. Mrs. Whetzel wanted me to think twice: "The house about which you write sounds attractive and I can see why you'd like to buy a place and fix it up to suit your fancy—but I still say 'Go easy.' Of course, you are having your brother's advice and he'll know whether it is a good buy or not. But it does seem to me that it is taking such a big chance. You *are* so good at laboratory work and times will change so there will be openings in things you *know* you can do and if you get all your resources tied up in property you won't be able to get away to take any position without financial loss. I *still* say that you should rent a place, if you are sure that you want to start on your own. Well, that's enough cold water."

I didn't want to rent. I had to get in so deep I couldn't get out; it was the only way to make myself see it through. Besides, I had to have a place to grow roses. The house was mine. Irene and I formed a formal partnership for the business and registered our name, THE PLANT DOCTOR, in Essex County. We also opened a bank account under that name. I was still at Rutgers, but buying a little equipment and doing a little doctoring there, at the Campus Inn and for Dr. Waksman. I had not thought of it before but I guess the discoverer of streptomycin was The Plant Doctor's first client.

Dr. C. H. Connors in Horticulture, Dr. C. C. Hamilton in Entomology, and Dr. R. P. White in Plant Pathology were all interested in this venture. When Bamberger's store in Newark wanted to put on a Plant Clinic in June the New Jersey Experiment Station decided it could not participate officially but suggested they try The Plant Doctor. Because my resignation had already been accepted they felt the Station would not be too much involved. They gave me a week off and Irene came from Yonkers.

The Clinic was really a promotion for Hammond insecticides and fungicides but we were not required to recommend any specific product. The sponsor's original idea was that all specimens should be presented to a registration clerk who would clip them into moistureproof bags with identifying labels and our diagnosis was to be made as rapidly as possible through the cellophane without removal of the specimen. I protested that looking at specimens through an unopened bag savored of quackery (though with present experience I could probably do ninety per cent of the material that way), so Irene and I were dressed up in white lab coats and stationed, each with a microscope, at opposite ends of a long table. Bamberger's had put a cute ad in the paper, with plant patients on stretchers and a couple of surgeons and a nurse bending over, and we did get quite a lot of customers.

We were greener than grass in practical lines, but we didn't know it yet and some of the time we stumbled on the right answers. Irene had to tell one man that the insect he brought in for identification was a human rather than a plant louse. I had a strange case of "mildew" on a moss rose which turned out to be white, fuzzy hair, the rose being grown under a window used for shaking out the dust mop.

We signed in and out each day as Bamberger employees, used their lunchroom, and could have made purchases at their discount. We didn't have money to buy anything for we were doing this for EXPERIENCE and expenses. We didn't even pad the expense account. I have the carbon of the bill I presented for hotel room and meals for five days—$21.80.

Along with experience we acquired a few prospective clients and on June 20th gave our first consultation, in West Orange. We provided an Entomologist's report and a Plant Pathologist's report, all neatly typed out for the huge fee of three dollars. The entomologist found on that day: willow leaf beetle, European pine shoot moth, birch leaf miner, pear leaf blister mite, and assorted aphids. The plant pathologist found rose mildew, hollyhock rust, laurel leaf blight, weather injury on rhododendron, crown rot on delphinium and sweet william. In another garden that day I got out on a limb

and declared that the leaf spots on the cherry tree were not disease
but came from the tree being sprayed with the same lead arsenate
mixture used on street trees. I was quite relieved when the Experiment Station confirmed that diagnosis.

By this time I had another Ford, the old model A having been
left in Ithaca. Frank had told me that if I wanted to get the new
Ford in Montclair, where he had a hundred dollars credit left over
from his work on the Reservoir, I could have half of it toward my
car. I journeyed back and forth from New Brunswick to Montclair,
by train and trolley, until I had learned to drive a gear-shift car and
had obtained a license. The last day of July, 1933, I loaded all the
New Brunswick paraphernalia into the Ford, Irene brought her load
from Yonkers, and we moved in with the painters at 96 Essex
Avenue, Glen Ridge.

CHAPTER 3

THE BIG CHANCE

S omeone once remarked to me that I must have an excellent press agent to get so much publicity. Irene and I never had a press agent and we never did any advertising as plant doctors, for we were determined to operate exactly as a medical doctor, but we did have friends interested in our welfare and reporters were naturally curious about this new profession for women. I had no illusions about making money right off; I planned to rent rooms and do anything else necessary to keep my head above water without sacrificing professional ethics.

We got the house livable as quickly as possible, using the antique furniture I had in Ithaca, a little new maple furniture to go with the old, and a lot of second-hand tables, desks and files for the office. Within two weeks the Dutch elm disease brought us our first paying guest. Our friend Anna Jenkins in Washington told Neil Stevens, Senior Pathologist for the Plant Disease Survey (and also a friend), what we were doing. He immediately sent us a carbon of his letter to the men scouting for the disease from East Orange.

"Gentlemen:

My attention has been called to the fact that Miss Cynthia
Westcott is now operating at 96 Essex Avenue, Glen Ridge,
New Jersey—Telephone 2-8424-J—a very high class tourist home at
which plant pathologists, when properly introduced, will be given
special consideration. Please consider this letter as an introduction.
I wish to blazes I was with you."

But Neil soon was with us, for the night of August 14th. We
bought a Guest Book with his lodging money and had all the boys
over from East Orange for tea so it was more fun than profit.

When someone advertised kittens in the Glen Ridge paper we
acquired black Graphium and gray Ulmi, *Graphium ulmi* being the
name of the Dutch elm disease fungus at that time. It has another
name now. Graphium had too many kittens and eventually was given
up but Ulmi was master of the household for many years. He hated
visitors and would glare at anyone who sat in his favorite chair. I
polticed his swollen limbs with Epsom salts every time he got infected
in a fight, I nursed him through a hard bout with pneumonia, but
I finally lost him to jaundice.

Kittens sleeping in the window brought us our first permanent
roomer that fall. I believed what I read about the ways to get acquainted in a strange place and was becoming a joiner. Of the two
churches in Glen Ridge, the Congregational was nearer my original
Universalist creed, so I transferred membership there. Stopping at
the Church office to see if they knew of any schoolteachers or other
women wanting rooms, I learned the Church Secretary was herself
looking for one. When she saw Graphium and Ulmi she decided that
if we were kind to kittens we might be kind to her. Ruth was a
wonderful addition but if she could have foreseen her hard lot that
winter she might have decided otherwise.

Anna Jenkins wanted to give us our shingle and have it painted
by an artist but Irene and I decided on a plain green board, to match
the trim of the house, with nothing but THE PLANT DOCTOR
in black letters.

My house, a two and a half story affair with peaked roof, was nothing I would have chosen had it not been for the land. Its chief redeeming feature was the screened porch on front and side, the only thing that helps me survive New Jersey summer heat and humidity. We did brighten up the inside. The front room was the office. The old dining room had the big colored glass dome removed, shelves built under the bay window for a combination window seat and bookcase, the dark woodwork painted ivory, and became a living room. We planned to use it for small garden groups and soon entertained the Garden Department of the Millburn Woman's Club. I tried to explain plant disease and Irene talked about insects. We were too technical, as are most people fresh out of a university, but this was promptly remedied. A frequent comment since then has been, "She talks so we can understand but she doesn't talk down to us." People hate to be patronized; we are all gardeners together.

GETTING STARTED

We were getting extremely favorable publicity in the newspapers. The New Jersey Experiment Station sent out a news release the day I left for this new work and arranged various interviews that were reported at length in Glen Ridge, Montclair, and Newark papers. The Station had a Radio Garden Club program and on October 13th we talked on "Giving Your Garden Its Fall Examination." We met The Proxy Gardeners in Glen Ridge, two women who helped other people garden, and they arranged some work for us. Irene spent an occasional day going around estates in Westchester and advising a tree concern there. I renewed friendship with Clara Hires, a Wellesley classmate, and thus got a foothold in Short Hills gardens.

We met a couple of young men starting out with a landscape service. We threw a little work their way and they helped fix up our back hill with a path wandering between boulders. I planted the hill with wildflowers and many plants donated by fellow gardeners. For a year the landscape company maintained my place. Their efforts were supposed to be confined to mowing the lawn, doing a little edging. I came home one day to find they had had a little extra time and zeal and had "weeded" the back hill. Practically everything I had planted with such loving care was gone. I never employed a maintenance firm again.

Roses went in that first autumn. I drove back to Cornell, dug up some of the Dr. Van Fleet climbers used in the brand canker experiments, brought them home bare-rooted, and set them out along the privet hedge. They have flourished practically untended ever since.

My next-door neighbor, who sometimes gardened for others, helped me prepare rose beds according to the formula considered best at that time. We dug out the soil nearly three feet deep and put in a drainage layer. When I bought the property the front lawn had been decorated with a life-size china Dalmatian dog and big round pieces of tile in which petunias were growing. The dog went with the owners and I smashed up the tile for drainage. I wielded the sledge hammer with extra vigor one day and a bit of tile flew into a wasp's nest in the lawn. The yellow jackets and I raced for the house. They won, and got inside my clothes before I could get them ripped off. I spent the next several days in bed.

The rose bushes came from Bobbink and Atkins, thirty cents apiece wholesale in those days. The nursery told me to put brush on top of the drainage layer, upturned sod on top of that, then topsoil mixed with lots of manure, ending up with bottomsoil. There were six beds of fifteen hybrid teas each, the same varieties repeated in the beds for spray tests, and two beds of hybrid perpetuals. In addition to the roses purchased, I was given thirty others they considered too poor or too sick to sell. We put them along the shrub line in the back garden and most of them are still living today.

Another major event of the first autumn was the acquisition of a gallon of alcohol for our laboratory, for those were prohibition days. It took weeks to get a permit to buy alcohol, with "the maximum quantity to be possessed at any one time not to exceed one gallon for preserving plants and insects for scientific purposes."

Both our signatures were required and we had to swear that we would keep the alcohol padlocked at all times.

The rest of the fall was spent collecting specimens, making cultures, going to garden short courses, and meetings. I joined the Glen Ridge Women's Club, the Montclair Garden Club, the League of Women Voters, the Business and Professional Women's Club, the American Association of University Women, the Horticultural Society of New York, but later I had to secede from groups not strictly allied to gardening.

Ever-helpful Rutgers offered us winter work, under one of the depression projects similar to WPA. On December 1st we started commuting the thirty-five miles each way four days a week. That was the first day of snow and the beginning of New Jersey's hardest winter, with the temperature going down to fourteen below zero and staying well below zero most of the time. We alternated transportation but neither my Ford nor Irene's Dodge had a heater. We left before daylight and returned after dark. Poor Ruth Martin came home to a cold house after her work each day; sometimes she managed hot soup for our arrival. The service station did not put enough antifreeze in the radiator of the Ford and it froze standing outside our building at the Experiment Station. It was towed to a garage and thawed out but froze up again driving home. Such a winter!

A few clients had been lined up for spring and I made the mistake of taking gardens on contract, with the price too low to cover such extras as being asked to drive downtown and pick up a turkey when the client's three cars and a chauffeur were otherwise engaged. We gave various talks, mostly for free. My first lecture on roses was for the Montclair Free Time Guild.

Irene was approached by the Pennsylvania Salt Manufacturing Company and asked to test the effect of cryolite on bees. So we put a hive of bees in the attic and Irene insisted their stings helped her tendency to arthritis. By summer she was working full-time on this project. We dissolved our formal partnership but Irene continued to live and work at the house until marriage a year later. I continued to give garden inspections and make reports and had about fifteen regular patients where I did all the spraying and dusting myself each week. In addition I had taken in two more roomers and was preparing dinners nightly for five.

I went back to Massachusetts to a Wellesley reunion in June and gave my first *paid* lecture to the Topsfield Garden Club, to which a Wellesley classmate belonged. In July I acquired Solomon, a young colored boy who was quite unable to live up to his name. I bought him a white coat and figured on using him as a butler as well as a spraying assistant. I left him to serve dinner to the girls one night when I had an engagement but he tried to put on so much pomp and circumstance they didn't get much to eat. I put him at the door when we had a large party, to direct people upstairs to leave their coats, and one of the guests came to me convulsed, "Do you know what he's saying? He is telling everyone the lavatory is upstairs."

Solomon was with me four years, then sent his cousin to take his place. I have not seen him since but apparently he still uses me as a reference. Every year or two someone calls up and asks about his qualifications as a house man. I carefully avoid comment on that and say that he was my assistant in garden work.

Iris borers and crown rot occupied me most of that summer. One client got me to spend a day with her dipping iris rhizomes in carbolic acid because she heard that at a garden club meeting. It should have been corrosive sublimate (mercuric chloride) but she insisted on the carbolic and I did not want to antagonize her by refusing. Later I had no compunctions in this line. I lost another client because I could not perform miracles. I carefully explained that there was only a slight chance that I could prevent the cyclamen mite from crippling her aconite but that she would get her money's worth in other control work in the garden. When the aconite did not clear up immediately I was dismissed with a bang.

Along with bills I sent each client a detailed report of what I had done and why. That, too, was a mistake. One woman said she would not need me another year; she could just follow my reports.

Our own garden took time. Elizabeth Bodger had sent us seeds of lots of annuals, some new and very valuable. Liz wrote, "The very small packet of Scarlet Gleam (nasturtium) is a prize, no less— treat it kindly with the greatest respect. It is our pet for this fall and not many people have been favored with a trial packet of it." Golden Gleam, the first double nasturtium, had been a Bodger triumph. Now they and their competitors were in a race to produce more double hybrids, of which Scarlet Gleam was one.

The rose test plots gave such interesting results in 1934 that I sent a glowing report to Dr. Massey and invited Mr. Rosenbluth of the Rose Manufacturing Company, producer of Fungtrogen and Tri-ogen, to come look at them. I had used Fungtrogen at Cornell with poor results but now the new Tri-ogen spray was performing better than the standard sulfur-lead arsenate rose dust. Dr. Massey thought it too difficult to use and too expensive to be practical but I don't think I could have stayed in business without it. Ever since 1934 I have tested new dusts and sprays in my rose garden but I still use Tri-ogen for clients. It takes care of most pests with one mixture and is safe in our hot New Jersey summers.

Anna Jenkins sent an SOS from Washington, asking me to meet the boat when Dr. and Mme. A. A. Bitancourt arrived in New York from Paris. He was head of plant pathology at the Instituto Biologico at São Paulo, Brazil, and negotiations were under way for Anna to work there with him on Sphaceloma, a genus she had been studying for years. I was a bit miffed for I had neither time nor money for entertaining strangers but I went. They were a charming couple and we took to each other instantly. Dr. Bitancourt went Americans one better in the speed with which he accomplished things. Inside a day he had purchased an automobile, passed a driver's test, obtained a license, and had negotiated the Holland Tunnel traffic out to Glen Ridge. They were house guests but I had no entertaining to do. They took me out to dinner and to the theater. They were much interested in my new profession and when they went to Washington for a week before sailing back to Brazil I kept a diary of a few plant doctor days to send as a steamer letter. It is as good a record as any of what I was doing in those early days.

PLANT DOCTOR DIARY
(*Late September, 1934*) *Wednesday*

"*7:30.* Start breakfast and Solomon arrives. I set him digging a rose bed, two spades deep. He does not understand that so I tell him to dig a ditch. I tell him about drainage on the bottom, sod next, and humus incorporated into the soil but he looks so blank I say, "Come and tell me when you have the ditch dug.""

"*8:30.* The plants are too wet to work with so I stay home and write business letters, dashing out every fifteen minutes to superintend the next step in the rose bed. I write a report for a garden inspected ten days ago. Luckily it had been serviced then so its crying needs have been taken care of. I blamed the delay on official duties in connection with Brazilian scientists. Write and tell Anna that the Bitancourts are nice people—grand people—but that she cannot possibly do anything for them without having it returned twicefold.

"*11:00.* Mr. A's garden, still soaking wet but there is no help for that. Put Tri-ogen on about 200 roses. There is some blackspot because I was not given charge of the garden until the first of July and that is too late to control. There is a small locust tree simply covered with gray aphids. Did I miss that last week or have they suddenly arrived in such numbers during the bad weather? A dogwood looks very sick; it may be borer but the slits in the bark can be injury from last winter. If I cut to find the borer I may kill the tree anyway so I paint the trunk with some new stuff supposed to penetrate the bark enough to kill borers. Two peony plants are simply covered with Botrytis spores and sclerotia. I remove the stalks and keep them for specimens; they are excellent. Put sulfur dust on lilacs, zinnias, and phlox for mildew. The dust gets in my eyes and I know from experience I'll have to cry every particle out before I can sleep tonight.

"*12:30.* Home for lunch. It is hot and I am too weary to get anything but fruit and iced coffee.

"*1:30.* Mrs. B's garden. I have been going here twice a week, once to put on a spray for aphids and once to dust the roses. Last week I thought I would change to Tri-ogen and have to come only once a week the remainder of the fall. But I see some yellow leaves on the roses—can it be that following sulfur dust with a copper spray would cause injury? I do not think so but it makes me uneasy. Earlier in the season the Eupatorium was infected with *Sclerotium delphinii* and there are faint signs of a recurrence; I scatter naphthalene flakes around. Azaleas and lilacs are dusted for mildew. As usual, Septoria leaf spot is turning the lower leaves of the chrysanthemums black. I wish someone knew something definite about the control of this. Would you have to use a copper spray all season or would August and September do? There are fine examples of Plasmopara on the grapes so I collect specimens. Mrs. B. is a charming woman; she is a true gardener and does not expect the impossible. She offers plants for my garden, as she has done before, and I accept gratefully. But I wonder if it is good policy to do that sort of thing with clients.

"*2:30.* Home to put in the new plants and get into respectable clothes.

"*3:30.* Order notebooks and paper in Montclair and open a charge account for The Plant Doctor to pay for same. Here's hoping enough money comes in to cover it. These are for outlines for the class I am giving at home in "The Cause and Cure of Plant Disease."

"*4:00.* Mrs. C., over the telephone and by letter, has several times asked for free advice, each time saying she would probably call me in next year. I decide to look at her garden now to see what its troubles will likely be next year. She informs me she has no trouble and that her flowers took all the prizes but I find plenty of work, some of which should be started this fall.

"*4:30.* Mr. D. wants to know why all the maple leaves are falling off while they are still green. I improvise on the theme of physiological conditions causing a premature abscission layer.

"*5:00.* Mr. E. thinks he has some new disease on his marigolds, does not believe me when I intimate it is ordinary Botrytis blight. He pays no attention to the really serious iris borers, blackspot and mildew on his roses, and, when I congratulate him on getting second prize in the Garden Contest, grumbles that he doesn't know how the judges did their work—best garden anywhere around.

"*6:30.* Scramble up some dinner (my roomers are out) and read the new *House & Garden.* Dr. Guterman, colleague at Cornell, has an article on 'The Plant Doctor Looks at Lilies.'

"*8:00.* Someone telephones to inquire if he can weatherstrip my house. This happens at least once every day—usually they try to convince me the world will come to an end if I do not put on a new roof or install a new oil burner immediately. I work on the specimens collected today.

"*10:00.* Ruth telephones she has finished the mimeographing she was doing for me, a notice about the forthcoming class, so I drive over after her.

Thursday

"*8:30.* Test pH of a soil sample. I use a crude colorimetric method with a spot plate and set of indicators but it seems reliable. Most New Jersey soil is acid but the public has learned the idea of putting on lime only too well, for many gardens now err on the alkaline side.

"*9:00.* At Montclair Library to arrange for an exhibit on Saturday.

"*10:00.* Arrive Short Hills. Try to work in gardens but find every plant dripping wet from dew and fog. Plant pathologists who sit in offices and write articles always advise dusting plants when the dew is on but if I tried it just once I am sure I would lose every shred of my reputation. Dust a plant when it is wet and the stuff goes on in thick mats which do not wear off the entire season. Dusting potatoes and dusting ornamentals are in different worlds. I had planned to make four visits before noon but return home with nothing done, disgusted with the time and gasoline wasted.

"*2:00.* Collect Mrs. F., client and friend, and drive to Paterson to

call on her cousin whose roses have not bloomed well. Find she
bought them from a department store with the usual result. They
need surgical treatment, which I apply. I sell a 75-cent duster, charge
for a half-hour of service.

"5:40. Read the evening paper and start dinner. This over I can
settle down to make some potato dextrose agar. Nice economy measure, use the water for agar and have the potatoes next day for lunch.

"9:30. Get tubes and flasks in the pressure cooker and type these
lines as I watch it.

Friday

"8:00. Instructed Solomon in the art of washing petri dishes. I am
going to try to make a lab boy out of him. Put dishes (wrapped in
brown paper) in the oven to be sterilized.

"9:00. Get off letters and circulars about my course; spray my own
roses.

"11:30. Mr. G. comes to see my rose experiments and unexpectedly
I make a contact I have been wanting for months. A wealthy woman
has a lot of expensive boxwood that looks to me, as I drive by in the
car, to be seriously infected with Nectria canker. When I showed
box specimens to Mr. G. he said that Mrs. X had been in his store
that morning and that he, from her description, had recommended
O.K. Plant Spray. That is entirely the wrong thing for canker so he
made an appointment for me for tomorrow. I only hope it amounts
to something; at least I'll have a chance to satisfy my curiosity. Start
to Short Hills. Collect our local weekly on the way and find out
that the interview given a reporter a week ago is splashed on the
front page.

"1:00. Dust roses and lilacs. Mrs. H. is just back from vacation and
the garden is so overgrown it scarcely pays for me to do any control
work. She is a vague person who likes to talk about gardening and
is president of a garden club but someway never manages to do any.

"1:30. Mrs. I. The gardener says that madame is much distressed by whiteflies on the hollyhocks, ageratum, nicotiana etc. I sprayed for these on Monday but it did not do any good; might as well try to stem the Atlantic Ocean. Mix up a lot more expensive spray. The weather this September has certainly spoiled things for the gardens I took on contract. This place, my largest, I took for a hundred dollars. I have already spent thirty dollars for material and much more than a hundred hours in time, to say nothing of gasoline, and I still have to work several hours a week for another month. I dust the roses; take out diseased peonies; observe anthracnose on the snap-dragon and wonder if I should have sprayed for it; dust lilacs and dahlias for mildew. Collect excellent specimens of mildew on grape. "*3:30.* Since I was here a week ago half the zinnias have gone down with Botrytis, due to the rain, and others have Cercospora on the leaves. I have been dusting with sulfur for weeks to prevent mildew and now look what I get instead!

"*4:15.* A box of a garden which needs only a few minutes twice a week but I have to make the extra stop and unpack all equipment. "*5:30.* Get a light supper and read a story while I eat it from a tray (boarders away). Build a furnace fire to dry pressed specimens more quickly. Fix up the exhibit for the Montclair Library and am quite pleased with it: an assorted collection of mildews, fresh and pre-served, grand rose blackspot showing lesions on the canes, all kinds of Botrytis material, a poster of boxwood canker that is quite striking. I have selected for exhibit only those diseases rampant locally at the present moment. I pour agar plates and can at last make cultures.

Saturday

"Terrible weather for a plant doctor. I wake to the tune of pouring rain. It is all I can do to get the exhibit to Montclair; there can be no work in gardens. One has been waiting since Thursday and my own roses have their experimental treatments three days overdue. The appointment with the boxwood lady is postponed to Sunday. I do the Saturday marketing and first-of-the-month accounts.

"I think I can show Solomon a little about cooking and waiting on table but he comes and says, 'Mis West', yo goin' to let me go home now?' I inquire for the reason and he says that the work I sent him to do down cellar made him sick. I think it a put-up job to get Saturday afternoon off (he took all Thursday off and asked to work Saturday instead) but I finally let him go. I alter a dress bought for October lectures. I have no money for new clothes but if people have to sit and look at me! I wonder if I can get my hands clean in the next week; have not been able to do much with them since outdoor work started last March.

"Ulmi and I are alone for the weekend and we love it. Tonight is a great treat; lobster was cheap in market today. I eat the meat and Ulmi has a grand time crunching shells. Along with the lobster I consume David Fairchild's *Exploring for Plants*. I cannot think why I have not read this before. It was thrust upon me today by the librarian in Montclair. The first part of the book deals with so many people and herbaria I know in Europe I am quite homesick. (Can you be homesick for countries not your own?) I finally tear myself away and go back to the accounts. First of the month is a sad time, when I figure up how little I have taken in and how much I have spent for business expenses. I can hang on until next spring but if things do not break better next summer the plant doctor will be just another mirage. I would not worry if I had not been fairly busy this summer and charged what seemed to me right prices. I was evidently wrong.

Sunday

"Raining again, a good time for breakfast in bed with the Sunday papers. The boxwood appointment is postponed again and I spend the day making out bills. My cousins send for me to tell them about some plants. I walk over, for exercise and to save gasoline, but the calories walked off are regained by tea and cakes.

Monday

"*6:30.* One good thing about the change back to Standard Time; the sun gets you up an hour earlier and the plants dry off that much sooner.

"*9:00.* To Upper Montclair and back for a half-hour's work dusting roses and lilacs for mildew.

"*10:00.* Treat my own roses.

"*11:00.* Start out and stop for gas. Idly look inside my purse to see if the license is there and to my consternation find it is not. Hurry home and find it in the purse I took to New York last Tuesday. There surely is a Providence that watches over fools. I'm glad it was not this week the Glen Ridge policeman stopped me for speeding and demanded to see my credentials. When he found I was a working girl and not a society matron hastening to a luncheon he let me off with a warning.

"*11:45.* Stop to work 15 minutes and listen to the woman the rest of the hour. I never can get a word in edgewise, even to leave. She raves on about how much she pays for stockings, how many shoes she buys per year, how much her husband leaves for tips which is why she had to give him all her change and cannot pay my bill to-day. Sometimes we touch on gardening topics. When I express incredulity in what the county agent said (she probably did not understand him) she says, "Well, even doctors disagree, don't they?" I assure her fervently that they do and beat a hasty retreat.

"*12:45.* I drive on through the reservation and stop at my favorite spot to eat lunch. It is a perfect October day; the life of a plant doctor is not so bad if it keeps you outdoors. I wander through the woods and note interesting Discomycetes, the kind I used to collect with Professor Whetzel.

"*1:30.* Purchase more spray and tree paint. The wet September has made bug control expensive.

"*2:00.* Not much to do—a little sulfur dust and a few diseased blossoms to pick off.

"*2:30.* Lots to do here. I spray all the roses for aphids and the hollyhocks for whiteflies. Slugs are chewing up the new growth of the primulas so I mix up lead arsenate. Something is chewing funkia and saxifrage. I spray the chrysanthemums.

"*4:00.* Not much needed in this garden except a spray for aphids on roses. The butler is sent out with a ten-dollar bill to cover August work here. I was so glad to see it I could have kissed it.

"*4:30.* Ten minutes is enough here.

"*5:00.* Pick a dishpan full of my own flowers in case frost, which seems inevitable tonight, spoils everything; take fresh specimens to the Montclair exhibit, trading for those too far gone. Stop by the church to pick up Ruth and serve dinner in more formal fashion than the weekend dining by myself.

"*7:30.* So many things to do, I can't decide which. I read *Science, Mycologia,* the *Rural New Yorker* and New Jersey bulletins in to-day's mail, answer letters, visit the furnace. From now until June my comings and goings will be planned around the furnace as a task-master. I must get up at six on winter mornings to have the house warm for the roomers and in below-zero weather I will almost literally sit up with it all night to make sure the plumbing does not freeze.

Tuesday

"*9:00.* At last it is a good day for the boxwood lady. I am neatly dressed in a suit, not the wash dress I usually wear for dirty spraying operations, and present myself promptly for the appointment. Mrs. X is not in. I inspect the box, never saw so much before in one New Jersey garden. Before last winter's cold it must have been worth a mint of money; now it has much dead wood and some Nectria canker which will become more without immediate attention. I wait until 10:15, then Mrs. X can give me only five minutes; she is off for New York. I point out the troubles and discuss remedies, indicating my expert guidance could be used in removing cankered material. She assures me her gardener is perfectly capable of doing anything necessary. Capable, my eye! He thought the spore pustules were mealybugs and wanted to spray with nicotine! I withdraw gracefully, thinking of the difference between a three-dollar inspection fee and the hoped-for week's work. Next year I'll charge more for inspection but this will scare out the small homeowners I'd like to help. A graded fee is scarcely possible in communities where rich and poor belong to the same garden club and Mrs. B. already knows how much you charged Mrs. A. before she calls you in.

"*10:30.* Home to change into washable clothes and off to spray chrysanthemums and roses. This is the first year I have noticed mildew on azaleas; the backs of the leaves are completely covered with perithecia. I dust for this (too late) and for mildew on lilacs.

"*11:30.* My nice Mrs. B. After dealing with a few other women I wax lyrical over her. She always understands situations and always pays her bill promptly. I treat the roses, then discover all the new hollyhock leaves are simply covered with rust pustules. Did all this happen in the rainy week since I was here last or is it another case of not observing accurately and quickly enough? All the early part of the season I kept sulfur on hollyhocks which, after blooming, I thought safe until next year. I remove the worst of the leaves, plaster the rest with sulfur.

"*12:20.* This garden near home has so few plants in it I visit it only when there is some spray left in the tank.

"*12:30.* Home for lunch. Try again to teach Solomon something about cooking but he merely succeeds in burning the toast.

"*1:30.* Dress up again and walk to the Glen Ridge Women's Club. I joined for personal reasons, to get acquainted in the community where I live, and for business, to be known to the gardening women of this community. I am to be guest speaker at the Garden Department this month which will surely bring to their attention the fact that a plant doctor is available in their midst. I was surprised when they offered to pay for the talk; I thought as a club member I would be expected to do it for nothing. This afternoon I heard Albert Wiggam, author of *Decalogue of Science,* talk on the marks of an educated man in this changing world.

"*5:30.* Collect the car, deliver a dust gun and some dust, take more specimens to fix up the exhibit at the Montclair Library."

SIDE LINES

Somewhat to my surprise the little class in Practical Plant Pathology that started in October attracted schoolteachers rather than gardeners. For a five-dollar fee there were five two-hour sessions, with tea or coffee provided during the question-and-answer period, so it did not add much income. It was a lot of fun and I learned more than the students. I had discovered dodder in the perennial border. Dodder is that parasitic plant with orange tendrils and pretty little white flowers that wraps itself around, and sends suckers into, self-respecting plants. Thinking it a fine example for the class I let it set seed in the garden instead of immediately cutting out all the tops of chrysanthemums and other plants it had latched onto. I fought dodder in my garden for the next ten years.

The course that I took that fall was bookkeeping, at a business college in Newark. All I learned was that I could not possibly afford the time to keep books myself in the approved fashion and there would certainly never be money enough to employ a bookkeeper. I evolved a simple, almost-no-work system which I still use. The time spent for each client and the amount of materials used are put in a field notebook at the end of each job. On the last day of the month, I put these visits on 3 x 5 cards, one for each client, then sort them out alphabetically. Bills are made out directly from the cards, with carbons for my records; addresses are taken from carbons of previous month's bills. All incoming and outgoing money is listed in the checkbook and on the last day of the year copied into a ledger in the various categories. Not until then do I know whether I have made anything over expenses nor how much I owe the government. If I did enough bookkeeping to know where I stand each month I would have been out of The Plant Doctor business long since.

The November 17th issue of *Florists Exchange* carried an editorial, "Women Scientists Pioneer in Plant Doctor Field," by E. L. D. Seymour, who has been mentor and friend ever since. Ned Seymour touched off the writing side of my life when he asked me to contribute the material on plant enemies for *The Garden Encyclopedia* he was editing for William H. Wise and Company. The pay was not excessive, supposedly $7.50 per 1000 words, but I ended up with so many words (100,000) it was reduced to $5 per thousand. Separate paragraphs had to be prepared for all the plants on which I could find any information as to pests. The files of abstracts I had been accumulating through the years and my personal subscriptions to many scientific periodicals now paid off, I could work at home rather than journey to scientific libraries. Even so, it took a vast amount of time. I'd sometimes spend a day digging out facts that were condensed into seventeen (or perhaps only seven) words.

I went to Pittsburgh to the A.A.A.S. (American Association for the Advancement of Science) meetings that Christmas to learn what phytopathologists were doing that could be used for the Encyclopedia. I traveled by bus to save money and returned exhausted to find Ruth Martin in bed with flu. After nursing her for a day or two I went to bed myself, where I decided that if I were to complete those 100,000 words and carry out other commitments I'd have to have a housekeeper to keep the boarders happy and fed.

Slavia, who used to work for Ruth's uncle, came to see me and we worked out a rather unusual arrangement. I wrote to Professor Whetzel, who had told me in Pittsburgh I must have more help, "I will pay Slavia $15 a month to keep the house clean and to answer the telephone when I am out. I will give her a good room and the use of the kitchen for getting meals. Then we will all board with her and pay extra for personal laundry, mending, and the like.

Slavia now has a good position paying $60 a month but she is lonesome and has long hours. I am underwriting her to the extent of $50 a month for six months. That is, I am betting the scheme will work; if it doesn't, I will make up the difference personally. It means that I pay Slavia for my own breakfasts and dinners but it will keep me from being imposed upon. The roomers will realize they have to pay for extra service and Slavia will be on her toes to keep costs low. If anyone is sick, she can take charge."

The system worked fine; Slavia was quick and intelligent and an excellent cook. She made well over the minimum pledged and still had lots of free time for herself. In fact, she was making stacks more than I was by writing but again I was getting experience.

I was still in bed with the flu when I added up plant doctor accounts for 1934, the first full season. Income $977.18; expenses $942.43; total profit $34.75. I was not dismayed; to break even the first year seemed about all anyone could expect but the roomers were sure coming in handy. So was a temporary job I took in Bloomfield. One of the concerns whose legume inoculants I had tested in New Brunswick (and often found unsatisfactory) suggested that I oversee operations in their laboratory for a month or two that winter. The dollar an hour pay was most welcome.

All the lecture money received in 1935 went for illustrations. In February, I went to a Garden Department meeting and heard Meta Shirrefs lecture on "Any Woman's Small Garden." Her illustrations were poster-size water colors of plants, and some insects, strikingly painted to show up well in a large auditorium. I asked the speaker if she sold her paintings. She had not, but agreed to do some for me, working from fresh specimens of diseases and pests as I ran across them in gardens and brought them to her in Elizabeth.

Such success as I have had in lecturing is largely due to Mrs. Shirrefs' water colors. They are clear, bold, and accurate. Everyone comments on their beauty, even those who think the subjects unpleasant. They are a welcome change from lantern slides in a dark room. People can take notes and I can watch faces, enlarging on items that seem to strike home, sliding over those that elicit no response. The pictures are a foolproof method of remembering what I want to say; I need only sort out those suitable for a particular time and place.

Because I was a struggling plant doctor Meta kept her fee ridiculously low. I was ashamed of taking so much work for such a small recompense but I needed lots of pictures and Meta liked to paint. She was for many years head of the Elizabeth Garden Center, now the Meta Shirrefs Garden Club, and has always been interested in insects as well as flowers. Despite being carried around the country for hundreds of lectures, most of her original paintings are still in use; a few have been replaced with fresh copy. Everywhere they have delighted audiences that expected to be bored with garden pests. I hereby tender a public "Thank you" to Meta P. Shirrefs for all that she has done for me and for the promotion of garden pest control.

I also obtained a liberal education from Meta's garden, for she grew practically everything she talked about in lectures. Tommy, the bull frog, and I were great friends. He started croaking every time he heard my voice but not when others talked. There must have been something in my New England twang that set him vibrating.

The first paintings went to illustrate an exhibit requested by the School Nature League at the Natural History Museum in New York and later to the Children's Science Fair. It takes an extraordinary amount of time to prepare, set up, and take down exhibits; yet I never seem able to refuse.

BACK TO WORK

Solomon and I started doctoring gardens again in March, beginning with a dormant spray. Charging by the hour, though only $2.50 for us both, was much better than taking a garden for a set price for the season. I stipulated that I be allowed to come as often as necessary to take care of the more important problems but said I would not waste time where the expected control would not be worth the cost of treatment.

I was fairly cautious in using chemicals and seldom had a case of spray injury. Once the weather turned unexpectedly cold right after putting a dormant oil spray on a spruce; there was considerable browning. Once I was unwise enough to feed a tree when it already was on its last legs; when it died, I got blamed. Generally, however, results were pretty good and clients quite satisfied.

I did pull one awful boner in replying about a specimen sent by mail. I had never met, in 1935, the Vespa hornet, nor seen the way it can tear off bark around a lilac branch. When a chewed-around lilac twig came in, I wrote that it was the work of a squirrel and had nerve enough to send a small bill. It wasn't paid, thank heavens, and when I later realized my error I vowed never again to charge for advice given by mail, or over the telephone, when I had no way of knowing all the circumstances or time to dig up pertinent information. Usually people don't offer to pay, they don't even send a stamp for reply, but occasionally someone encloses a check or asks me to send a bill. When I returned payment to a doctor in Vermont after answering a question on roses, he sent a gallon of maple syrup back. I kept it in the refrigerator and used the syrup as a special treat over many months, blessing the good doctor each time. Another unexpected pleasure was a rosebud cup and saucer, of English bone china, sent from California by a woman who had read the rose book in a hospital and had written to ask where she could get certain varieties.

All the plant doctor money that spring, after paying for supplies and labor, went toward an oil burner to keep the housekeeper warm. In those two terribly cold first winters I had never once let the furnace go out, for it was banked during the day when we were all away. Now with someone at home to open up the furnace and forget to add coal later I was having to dump ashes and start a new fire when I came in exhausted at night; hence the oil burner.

I can't figure out how I have kept in business all these years for I continue to operate in the same unprofitable manner, each new step leading to greater expense. The Wellesley Botany Department asked me to come back that spring and talk to the girls about my new profession, but I could not scare up the travel money. I wrote them, "I still think Plant Doctoring is a fine field, after I get the public educated. However, it would take someone overwhelmingly interested in this sort of thing to battle against the odds at the present time."

Professor Whetzel seemed to think I was doing well enough to take on a girl apprentice. Margaret was a Charleston debutante turned serious and taking plant pathology at Cornell. Prof wanted to send her to me to determine if she should do graduate work in this field. Feeling as I did about the prejudice against women and willing to do anything for Prof in return for his many kindnesses to me, I agreed to take her on for spring and summer vacation. Margaret was a most attractive girl and a willing worker but I was crazy. I had my hands full trying to earn enough to pay Solomon and Slavia. Despite interest in helping women I have no work for a woman. I need only the husky right arm of a man to pump the sprayer, to load and unload the car. We can't use more than two people on a job efficiently and trying to teach a third person means slowing up the work and doing half as many jobs as usual in one day.

I tried turning over some of the experimental work in my own garden but I learned then, as I keep learning whenever I am rash enough to hire someone with a little knowledge of this subject, that the college-trained person will do what they think you *meant* (according to what they have been taught) and not literally what you *say*. An untrained person can be trusted to follow directions literally. In my work it is vital to have directions followed to the letter even if they do not agree with some of the teaching in academic halls. I could not dictate letters to Margaret because she had no shorthand. She could type and I finally kept her busy abstracting information needed for the Encyclopedia.

All that hot summer I sprayed all day and wrote up Plant Enemies for *The Garden Encyclopedia* all night. It was so hot that even at midnight the sweat would be pouring down my face and my fingers sticking to the typewriter. Like most writers I wanted my stuff used as written and of course all editors feel they know better. It is a tribute to Ned Seymour's forbearance that we remained friends for I battled furiously for every point. He conceded a lot of them and acknowledged courteously and immediately every batch of copy sent in. That is unusual. Sometimes I don't know an article has been received until it appears in print. On September 5th I still had 17,000 words to grind out before the September 13th deadline but I made it, then celebrated with a few days' vacation in the Poconos.

Irene had been married in June to her apple farmer and had moved to the Hudson Valley. We had had a garden luncheon and shower for her when the lilacs bloomed on a sunny Sunday in May. Solomon dressed up again in his white coat and condescendingly asked Slavia, who was doing all the work, if she would help him serve. The effort was too much; the next day he sent around Justin with a note stating he was an "onest boy."

After Irene, the head of the Glen Ridge Library was here until she found an apartment and a woman in social service. We had two permanent guests connected with a publishing firm and, for a few weeks, a woman from the West Coast to complete some children's books. She was A AUTHOR, not just an author. I have no recollection of the name of this children's writer, nor did I see her books, but I remember vividly their importance. She had to have meals in her room; she wouldn't take time for exercise so in place of it I had to drive her to a doctor twice a week for injections with some medication brought along from her home physician. Any time I have delusions of grandeur and think of myself as A AUTHOR I can quickly cut myself down to size by remembering the time one lived in my house. Then it is easy to know that I am merely a pedestrian writer passing along factual and technical material.

I was doing a fair amount of lecturing. Talking to a group of

college women in New York in early May I learned that spittle bugs
and some other insects, commonly met in suburban gardens, also visit
penthouse gardens on top of tall city buildings. A lecture date in
late May, at Millbrook, New York, proved a red-letter day indeed
for I met Mrs. Oakleigh Thorne. Staying after the lecture to give
a few garden consulations the next morning I was invited for lunch
at Thorndale, one of the finest estates in the East. From that day
until her death Mrs. Thorne was extraordinarily kind to me, her
first gesture being to telephone the Garden Club of America office
in New York and say I *must* be on their approved list of lecturers.
I must have talked to at least half of the member clubs since 1935
and have enjoyed every one. To qualify for membership a woman
must be a real gardener and not just a flower arranger.

In November I wrote my Brazilian friends, "I talked to the Montclair Garden Club this week about Garden Sanitation and afterwards
several people said my lecture was most *inspiring*. I thought that a
queer adjective for such a practical subject but when others told me
I was the most discouraging lecturer they had ever heard I thought
that was worse. Lots of people are like ostriches and think that by
ignoring garden pests they do not exist."

I kept hearing that discouraged angle, with people telling me
they might as well stop gardening, so I started repeating the discouraging elements at the beginning of a talk and then proceeded
to try to cheer up the audience. People differ in their reactions to
insects. Once I had what I considered a very fine educational exhibit
at a Flower Show. A woman came along, shuddered, averted her
head, and sailed past saying, "I'll send my husband to take this in;
I can't bear to look at it."

MORE SIDE LINES

The money from the Encyclopedia was gone but Slavia was still
on deck. I took a tearoom to tide us over the next winter. It was a
tiny one, in the single business block Glen Ridge possessed at that

time. The work was mostly providing lunches for nearby workers, an occasional tea or supper, and producing some home-baked products to sell. Ruth, who got her lunches there, had persuaded the owner to let me run the place while she went to the hospital for a serious operation and subsequent recuperation. The tearoom was far from profitable under my management but it was another kind of experience and fun as well as hard work. With another coal furnace to keep stoked I arrived before 7 a.m. and left long after 7 p.m. I gave too good meals for the prices charged. Slavia helped some of the time and we featured her delicate little melt-in-the-mouth fishcakes on Fridays. Saturdays I baked beans for people to take home, also butterscotch rolls. All during the week I made little cakes and cookies on order for tea parties. It would have been a lot simpler, and more profitable, for me to have stayed at home that winter and cooked for my own boarders, but I wanted to keep Slavia.

Then in the spring she left anyway. She claimed insomnia and said our quiet street kept her awake. Actually it was a sort of asthma and I thought Ulmi might be responsible. I wanted to park him elsewhere for awhile but Slavia insisted on leaving. She was better in the new place; it was on a very noisy street but there was no cat in the household.

Next we had Jessie, convert of Father Divine. She highly disapproved of me if I stayed home from church on Sunday to answer inquiries and she disapproved of most of my friends but she was a good cook and kept us fairly comfortable.

March, 1936, was marked by two events: publication of *The Garden Encyclopedia,* which seemed to be well received, and a visit to the New York Flower Show. It was not, of course, my first visit. That had been a time of unbelievable ecstacy, of being overwhelmed by the magic that turned old Grand Central Palace into spring. This visit had more effect on my life because I acquired a cabin. Yes, literally, I bought a one-room shack at the International Flower Show in New York. I fell in love with the model, a shingled affair with a studio window, and with the name of the Colony, Artists and

Writers. I was going to be a writer, wasn't I? I had to get away from all those boarders at home to have a chance to write, didn't I? If I were going to continue plant doctoring I would need to broaden my field, wouldn't I?

I can always give myself the most plausible arguments for the most implausible acts. I thought of them all the way home from the Show. I went back the next day and plunked down $25 to bind the bargain. The Colony was out on Long Island, a couple of miles beyond Port Jefferson. I bought it as Miller Place; I've been told since I live in Mt. Sinai; the Town of Brookhaven collects taxes. All the way driving out on the Island that windy March Sunday I told myself it could not possibly be any good for the low price, the land must be a swamp, the cabin jerry-built.

It truly was a bargain, and I could have more than doubled my investment in no time had I been willing to sell. For $375 I acquired a 75 x 150 foot lot in the woods (later I added a little more land) with white birches, laurel, huckleberries, pipsissewa, ground pine, even a seedling chestnut, as well as lots of scrub oak; all kinds of birds, with whippoorwills singing every night at dusk; a well-built cabin, with location, color of trim, position of 5 windows and door according to my preference; two built-in double bunks, shelves, window seat, screens, stove and enough wood to last a lifetime. There was also a "necessary house" as they call such structures down in Williamsburg. Two miles away there was a fine beach restricted to residents.

The chief thing I purchased was solitude. I like people and love talking to groups but I can't live with them continually and keep my balance. When I had a couple of roomers in the beginning they went away weekends and I had a chance to get recharged but with more boarders and a housekeeper I was getting smothered. The cabin meant escape. It also meant lecture dates and consultations on Long Island and soon paid for itself.

The whole Colony was quickly sold to city dwellers. So far as I know there isn't an artist in the lot, nor another writer. All the rest have "improved" their properties, cut down trees, put in gardens, added rooms, electricity and wells. Originally water was pumped to the corner of my lot from a community well but the system soon broke down. Unwilling to pay for electricity, well and pump, I now carry water from home on the few weekends I presently manage to get out on the Island. I still have the wilderness of trees and undergrowth. Gardening and plumbing I leave for Glen Ridge.

One of the lecture dates resulting from the purchase was presided over by the woman who had owned the land developed into the Colony. I sat through a long, long business meeting of her garden club but as soon as I was introduced the president stalked out saying that she never listened to lectures.

Another talk that season was to the Westhampton Garden Club at the home of Mrs. Harold R. Medina. Judge Medina was present and most kind, showing me his famous library, ordering a duster and some dust. He asked about some sick pines but I did not know the answer.

That spring I did manage a trip back to Wellesley to talk to the botany students, combining it with a Massachusetts date which paid travel expenses. I felt very grand to be a guest of the college for overnight. It was also soothing to my ego to be asked back to Cornell to give a seminar on practical plant doctoring to all those men graduate students.

The talk which proved most important to future work was on a hot, hot day in Nyack. As I spoke, I was almost mesmerized by the sea of waving fans. Before that, there had been a morning tour of gardens. I make it a rule, when speaking in a new place, to visit a few gardens and collect specimens, so that club members will know I am talking about their own problems, not some encountered elsewhere. This morning a dozen or so members, some of whom had been studying butterflies and such, asked to go around with me. They expected me to swing a butterfly net but I was expounding the effect insects have on plants. I showed spruce galls caused by aphids; the stippled pattern leafhoppers make in rose leaves, the windows made by slugs; margins notched in rhododendron leaves by weevils; the lacy pattern of elm leaf beetles and the quite different lace work of Japanese beetles. Such an approach was entirely new to the group. It led to my meeting with the Diggers in their own gardens all the next season and to spending at least one day a week in Nyack gardens for the next twenty years. More about this later.

Another lecture was at the New York Herald Tribune building for their course in gardening. I brought in a lot of spraying and dusting equipment and personally lugged it up in the elevator and set it up on the stage. I snagged my stockings in the process and just before being introduced looked down and saw a two-inch wide run from knees to shoes. There was nothing to do but stand up and talk. I may have appeared unconcerned but I was squirming inside.

WRITING AGAIN

Early that summer Dan Walden of Frederick A. Stokes Company wrote asking if I would consider doing a book for them. He had helped edit *The Garden Encyclopedia* and liked my style (first time I knew I had any). I put the typewriter in the Ford and drove down to the Cabin. One weekend produced an outline and a first chapter which was delivered on the way home Monday. By August we had settled on a short book, about 40,000 words, priced at $2.00, on "Disease Control and Garden Hygiene." When the contract was signed the book was called "The Plant Doctor Visits Your Garden" and it was finally published as *The Plant Doctor,* subtitled "The How, Why, and When of Insect and Disease Control in Your Garden."

I was still spraying every day and did not try to write more during the summer. I did take some photographs. I had never taken pictures except a few snapshots with a Brownie when I was a child. Again it was a case of having to learn fast while doing. Because this was to be my own book, not a distillation of reference material,

I felt the photographs also had to be mine, not borrowed from text-books.

When I asked to see a good second-hand camera at a recommended shop I was obviously so inexperienced the clerk wondered why I did not buy a cheap camera to begin on. I had no time to lose. It was August already; if there were to be pictures for the book they had to be taken immediately. I was exceedingly fortunate in the Zeiss Ikon, with double extension bellows, they sold me. It had an excellent lens and I could take close-ups on my desk, suspending the camera from a chemical ring stand and lighting the leaf, caterpillar or whatever with a photoflood bulb.

Those were the good old days when a book could be conceived and published in a few months. I was busy doctoring until nearly the first of December. Then I settled down to write, in a blessedly empty house. Ruth had decided she could not spend another winter walking the icy mile to her church office, the publishing girls were moving with their firm to New York, so instead of trying to get more roomers I let the housekeeper go. I hoped that doctoring plus lecturing plus writing would keep me afloat.

The book was based on a calendar for the Northeast and I copied into a five-year Diary the dates on which I had done various operations for clients. This gave me the range of dates on which the different pests could be expected to appear and I worked out an average for the calendar. I did not have quite five years of experience but I had a few records for 1933 and plenty for the next three years. I wrote a chapter for every month, March through November, putting the calendar at the beginning, then telling what to do from my own experience.

It seemed easier to do the drawings than to tell someone else what I wanted, so I made seventy-five little sketches along with completing the text. The contract called for the manuscript by January 1, 1937. I delivered it the afternoon of December 31st, not realizing that everyone except the office boy would already be out celebrating New Year's Eve. I bought a hat as my personal celebration, then went home to a solitary New Year.

Luckily for me, Dan Walden believed in letting the author say things her own way. There was no rewriting, not even much attempt to insert the punctuation marks I had more or less expected someone else would provide. Dan decided it read better without too many commas. While I was waiting for the book to be set in type (which took less than a month) I gave a couple of lectures, the one to the Horticultural Society of New York making me feel as if I had finally "arrived" as a lecturer. I did a little packing and on January 29th turned in corrected galley proofs.

On January 30th the plumbers closed up my house, and the Ford and I started for the South. As usual, I had a good excuse for something I wanted to do. I had to see how much of *The Plant Doctor* was good for the rest of the country. I blithely left page proofs and index to Dan, not having enough experience to know the enormous favor I was so nonchalantly accepting.

CHAPTER 4

WANDERING

I HAVE NEVER BEEN ABLE to keep a diary for more than a day or two. I do sometimes write rather detailed letters and keep the carbons. On this first trip South I used my long-suffering editor as a sounding board, with the excuse that he might get some copy out of it for promoting the book, but mostly so I'd have a record of what I saw and did and felt. The first stop was at Williamsburg, where I spent the night in an ancient four-poster at the Richard Bland Tavern. The "diary" starts the next morning.

THE SOUTHEAST

"*Feb. 1.* I was the only passenger crossing the River James. The ferry had made three trips already and I was still their first passenger. Rain, rain and more rain—good roads but narrow with teacherous red or yellow clay shoulders. Slowing up for crossings I was frantic to realize I had no brakes; they were too slimy with wet clay. Finally Danville and Julian Meade, who wrote *I Live in Virginia* and *Adam's*

Profession and Its Conquest by Eve. Never did a fire look so good. We talked beside it, not about gardens but about publishers and the maximum return that could be exacted from a garden book. Finally I explained that I came to see his garden so out in the rain we went, Julian donning overshoes and explaining that he was really very 'puny' which seemed an odd adjective from a man six-foot-three. [Apparently true; this clever writer, who could satirize gardeners and make them like it, lived only a year or two longer.]

"On again in the rain—dark, slippery pavements, blinding bright lights, treacherous shoulders. Halfway to Durham I called a halt. Mud to my ankles as I got out of the car in front of the 'best' hotel. I took the 'best' room. A bath, yes, but cigarette stubs left on the floor, the bedroom shade pinned up with safety pins. The commercial travelers went to bed until all hours and about 3 a.m. the hounds and roosters started. At 5 a.m. the travelers were starting on again and by 6:30, still in the dark, I, too, was in the car and headed South.

"Durham at 7:30; a fine breakfast at the Washington Duke. By 8:30 I was at Duke University, well worth coming to see. The buildings remind me of Princeton. Visited the Sarah Duke Memorial Gardens—jasmine out, some periwinkle and crocuses. Then to the Woman's College and Professor Ruth Addoms, whom I had known at Wellesley. On to Chapel Hill where the old University of North Carolina was even more appealing than the new swept and garnished Duke. The professor I wanted to see was busy, so I contented myself with the Arboretum, admiring tall bushes of pink and white Japanese quince, wondering about numerous spots on leaves of a climbing rose.

"Sanford by noon, and a call on a cousin recently married to a North Carolinian. She is living with her in-laws and I was treated to side meat and greens and corn pone. It was good! Her husband wants to be a veterinarian to wild animals and has already been on a trip to Africa with Frank Buck.

"Pinehurst by mid-afternoon and I simply had to stop to see this resort I had heard so much about. Grandfather spent every winter here until he died. The air and sun are like the Poconos in October but the pines—! I remember that a cousin married into the family that owns most of this resort. A little investigation yields the news that Frances and her husband live now at Chapel Hill but that her mother, whom I knew best in childhood days, is now visiting here. Three tries, and I finally locate the country road to Pinewild and then the private road, well over a mile long, which leads through 2000 acres of pines to a most deluxe log cabin, a hunting lodge. The hostess comes from Massachusetts and has charming pictures of her elaborate garden there. She is interested in *The Plant Doctor* and another sale is, I think, assured; perhaps even a lecture date.

"*Feb.* 2. Ground-hog day and the sun is really shining but they say there are no ground hogs in these parts. I have fallen in love—with those long-leaved pines. I want one of the babies for a pet, to caress its sleek brushes. Again and again I stop to take pictures.

"Cotton field after cotton field, many not even picked. And peaches! I am told it is some of the best peach country in the world. The trees grow in sand and are pruned very low, so that all fruit can be picked from the ground. Contrary to principles about lifts, I pick up a couple of country girls and carry them for a bit. I ask them when the blossoms come and they confess they have lived with peaches all their lives and don't know. They do know when the fruit is picked, July, for that is when they work in the packing sheds.

"Arrived in Charleston around 3 p.m. and find the St. John Hotel, in the center of old Charleston, as delightful as I had heard. It is decidedly not modern—you walk a mile to the bath and then put a quarter in the slot to take one—but my room is big and high-ceilinged, with tall shuttered windows. In the mail waiting at the Post Office is a most cordial letter from Mrs. Felder, to whom I had written on advice of National Council of State Garden Clubs. Informing her by telephone of my arrival, she practically gives me the keys to the city. At 8 p.m., Mrs. Wilbur, president of the Garden Club of Charleston, makes a formal call and invites me to the garden club meeting tomorrow.

"*Feb. 3.* Breakfast with Margaret Huger (the Charleston debutante who worked with me one summer) before the fire in Mrs. Bamberg's tearoom, then out to Margaret's headquarters at the South Carolina Experiment Station and then to Magnolia Gardens where entrance under her wing saves me two dollars. Margaret is working there for the government on the Sclerotinia disease of azalea flowers. Luckily for me, the season is early; Banksia roses, jasmine and many azaleas are in bloom as well as camellias. We went on to Middleton Place. The owner is 'Cousin Pringle' to Margaret but we did not feel like asking to have the entrance fee waived. It is well worth it—huge live oaks, festooned with moss, hanging over quiet lagoons (the big oak is 900 years old) and giant camellias.

"*Feb. 4.* Mrs. Wilbur took me to gardens between showers and into a few lovely Charleston houses as well. Everything blooms at once, pussy willows, daffodils, iris, azaleas, and roses. How can one prescribe for seasons here? But they do need a local plant doctor, someone to keep notes for several years. They have lace bugs galore, especially on pyracantha and azalea. The eggs are there but I have no idea when the young hatch or how many broods there are. Scale is particularly awful, hard and soft, of all colors. Snapdragons abound in rust but hollyhocks seem to be rust-free. Mildew, not present now, is said to be particularly bad on crape myrtle. The gardens are charming—walled affairs tucked back of beautiful iron gates. I wanted a picture of a huge yellow Banksia but the suggestion met with a rather chilly response so I did not press the point. I understand Mrs. Francis King has photographed and written of this particular garden.

"This afternoon I was taken to the meeting of the Society for the Preservation of Old Buildings, held in the fascinating old Heyward Washington house (DuBose Heyward's family). The son of Dean Howells read a paper.

"*Feb. 5.* Left Charleston with great regret, after a farewell tour around the old streets, including Catfish Row of Porgy fame. Savannah was full of tourists so I went on, my only memory a city of streets with parks in the center and open squares full of flowers. I did take in Wormsloe Gardens, some miles to the south, which have been in the De Renne family for six generations. The gardens are lovely, part formal, part winding drives under moss-filled live oaks. The Negro guide was even more delightful than the gardens, every botanical name correct but such joyous slips as *wisterius* vine. I loved his introduction to the she-holly and yonder the he-holly which bears no berries.

"On through Darien, where I passed up the chance to talk to 117-year-old slaves, to Brunswick where, joy of joys, there was a comfortable new tourist house. In the morning ice was frozen on every window of the car and I drove to Jacksonville in heavy coats, a robe, and fleece-lined gloves. But on reaching there at 11, it was too warm for even a coat. My letter ahead was very useful, for Mrs. Cummer replied with permission to see her own garden, the names of several others and the address of a place to stay across the street. Entrance is not generally so easy and when I told the old ladies in the recommended boarding house (Florida is, of course, filled with people over seventy) that I had been walking in Mrs. Cummer's garden their jaws dropped and I am sure they thought I was telling fibs. Her gardener helped me collect specimens of a dozen different kinds of scale, told me of the depredations of whiteflies. His roses were free from black spot; he had been using Tri-ogen.

"At the 'Palm Olive' place, really two huge estates running together, I had my first sight of flame vine covering a house. The young head gardener confessed how much they needed plant doctors in Florida and how little help they could get from the state on ornamentals. That has been the cry everywhere, no literature available, no place to turn for help, but I can't help much either. They need their own local person. At another estate I made the mistake of asking the superintendent if he were the head gardener but, after putting me in my place, he took pleasure in showing me around, introduced me to more kinds of scales, and gave me his pet idea for whiteflies, adding citronella to the sprays. Azaleas were everywhere and there was a private orange grove. I wish you could see the oranges, miles on miles of trees laden with gold and full of blossoms at the same time. Again I am lucky, for the blossoms are usually later. The air is heavy with fragrance as I write.

"*Feb. 7.* A leisurely start for Mt. Dora but with detours to drink from the Fountain of Youth at St. Augustine, to visit an alligator farm and send a live baby home to my nephews. They showed me an alligator said to be 900 years old; I can swallow that about a tree but it is hard to believe of an animal. The rattlesnakes, collected from the vicinity, were not reassuring. I sat on the sand at Daytona Beach to watch the automobiles drive on that white expanse and finally went inland to the end of my journey. In the first five minutes my aunt started outlining the parties planned at the hotel; not even my stock excuse of not playing contract could save me. The idea of coming to this land of sun and flowers to sit indoors to play cards! The day ended with the unbelievable sunset you see on postal cards, orange and turquoise sky over a lake, palms etched on the skyline.

"*Feb. 8.* On landing here I found that a Wellesley classmate was visiting her parents at Winter Park and my aunt and I were just about to drive over when your letter came about X. We found her house and office easily but were kept waiting a long time before the lady finished dictating to her secretary and deigned to receive me. I think it was to make an impression, since she had also just had a letter from you. My friends say her self-confidence makes her a fine lecturer and I am sure it should make her book equally fascinating. It was only after I acquired this same armor of self-confidence that I was able to lecture at all and probably after this first book I'll be insufferable. Please do squelch any inflation tendencies.

"I discovered in the first second that my mission was as a reporter to interview the great lady and I regretted leaving notebook in the car. I did have camera in hand and was given plenty of opportunities for pictures. When I suggested that I include her she said it was just impossible *until* we got up on the balcony and what she thought was a proper setting. Then she sent her guest for a plant to put on the railing, her secretary for pillows and a manuscript (and the pillows had to be the right color though I protested I did not have color film) and her Negro man for oranges and grapefruit and lemons. When she finally got her attendants poised around her, I was allowed to take not one but several pictures. After that she wanted to be assured of copies right off. She marched me through the garden, naming every plant. I think she wants them in the interview and I will look up the spelling in *The Garden Encyclopedia* I brought along for such emergencies. Once or twice I tried to glance under the edge of a leaf to look for pests but she always caught me and said I could forget those for once and besides, everything she owned was healthy. As we were trying to get away to keep our luncheon engagement she said, 'Of course, I am interested in your work in gardens, too, but today was for something else, wasn't it?'

"The rest of the day was kaleidoscopic. Gardens and parks and nurseries, azaleas flaming everywhere, bougainvillea, flame vine so gorgeous it is dazzling though they say it has gone by, hibiscus, sweet peas 12 to 15 feet tall; grapefruit for the asking, oranges everywhere, papaya to eat for lunch.

"Tomorrow I'm taking it easy. A few gardens in the morning, a visit to orange groves in the afternoon, a party in the evening. Wednesday and Thursday Betty and I are driving down to Palm Beach and back. Her mother wants to order several books and Betty says she is using some as gifts. Nice to have friends. Betty writes the Wellesley notes for 1920 and maybe can advertise us through that. "*Feb. 13.* It was pouring cats and dogs when Betty and I started for Palm Beach, Miami and way stations and then it rained harder than that. They say it is the first rain this year but I wouldn't know. They advertise 359 days of sunshine so it would be my luck to get in on the rainy ones. Even through the rain, the vegetation along the Indian River was simply gorgeous: sansevieria, chandelier plant, shrimp plant, century plant fruiting through the telephone wires (honest), fruiting pincushions of Spanish moss along the telephone wires. By that time the Bauhinia tree, hibiscus, oleander, bignonia, and brilliant bougainvillea in purple or cerise were an old story. But the herons and funny pelicans were not, nor the egrets, and we could not believe our eyes when we saw the jumping fish (mullet). For a short while the rain reduced itself to a drizzle so we lunched on a pier in the Indian River at St. Lucie surrounded by herons and those crazy fish and a sweet hound pup whose ways were so ingratiating he got most of our dessert.

"Further south we met the coconut palms and saw Australian pine used in every way, as windbreaks, clipped hedges, trees meeting over a street, or as enormous specimen trees. We also saw many traces of the old Florida boom, houses, hotels, stores abruptly left to the ravages of the jungle, many never completed. Right in the middle of nowhere we passed under an enormous pink stucco arch labeled 'Atlantic Gateway to the Gulf of Mexico.'

"By the time we reached Palm Beach and looked up Mr. Wilson (representative of Andrew Wilson, Inc., in Florida) it was too late to see gardens. We decided to push on to see why all the world is crazy about Miami and come back in the morning. Well, we saw Miami, at least all of it I want to see, and it is a city plumb full of tourists who evidently do not know there is a lovely Florida elsewhere. I can't hand it a thing except its coconut and royal palms. We worked for two hours, in a city literally made of hotels, to get a room to sleep in that would leave us money to get home on. Finally, for a cot and a wash stand moved into the back parlor of a boarding house, we paid five dollars for six hours' use but no sleep. The wind lashed and howled through the palms and the rain came down in more torrents. We cannot conceive of living through a hurricane here. [That was before they became commonplace in New Jersey.]

"We had early breakfast with another Wellesley classmate who lives at Miami Beach. We had not had nerve enough to descend on her for lodging. She took us for a tour of the famous hotels, $26 a day minimum for a room without meals, and bath clubs. It was still pouring when we got back to Palm Beach but Mr. Wilson was game and drove us for two hours up and down drives and beaches, naming every estate, taking us into a few. He sprays as well as sells insecticides for scales on palms and other trees. He defoliates banyan trees so they will not look so disreputable when the new leaves come out, and sprays lawns with sulfate of ammonia when salt has concentrated on them after a long north-east blow. As a matter of fact, nearly everything has to be sprayed with sulfate of ammonia to counteract the natural alkalinity of the coquina shell which, by the way, makes a fine road surface.

"After being taken to lunch, where I learned that the Florida kingfish tastes much like our swordfish, we started inland to the Everglades. Both Mr. Wilson and the gas station man warned of a terribly dangerous road, with no shoulders, right along the bank of the canal, with a record of many fatal accidents. But we reached Belle Glade without coming through anything we ourselves considered dangerous and concluded that the accidents must have been from drunks driving 70 miles an hour, a pleasant habit down in this state that does not require a driver's license.

"I don't know how I had pictured the Everglades but I think as a swampy jungle rather than a flat plain stretching ahead for ten, twenty, thirty miles without a tree or gas station, a house or scarcely a bend in the fine coquina road. The glades have been drained into canals in which water hyacinths grow so rank it is a constant fight to keep any open surface. Truck crops are grown on the thick, black muck. Now when I eat tomatoes, beans and lettuce out of season I shall think of that broad expanse blooming with tall sunflowers, for they are planted every five rows as a windbreak, a completely unexpected effect. I shall also remember the driveway near Belle Glade with a sign on one post, 'Hunting and Shooting Club' and on the other, 'Animal Rescue League.'

"Near dark we got back in the land of lakes and orange groves. We spent the night at Avon Park, a town that boasts twenty-nine lakes of its own. The hotel was simply elegant and for our luxurious room with twin beds, bath, we paid only $3.50 for the two of us. Why, why will people go to Miami when they could have this—this including a gorgeous log fire in a large and pleasant lobby, a colorful bowl of fruit for the guests, very good meals served in a flower-filled dining room, orange blossoms scenting the air outside.

"We wanted to stay but I was trying to make Mt. Dora by noon so we dashed on to Lake Wales and the Singing Tower, of pink marble, faïence and coquina. I was impressed by the signs, 'Gentlemen may not remove their coats' and 'Please do not invade' instead of 'Keep Out.' I was disappointed to find that the pink flamingos were white.

"Then mile after mile of lupines blooming wild in the meadows. They are lighter in color, somewhat smaller, and with a grayer leaf than those I have seen in the Rockies but they are lovely, a welcome relief from the overwhelming colors of the planted hibiscus and bougainvillea. We tore into Winter Park just before noon to find a message from my aunt that the party had been called off and I need not hurry back to Mt. Dora. So I went shopping in Orlando, for tangerine and wild orange marmalades, kumquat preserves, roselle and guava jellies.

"I'm concluding that Wellesley is sort of magic. Another Wellesley friend, living near Atlanta, has heard of my trip and will take me to see gardens there if I will visit her. The mother of a Wellesley girl asked me to call on her friend down here and she introduced me to members of the Fairfield, Connecticut; Rumson, New Jersey; and Manchester, Vermont, garden clubs [which led to engagements to speak the next summer].

"*Feb. 17* (written from Mississippi). I went to church on Sunday. I thought it necessary after the unsabbatical performance I put on early that morning. Investigating the back of my car for repacking I discovered everything mildewed from the rain. In the middle of

Mt. Dora's main street I proceeded to clean out the Ford and drape wet blankets over the hood. By that time it had cleared up enough to take a picture of the pelican vine given me the evening before. I do hope the pictures come out; they were taken with the aid of half the population of Mt. Dora, all wanting to see and smell. I can remember the smell yet; it should be called carrion vine. I perched it on the hood of the car for its picture. The bud or blossom or what have you is over a foot long and looks just like a pelican, then opens along the 'breast' to disclose a rich red velvety interior and more rich odor, both, I assume, most attractive to insects.

"The sun came out to speed me to Gainesville Sunday afternoon and I stayed at an entrancing Spanish hotel built around many courts and gardens. Monday was spent at the Experiment Station (University of Florida). I met a plant pathologist first and one by one others were called in until we had a round table, not to give me the information I came for but for them to find out how the plant doctor game worked. They decided they would try it when the legislators put them out of business. I discovered that the entomologist and plant pathologist working especially on ornamentals were at Leesburg, which I passed through the day before, but I talked with another entomologist, collected a lot of bulletins, and had a conference with the acting Director, Dr. H. H. Hume, author of *Gardening in the Lower South,* still, apparently, the only garden book of much use around here.

"Gainesville was beautiful—streets with azalea-filled parks in the middle, lots of flowering dogwood which I had not seen further south, and a few orange groves but these were filled with wood, ready to fire at the first sign of frost. After that no more oranges as we went toward Tallahassee over desolate, though very fine, roads. Miles on miles of pines on burned-over land. It still hurts to see the trees slashed for turpentine but they say each tree lasts for some years, then is used for paper pulp. No one puts out a fire in Florida and lots of them are started purposely to clear out underbrush but I cannot get over being horrified by it. Yesterday I passed through smoke so thick I could scarcely see to drive and in one place there was a long line of wicked red flame but no one seemed disturbed.

"Have I raved to you about stock loose on the roadsides all through the South? It is your lookout not to hit them but you can expect any moment to round a curve and see a cow or steer in the middle of the road. This day there were hogs of all colors and shapes to add to the hazards and once in a while a few goats.

"I bragged too soon about the Ford's perfection. I picked up a nail and, before I could stop, ripped the inside of the tire. There was a farmhouse, though they had been many miles apart, and the obliging farmer tried to help me change the tire but we discovered one of the essential tools was lacking. I tried to flag a ride to a telephone but all the tourists went by with their noses in the air as is my usual habit. Finally a native took pity on me and swept me along at sixty miles an hour in his old truck. 'Aren't you afraid of hitting the cattle?' I asked. 'Yep, this is a terrible road, several cows hit just lately; I killed a nigger on here last summer.' I was more than relieved to be set down at a telephone. I might just as well have driven into town on my rim, for the guarantee was useless and I had to fork over $15 for a new tire out of slender capital.

"However, I reached Tallahassee in time for a Cornell dinner party and a concert at Florida State College for Women. I forgot to mention the beautiful orchard passed. I wracked my brains to think what the trees could be until I came to a sign—'Tung Oil Trees, experimental planting.' The blossoms are the most luscious shade of pink!

"All day Tuesday by the Gulf of Mexico. My first glimpse of it was blue; then when I crossed over a very long bridge it was burnished copper; sometimes it was turquoise, sometimes gray, sometimes sapphire. Sometimes there is no beach, sometimes white sand so dazzling it gives you a headache to watch it. There are many bridges, most of them free, but enough with tolls to make traveling expensive, along with gas at 24 cents a gallon against 17 cents at home. All day I was bucking head winds and although I had the gas tank filled some time before Panama City where I had lunch, by 3 p.m. the old Ford gasped and died. Fortune smiled and a man from Arkansas pushed me to the next gas station. The last that I had noticed had been about a hundred miles back but the next was close. It was brand new, opened for business just five minutes before we arrived.

"I had planned to stay at Pensacola but then started toward Mobile. Halfway were the Latchstring Cabins which looked wonderful to my weary bones and proved to be even nicer than they looked. For $1.50 I had a large, clean log cabin, private bath, most comfortable bed, fireplace with lots of wood to burn in it, the whole set in a pine forest with clear, crisp air. After a bowl of oyster stew I went to bed in great contentment.

"Great luxury; had my breakfast brought over to be consumed by the fire and spent Wednesday morning perusing the literature I had acquired at Gainesville and working up the lecture to give in New Orleans. I was sorry to start out again after lunch.

"At Bellingrath Gardens I looked up Mr. Bellingrath who turned me over to Mr. Hunt, his most intelligent superintendent. Mr. Hunt spent at least two hours taking me around and answering questions, even refunded my admission. The Gardens have azaleas and camellias in full bloom at present but later have many other things. They are the most extensive and magnificently planted gardens open to the public that I have seen. Only ten years old, as opposed to the several hundred years of Magnolia and Wormsloe, but you would never know it. Thousands of very large and ancient bushes have been moved in and a fortune spent. In such a place it was hard to realize that we did have things in the North to compensate. Mr. Hunt reminded me that we have lilacs, peonies, delphinium, and bulbs that do not grow here at all.

"It was late afternoon when I tore myself away. A few miles further on I was flagged down by people standing near a stranded Greyhound bus. Remembering my own recent plights, I stopped and took on a woman wanting to go to Biloxi, where I had decided to

spend the night. It was good luck for me for she paid the next bridge
toll and got me in her small and inexpensive hotel. Faded southern
style with much stained wallpaper but eminently respectable; already I have been introduced to half the people around. The lady
comes from Illinois and is going to see that the library in her home
town gets the book. Tomorrow she is going to take me on a tour of
this glamorous old Biloxi, founded in 1699. It is right on the Gulf
with the oyster boats practically in front of the hotel. I do like
traveling alone; you make such interesting and unexpected contacts.
"*Feb. 23.* 4 a.m. Curses on all modern hotels with steam heat in this
part of the country. My radiator is off but there is a big hot pipe
leading to the next floor which won't let me sleep, now that I have
gotten over the exhaustion of yesterday's drive. Three hundred miles
is not so much but when the last two hundred are on gravel which
throws you, on roads with deep canyons for shoulders, winding up
and down hills and around corkscrew turns, over bridges labeled as
dangerous, that's something else again. But I saw the country, as
you never do from a straight paved road. The vegetation all seemed
pretty dormant, no broad-leaved evergreens through these farmlands
but every now and then clumps of sweet tiny daffodils, some not
more than a half-inch across, around gray, weatherbeaten houses.
It was dark when I finally got here (Meridian, Mississippi). I pulled
up near a tall building that looked like a hotel and went across to
investigate. Seeing that it was not, I asked a policeman where I
could find a good hotel. 'Waal, now, you must come from the
country, to think that tall office building is a hotel.' When I found
one and the bellhop took my things out of the back I knew I had
come from the country. Everything was inches deep in yellow mud
and I am terribly worried about what may have gotten into the
picture case. When I paid for dinner the waitress asked, 'Have you
got any tokens, honey?' They have the darndest system here in
the Gulf States of taxes on the mil basis, each mil or token being
about as big as a quarter. When you think you have a pocketful of
real money you are worth less than two cents.

"To get back to New Orleans. The Bradleys, father, mother, and daughter, took this stranger into their home and hearts as if I were a lifelong friend. Camilla is secretary at the Garden Center maintained by the New Orleans Garden Society which invited me here to lecture. She also does some planting for people. The camellia she was having moved Sunday was perhaps eight feet tall and will cost the client, when planted, over a hundred dollars but that is considered very cheap. These people will just about pawn their souls for camellias and I would get the bug too, if I stayed down South. I want to say here and now that as a general rule Southern women are far more intelligent about their gardens than their Northern sisters. They are real dirt gardeners and pay much less attention to flower arrangement. They know intimately their plant pests and are doing something about them. A Junior League girl may spend all Saturday afternoon scrubbing sooty mold off her gardenia bush or show you with pride the cuttings she is making. Mrs. Bradley can make anything grow in her tiny backyard in the city. From flowers salvaged from a bride's bouquet she grew lusty plants to present to the bride on her first anniversary. She took cuttings from the gardenia corsage given the plant doctor at the luncheon and discovered with glee a mealybug upon it. Travel is good for deflating the ego; I never felt so humble as I did talking to these New Orleans gardeners.

"Camilla planned a houseparty at their farm. I brought my hoodoo along for the trip upcountry for we went through cloudbursts all the way. We read the next day of a tornado elsewhere in Louisiana so I suppose rain was much better. We went over the Spillway, some twenty miles from New Orleans, where the engineers are letting water into the countryside to divert it from the city. It is up to the middle branches of cypress trees but the road seems safe. At St. Francisville high water is taken as a matter of course. The railroad station was under water but the trains came through. One house had water up to the second floor but they just put a gang plank to the road and moved up, where there seemed to be a party going on.

"Sunday was clear and cold; I spent the morning getting drunk on camellias. One old woman was layering all her splendid old bushes, with four or five pails or tubs of earth around each one. She sells the tiny layers for two dollars up and wants twenty dollars for a bush three or four feet high. The finest bushes were in the church-yard. Camilla hid a blossom of an unusual variety under her coat so she could make a cutting. There may be hundreds of blooms on a bush but each is treated like a jewel. You are rarely given one for they are left to be admired on the bush or used to grace social functions. A tourist at Rosedown begged for just one flower, and was refused, though I know he would gladly have paid for it. Rose-down, one of the best of the old plantation homes, is hoary with age. Even the boxwood is covered with lichens. There are three 'girls' left here of the original family and they never leave the place. One showed me her mother painted by Audubon and other ancestors ad infinitum."

That seems to have been the end of diary letters for this trip. My next stop was Birmingham to visit a good Cornell friend. Her husband was in bed with a cold but honored his guest by getting up for dinner. I caught the cold. I was pretty rocky by the time my Wellesley classmate was showing off Atlanta gardens but I hated to give anyone in that family my affliction so I said I was better and drove on. I managed a day and a half of travel but finally col-lapsed at the Lincoln Hotel in Marion, Virginia. Again it was a tale of utter kindness to a stranger. The doctor sat around and told me stories; the bellboy brought magazines; they served meals at my bedside and did not charge for room service; when I was able to walk again they arranged for me to see nearby gardens. I had had just money enough left to get home but not enough to stay over a week. My checking account was bare but the hotel trusted me while I sent an SOS to the Savings Bank in North Attleboro.

HOME AGAIN

THE BOOK came out while I was getting well enough to drive home. I didn't know enough then to appreciate all the public relations work that must have gone on prior to publication. Reviews appeared in every sort of journal and newspaper across the country. They were unexpectedly favorable; I was supposed to have style and humor as well as down-to-earth practicality. A Texas reviewer liked my time budget and the "rare literary flavor" of the prologue. I wrote Dan Walden, "Now I'll be so smug I'll never be able to write well again." I groused because sales did not catch up with all the publicity. Garden books are not best sellers and *The Plant Doctor* continued to sell fairly steadily, if mildly, for many years. I suspect that the continuing sale was largely due to meeting Mrs. Sarah V. Coombs, whose *South African Plants for American Gardens* had been published by Stokes just before my book. She put *The Plant Doctor* on the required reading list for the Judging Schools conducted by the National Council of State Garden Clubs. It stayed there until quite recently and everywhere I go some woman comes up and says she *had* to read me.

I needed royalty money to pay for a new roof. While I was wandering through the South my good neighbors, a Lutheran minister and his wife, kept an eye on things. They had written that the roof had blown off. It wasn't quite that bad but a lot of shingles had come off in a windstorm and a new roof was imperative that spring. Another writing job helped out.

Jersey Life, a local weekly magazine, asked me to do a regular column, "The Plant Doctor Says." It was fun but it took some scrambling to take enough pictures for illustrations each week and sometimes the column had to be sandwiched in at exceedingly odd moments. I liked it because I could get into print what was happening right now, not what might be expected to happen in an average year. And I could drag in practically everything—reviews of garden books, unusual flowers, garden philosophy, as well as pests. A client started taking the magazine because of the column and I overheard her explaining to someone else, "Well, she just talks along—." A man was overheard to say, on going up to a magazine stand and asking for a copy of *Jersey Life,* that he would buy it if "that woman who writes about gardens so a man can understand has another article."

The column was very personal. I readily confessed my own sins. For example:

"Last June I promised a neighbor she could have some iris provided she would come and dig it herself, for I was too busy and probably would not be home. The other day I saw her out in the garden. I started to keep on at the desk but finally my New England conscience got busy, 'A fine plant doctor you are, after scolding every one else for giving iris away without treating it.' I went out and found, greatly to my surprise, shame, and sorrow, that the rhizomes she had dug up were covered with the sclerotia of crown rot. So I mean what I say more than ever; don't give away iris without cleaning off the rhizomes and treating them to a half-hour bath in bichloride of mercury."

I told the readers that they were at liberty to come to my garden and look around but reminded them, "Just realize that it does not pretend to be much but a back yard. A landscape architect looked at it in scorn once and said, 'You don't call this a garden, do you?' And I really don't, for it is chiefly a place to experiment, though I have tried as best I could to get a little privacy and comfort on a budget of no time and less money. You can expect to find weeds, but you may also compare beds treated, this year, with Tri-ogen, Kolotex, Sulrote, bordeaux mixture, and a red copper oxide combination."

Along with the weekly column and an occasional story for the *New York Times* I did a series of four illustrated articles for *American Home,* entitled "One Hour A Week Enough." These had repercussions and I began to see that it was a lot easier to write a

book than an article for a magazine with advertising. We ran a
picture of the time-tested sprayers and dusters actually used in my
own work. The editor was inundated with irate letters from manufacturers wanting to know why he had not asked them for pictures
of their own up-to-date apparatus, not my antiquated stuff. In listing
items for a simple medicine kit I included "Soap—10 cents." In
editing, the word white was inserted merely as a reminder that it
should be a mild soap. The manufacturer of a yellow soap threatened
to take out all his advertising, even though it related to soap for
clothes and not plants, unless there was a public retraction.

I read a novel once, *Time at Her Heels,* and that was the way I
felt all through the spring and summer of 1937, with the book leading to various extracurricular activities. Here's a typical weekend in
May, salvaged from a letter. On Saturday Solomon and I sprayed
five gardens, including roses and a molasses spray on boxwood for
leaf miners, before 9 a.m., then sprayed my own experimental
roses. I cleaned up, set up an exhibit at the Montclair Flower Show,
went to East Orange to answer questions at a Plant Clinic for three
hours, then back to Montclair for four hours of duty at the Show,
after which I returned to East Orange to collect remaining books.
They had been selling them for the benefit of the Garden Center
there. Someone brought me a sandwich for lunch and I had dinner
about 9 p.m. On Sunday I breakfasted in bed with the Sunday papers
and a scratch pad for ideas for the column, then went out to spray
a garden. I did not usually work for clients on Sunday but it had
rained on the scheduled day and this garden had to be spiffed up in
time for a garden club meeting there on Monday. I came home to
type out the column, talked to friends who dropped in to see the
garden. I answered questions at the Monclair Flower Show all afternoon and took down the exhibit when it closed, going home to a
kitchen full of unwashed dishes, chemicals, and specimens.

I don't know why I tried to have a party that crowded spring,
probably in return for one given for me after the book came out. I
followed Cornell tradition by making it a breakfast on another

Sunday in May, feeding people on the porch on the installment plan, shooing one bunch into the garden as the next arrived. I added cinnamon buns, rolls, bran muffins, Canadian bacon and fried pineapple to the usual waffles and sausages. The garden never looked better; I don't think it had ever been all cleaned up at once before.

The Nyack lecture of the previous summer had resulted in a course for the Diggers, a dozen women with special horticultural interests. We met every other week at a different house. I talked indoors for an hour and then we all went outside to work in the garden of the hostess. The idea was that the students would learn to do their own pest control but it didn't work out that way. The lessons were continued. They loved those but they thought it lots easier for me to do the actual doctoring. Thus I was spending one or two days a week near Nyack, too far from home to be practical but with awfully interesting places and people.

Madame Mouquin was a member of the Diggers and because we were to meet at her place later I stopped in one spraying day for some advance information. I had been told she had a marvelous rock garden but that was decidedly an understatement. The whole place was fairyland from the meadow path lined with white birches and primroses up the hill to the frog house and dogwoods and silver-bell tree (new to me then), through the formal garden, along the long path of lily-of-the-valley and finally to the rock garden where every plant seemed to have its special environment. They had also told me that Madame Mouquin would never see 75 again yet she was working out every minute of every day, now raising seedlings, now turning a whole mountainside into more rock garden. Her place seemed to me infinitely more beautiful than elaborate estates with twenty gardeners. She had one, half a day. It was the most loved and cherished garden I had ever known, so well and tenderly loved I could find scarcely a single diseased specimen. Madame was, of course, pleased when I said I would bring class material up from New Jersey rather than getting it from her garden.

The Mouquins were the original proprietors of Henri's in New

York, a place I had visited occasionally for tea in the old days when I had a salary. It was nearly 2 o'clock when I started to leave but Madame found I had not eaten my lunch and asked me to have it there. Thinking I could enjoy the garden, I agreed, only to have them insist on my coming into the house. So there I sat, acutely embarrassed, my hands filthy with all kinds of poisons (and they made no suggestions about washing), eating my lunch out of a paper bag on their typical green plush table cover. Madame and Monsieur, of such culinary fame, hovered over me, offering white wine and chocolates, as I tried to swallow those hastily-put-together sandwiches, crusts left on. My meals were usually peculiar those days. Tuesday dinner had consisted of an ice-cream bar and crackers purchased on the Yonkers Ferry on the way home from a lecture in Stamford; the next night I dined on a hot dog collected along the road, but the Mouquin affair was the strangest yet.

I invited the Diggers to Glen Ridge for a Rose Party in June, with games devised to find out if they had learned anything about roses from me. When those women arrived from their fine gardens, took one glance at my small back yard and raved, "Look at your Roses!" I began to appreciate these guinea pigs. Such admiration led to an annual Rose Day but it was some years before I did more than invite residents in my own and neighboring blocks.

There were many lecture trips that summer, all hectic, some more than others. I talked on Long Island one afternoon and stayed over night with a client who had a summer place at Quogue. I left at dawn the next morning to drive more than a hundred miles home. The boy who was supposed to substitute for Solomon either didn't show up or got tired of waiting, so I parked my suitcase, changed clothes, and drove alone to Nyack, to spray all those roses with a knapsack sprayer on my back. It was fiendishly hot and coming home about 8 or 9 p.m. the Ford gave out. I think it might have started again had I let it rest a little but the gas station man said it needed a new timer and none could be gotten until morning. The tourist places in the vicinity looked horrible so I telephoned a friend in

Hackensack who took me home with her, dirty spray clothes not-withstanding. Why did I leave that suitcase at home?

As soon as the Ford was repaired the next morning I did a day's work spraying around Montclair, still by myself. Then I came home to clean up, repack the suitcase, collect the typewriter. I drove a hundred miles north before stopping at an Inn for the night, completing the journey to Vermont the next morning. In pulling off the road to read a signboard one wheel went down into a concealed ditch. A truck with a tow rope happened along almost immediately and I was able to be on time for the afternoon lecture. Before starting home next day I typed out the weekly column and visited many gardens.

I kept up the same dizzy pace all summer but lecture jaunts were actually vacations from more arduous spraying. One trip was to Cooperstown and I stayed at the Fenimore Cooper estate, one of the first places landscaped by Ellen Shipman. It was so beautiful I took reams of pictures.

On October 1, 1937, I totaled up what I had been doing since April 1, six months. I had made 478 service visits to gardens, given 22 lectures, written 33 articles (including the weekly column), taken 500 photographs of pests, of which about 50 had been published, donated four days for garden club exhibits, had opened my garden, with a spraying demonstration, for the benefit of the College Women's Club, and had attended four conventions—the American Rose Society in Cleveland, the Men's Garden Clubs in Lancaster (they invited me because of the book), the National Shade Tree Conference in Baltimore, and the New Jersey Florists meeting in New Brunswick. I had also answered many, many letters, carried on experiments in my own garden, tried to read most of the garden and scientific periodicals that cluttered up the house.

That autumn I cleaned up gardens, planted roses for clients, appeared at the New York Times Book Fair in company with really illustrious authors like Richardson Wright, and wrote letters about the next trip. We were wandering again, the Ford and I, this time to the Southwest. To save a little energy we went by boat to Galveston, leaving New York on December 8th. Again I resorted to diary-letters, but I was sending back the column, too, having talked the editor into believing that *Jersey Life* readers would be interested in a travelogue.

THE SOUTHWEST

"December 11, 1937. Lights of Miami Beach shining through early morning darkness and breakfast at dawn as the boat docked. Spurning the three-dollar bus trip to all the points of interest, including Al Capone's house and the one where the boy in the iron lung lives, I set off by myself. Did you ask if I have warm clothes? Yes, I have, and I was bundled in a wool suit and a top coat and shivering at that when I stopped at the first fruit stand to get all the orange juice I could drink for 5 cents.

"I had planned on buying Christmas cards here and was directed to Miami's best store. Wouldn't you think with all the tourists you could get some tiny etchings of palm trees or something distinctive without its being all tinseled up or GREETINGS FROM FLORIDA scrawled over a crocodile swallowing a nigger baby? Here's hoping Texas will do better by me.

"As I rode the streetcar over the causeway and the bus to Miami Beach I jotted down the number of things in bloom—oleander, sleeping hibiscus, and the scarlet wideawake kind being sworn at by purple bougainvillea, poinsettias just starting, a little allamanda, lots of things I don't know, and an ordinary yellow marigold. In every dooryard gaudy crotons and succulents of various sorts. I love the coconut palms, which make me think I am walking in a movie scene, and I am still thrilled by Australian pine. There are miles of hedges of it, clipped like privet, columns of it trimmed like arborvitae.

"The beach and a swim. My only claim to fame on this boat is that I did go for a swim, the one intrepid soul on all that sand. The water was warm and a heavenly turquoise blue. All that was necessary was to stay under and not get exposed to the chilly air breezes.

But by afternoon the sun was really hot and folks were lying on the sand clad in next to nothing. I curled up under a palm (they grow right out of the sand on the beach) and lazily wondered what the soft brown blotches were over my head, discovering, when my plant doctor curiosity got aroused, that they were not soft scales but bristly empty pupa cases of some insect I don't know.

"A walk along the Avenue yielded the following appropriate signs: Harbor of Lost Soles (for a shoe repair shop, of course) and Adam and Eve Solarium (nude sun baths). Another 5-cent drink, this time coconut milk.

"Sailing again at 4:30 I attempted pictures of that transplanted Manhattan skyline. There was a red sun sinking into the sea in a pool of molten gold.

"*Dec. 12.* Sunday. Lifeboat drill again at 10:30. No *Morro Castle* disaster for the Clyde-Mallory line. There's drill after every port and they actually get the boats over the side so you know they are O.K. With the handful of people left after the Miami exodus it looks as if we could have almost a boat apiece. Divine service at 11:30, led by the purser. He has to be a man of parts for he headed the variety show the other night as well. Tonight the sun set on the side of the boat where it has been rising heretofore for we are heading northwest in the Gulf of Mexico.

"*Dec. 14.* Galveston is actually an island, about thirty miles long and two wide, with fortifications at both ends. Fort Crockett has stunning Spanish houses for the officers. A girl from the boat and I decided it was too rough for swimming (I had no idea the Gulf could produce that high a surf) so we drove up and down the boulevards. This is a lovely town with many streets centered with palms and oleanders and green grass. It is old and Southern and sleepy, a little down at the heel (except for a few immaculate and enormous public buildings) and wholly charming. The beach is sort of Asbury Park or Atlantic City in winter but not as pretentious, really more like Bournemouth, England, and probably nicer in its deserted winter aspect. A wide, wide boulevard of brick goes along the sea wall and when you get to the end of the paved road you can go for miles directly on the hard, sandy beach. I tried and tried to get camera shots of sea gulls at the water's edge but every time I was almost in focus they were off. At the edge of the sand are brine-burned feathery salt cedars and yellow flowers, about a foot high, sort of a cross between a dandelion and a daisy.

"To get to Houston you drive over a long causeway and then for fifty miles on a concrete ribbon through perfectly flat country, dotted with many oil tanks, a few wells, and occasional flame spouting from upright pipes (I suppose some kind of safety device).

"Houston is a big, big, big city, full of hotels and traffic, not by any stretch of the imagination a place for tourists but a bustling, thriving place for its own inhabitants. Downtown here you are farther from a flower or a bit of green than you are in New York for there we at least have the public squares and Central Park. The skyscraper Gulf building which I see at night from the window, its top bathed in Christmas red and green lights, is as grand as anything in Manhattan except the Empire State.

"*Dec. 15.* My hoodoo follows me. Rain is inevitable when there are gardens to visit. Mrs. Neff was a good sport, sent her chauffeur for me at 9:30 and walked around with me all morning in the mist, despite having a young son ill with a trained nurse and herself lately out of the hospital. She had a luncheon party at noon, provided another escort for garden visits in the afternoon, then had me back for dinner and the evening. I cannot get over how marvelously kind people are and think who am I to deserve all this. Of course, it was Mrs. Oakleigh Thorne's letter that evoked such a welcome. One of the luncheon guests brought a brown and gold orchid for *me,* simply because Mrs. Thorne had been kind to *her*.

"Texas, at least hereabouts, grows every kind of southern plant and has our northern elms, a few, and oaks, quite a lot. Deciduous trees are not as common as the others and dried oak leaves lying on the ground seem to fill people with delight. In the morning we saw so-called small gardens, in the afternoon, large estates. In both cases the houses are comparatively new and not of the 'modern' type, with gardens and house together forming a perfect unit. Never anything flamboyant or ugly but I have to remember that these all belong to Garden Club of America members.

"Camellias are coming into bloom, the white *Alba plena* and the shell Pink Perfection, carved from alabaster, and a few azaleas. Roses are still in bloom, the flowers enormous. A favorite hedge is the yaupon, with stunning red berries. Gardenia is often used and another gardenia with small glossy leaves is a ground cover. In many gardens a huge, spreading willow was in the background; there were also large ferns, with maidenhair in shady corners. Most of the larger places have a sort of courtyard with the drive curving around a central planting. The most effective was a large circle of grass surrounded by a low hedge but the most interesting had a central Spanish well and four quadrants, edged with box, filled with maidenhair fern, oxalis growing through. Plumbago, lovely soft blue, massed under purple bougainvillea falling down over a house is heavenly, especially when there is silver-gray Leucophyllum somewhere near.

"Some of the larger places have natural woods running down to the bayous and paper-white narcissi are in bloom by the thousands under the trees. Bulbs are planted in September for Christmas flowers. We went to the Neal Estate (Maxwell House Coffee) and to the Cullen Estate (oil). Mr. Cullen is having the time of his life with his garden. Right now he is experimenting with a heating system for outdoor camellias. The garden cost half a million just to start and there are camellias of great antiquity thickly edging a square the size of a city block. I was told some of the finer specimens cost $1000 apiece. I am sorry for the old plantations they must have been taken from but think of the comfortable old age they must have provided for impoverished gentlefolk.

"Grass is interesting here. Because it stands up better in summer they are planting coarse St. Augustine grass at great expense. It looks about like the crabgrass we dig up at great expense. The garden club is paying $1000 to get this grass planted around the Art Museum, a gift to the city. This is a rich metropolis; it is fun to know one Southern city you don't have to feel sorry for.

"*Dec. 16.* I went to the post office to mail a book. I always said there should be some agency to wrap packages and here they really do it for you at the post office, an idea worth copying.

"*Dec. 17.* Real sunshine. Mile on mile of rice fields, empty, then cattle country, but you can't see anything but wire fence. Victoria is a nice Western town with old-fashioned roses blooming in every dooryard. I got a lariat for John (my nephew).

"*Dec. 18.* I did not want to stay in Laredo and was delighted to find there was a sleeper to Monterrey (Mexico). I could have taken the Ford by paying for special permit and insurance but the train fare was less and without the bother of having everything in the car inspected. So I locked it up in a garage and arrived at the station at 8 p.m. only to be told they could not get the promised reservation but there would be plenty of room on the train. I waited and waited and the train came lazily in at 11:30. I was sort of catapulted into a Pullman overflowing with students going home to Mexico from the States. For two hours we struggled with inspectors and baggage. Then I finally got the conductor to listen to me and learned everything really was sold out. Eventually, about 2 a.m. they found an upper in another car. That one had not been inspected so I was awakened at 5 for a second round with the baggage. There was something of a struggle in the dressing room surrounded by sweet senoritas who were applying mascara and war paint and fixing elaborate hair-dos but by 8 I was having breakfast in the very Gran Hotel Ancira—delicious pan dulce (sweet rolls) and coffee.

"This is a place of vast marble halls and murals. By paying a peso extra I got a room with a view, through tall and wide French windows, of range on range of mountains. They look something like the Romsdal Pass in Norway.

"On starting out to see the sights I was picked up by a guide and decided to trust him on sight. I learned during the day that such guides are licensed and regimented within an inch of their lives. They are bonded to drive clients' cars, thumbprinted, not allowed to drink on duty. They are graduates of a guide school that teaches them English and history and how to act toward tourists. They usually drive the owner's car but since the Ford was not here the guide escorted me by bus, at a cost of one peso (28 cents) an hour. We went through a brewery with an assembly line system, watched serapes being made, went out to the modern fort, ate enchiladas and drank frothy cinnamon chocolate, inspected the beautiful garden, chiefly poinsettias now, of the one and only grand night club here, and climbed step on step to the Bishop's Palace where Pancho Villa made his stand. And now I am waiting for Mr. Jesus Segura to take me to a vaudeville show to see some Spanish dancing and because I was nice to him (so he says) it is almost a date. At least, he invited me to go, paying only the admission and not his time. Little did I think I had come to that gigolo period of a woman's life.

"*Dec. 20.* It was an exciting evening; the theater was packed to the rafters with humanity—all Mexican, not tourists—to see a beloved variety troupe up from Mexico City. The show was great fun, though I knew no Spanish, and then Jesus guided me most expertly through the crowd, made discreet love in the taxi, took me for coffee at the Foreign Club at a late hour, and I'm sure spent more than he made on me as a guide during the day.

"All the things you have ever read about Mexico are true: the late trains and the filthy urchins and old women selling violent tomato and meat mixtures wrapped in tortillas (one man had a furry black kid with its feet tied together slung over one arm while he passed out food with the other); interesting and unsanitary candy sold on the plazas; a man doing a pink spun-sugar arrangement in front of the cathedral; Sunday morning market with meats and flowers and straw baskets and serapes and pottery all jostling each other; huge pink paper Santa Clauses; evening promenade in the plaza, lively music from the grand stand in the center, the girls, hundreds of them, walking by twos and threes around the square in one direction and the young men in the other, the rest of the city sitting on benches watching.

"*Dec. 21.* Laredo. It seems I'm going to recover (from the usual Mexican sickness) though I had the doctor as soon as I got here to make sure. I am spending today in bed but the column had to get in the mail so the typewriter is on my knees. Last night I thought this room was the most gosh-awful place to be sick in. I had a choice between a pretty, modern room and steam heat that could not be turned off and this room in the old part. I couldn't stand the heat while running a temperature so I took this, damp and cheerless. The gas heater leaked so I had to turn it off; the window is frosted so I can't see out; the only light is a glaring ceiling affair; the wall telephone is on the other side of the room.

"*Dec. 22.* San Antonio was looking its worst when I arrived in the rain. Having seen no place to stay for the night I decided to get the mail and then hunt. I drove three times around the most likely looking building and paid my nickel in the slot, when I finally found an inch to park the car, and then found it was the courthouse. I asked a girl clerk where the post office was. 'Do you know Houston Street?' 'No, I'm a stranger here.' 'Well then, I'm sure I can't tell you, if you don't know where that is.' My next contretemps was with a policeman, the same one twice. He first bawled me out for stopping the car to ask him a question and when I came back he yelled at me to step lively and tried to make me drive into a living wall of pedestrians. And that's your polite South, though I must say it has not been so in other places. I think they are just worn out with Christmas and crowds and rain and the awful traffic.

"I cheered up when I finally reached the post office for there was a whole fistful of mail and an enormous Christmas box from home. And after another hour of wandering I found quite a nice place to stay, a motor court, advertised as 'America's Finest Tourist Quarters.'

"*Dec. 23.* I'm still in the moronic stage and never did grow up. Witness the fact that at 8 this morning my feet were making an unerring path through the park to the San Antonio zoo. After I had gazed for an hour at the llamas and monkeys and heard the lions roar and seen the pink flamingos I thought I should visit the reptile house (I always do snakes for penance) but a voice inquired, 'You looking for the sunken garden?'

"I thought that might be a slightly more appropriate destination for a plant doctor. (It is increasingly difficult to remember that I am one and that this trip is supposed to have some raison d'être). The sunken garden was a monstrosity but my guide was most anxious that I do justice to San Antonio. 'You seen the Missions?' 'You want to take me?' 'Yes, but I gotta go home and dress up.'

"So he went home and dressed up and made his debut as a city guide. I think he was really a day laborer in the park but under his care I saw most of San Antonio in two hours and it would have taken three days by myself. I decided three Missions were quite sufficient. I have to confess they do not interest me too much except for the gardens and the gardens of the California missions are much nicer. So then I wanted to see the residential section and we went to Alamo Heights, 'where the rich people live.' The quite beautiful new Spanish houses have good foundation plantings but not much color in them.

"You know, I'm the eighth wonder of the world out here, traveling alone. They don't do it in these parts. My Mexican guide tried to get the rights of this unknown phenomenon. 'Your hosband in New Jersey?—You ain't got no hosband?—Howcome you can live all this time without you got no hosbond?—Are you a girl?'

"I explained that we called it old maid and he confessed, shameful fact, that he had a sister in the same boat. 'You got a house in New Jersey?—You got a father and mother?—You live all alone?—Ain't you even got no one to work for you?'

"At that I brightened and boasted of Solomon in all his glory. I should have told him that I also had an editor who was a father confessor.

"Having shaken as much of the mud of San Antonio from my

feet as possible I did 220 miles between noon and 6 p.m. Driving in the country is far, far better than sightseeing in a city. The sun was out at last and my spirits rose with each passing mile. I am on my way to Carlsbad, New Mexico, for Christmas.

"Coming north (I have traveled lots more up and down the map than across it) the land changed rapidly from adobe mud and Opuntia cactus and cattle raising to quite tall trees, oaks live and regular, and then to sheep country with hills and almost mountains. It was also Dip country with every mile or so a sign, 'Dip—400 feet,' which means a depression where the creek can flow over the road in rainy weather. Sometimes there is a pole marked so you can tell how far your car has to swim. Today the dips were mostly dry but if you did not see the sign and slow down the effect was worse than a roller coaster. One had so much water in it I waited for another car to come along and go through before I took a chance.

"There was a splendiferous sunset. This is the part of the West I love, where you can see the whole horizon in a great circle around you, unmarked by human habitation, and you can see the reflected glory of the sun's setting in every direction, rose color, above a strip of deepest blue. The air got better and better as we approached Ozona, "the Biggest Little Town in the World" according to the electric sign in the square. At any rate it is a pleasant Western town; the streets are dry and paved and there are sidewalks! I felt like apologizing for me and the car both in our muddy state. There is a square hung with Christmas lights and rather nice window decorations. I don't think they go in for as much street trimming as we do but I saw one town with Spanish moss hung across the streets and San Antonio had red and green stars on white backgrounds to represent the lone star state. They have fireworks in the South for Christmas; one boy was setting some off prematurely. Maybe they don't need to decorate with every tree along the highway having great balls of mistletoe. I stopped to take a picture and gathered a sprig to take with me.

"*Dec. 25.* Christmas Day at Carlsbad Caverns; could there be a more unique way to celebrate it? My queer one-sided mind thrills more to a cactus a hundred years old than to glistening stalactites and stalagmites with years numbered in millions but that six-mile walk through enormous subterranean halls made an unforgettable impression. The best moment was when Rock of Ages was sung as we rested in black velvet darkness beside the pillar of that name—a pillar formed drop by drop during the past fifty million years. There was one other New Jerseyite among the 372 visitors this day and we just happened to drive up and park together, much to the amusement of the ranger who drawled, 'Looks like you New Jersey folks ought to get together instead of driving all the way out here in two cars.'

"*Dec.* 27. Yesterday was my first experience with real mountain driving. The other two times I've been West someone else has been at the wheel. The bad roads were slow but very beautiful. El Paso is far and away the nicest city I've struck yet (on this trip). Not quite so big, and in the mountains, yet with a livelier, gayer air. There is much more Christmas decoration and in the Plaza a community tree, very tall, silvered, with round green, red, blue and white lights. They go on all together and then one color at a time. Somewhere underneath there is the mechanism for a continuous program of Christmas carols and the tinkly Swiss music box melodies.

"My Wellesley class paper told me I had a classmate living in El Paso so I called her up. It is strange, seeing people you have not met since college. Ruby's husband asked her what I looked like and all she could remember was that I was terribly thin. It seems incredible to me now that I was once that thin. The Tappers drove me around town—trim bungalows everywhere, Spanish, modern, and Californian in type, with oleanders and pittosporum. I was taken to lunch and until you've been a female traveling day after day with 'Alone?' uttered with the most peculiar inflection every time you ask for a room or a table in a coffee shop you cannot imagine the relief of eating with friends.

"We went over the border into Juárez. I had just had a letter from

Liz insisting that I procure there and bring along with me two
bottles of Pavon and three of Barreteaga. Nobody had heard of the
Pavon so I got all Barreteaga, a kind of brandy. I felt so foolish declaring it; I wanted them to know it was not for private consumption.
Visitors from wet states outside of Texas are allowed one gallon
every thirty days. I had to prove New Jersey residence.

"*Dec. 29.* The last two days have been very full and I only wish I
had hurried to this part of the country sooner. Not Phoenix! That's
another great city, lined with auto courts for five miles out, traffic,
four-lane highways, scads of hotels, all expensive. I drove up and
down trying to find one shabby enough so I could afford a room. I
can't get used to the swift transition from desert to bustling city.
Just a few minutes before I had been alone with God and the mountains, and giant cacti dark against the sunset afterglow.

"Yesterday the first two hours were through a thick gray fog.
Once I stopped to avoid running down two coyotes, beautiful crea-
tures who stared at me as I was staring at them. After a brief stop at
Tombstone I reached Tucson in time for late lunch. It was the first
time in ages I had had fresh vegetables and the first time I had had
the hot, dry heat I have been expecting. I can understand why
anyone with T.B., sinus trouble, or arthritis comes out here but
the various mortuaries and funeral chapels are eloquent testimony
to the number of people who arrive too late. Also, since the sick
seem to be harbored anywhere in town, it is a sobering thought to
wonder what illness the last person who occupied your room may
have had.

"My first objective was the entomology department, for Dr. Wehrle
had been at Cornell when I was. We talked bugs fast and furiously,
then went down to plant pathology to learn about root-rot fungi
from Dr. Brown and Dr. Streets. I collected all kinds of literature.
It was nearly dark when we got outside to study plants—the cactus
garden, the avenue of Canary palms alternating with columnar
cypress, the lovely gray Arizona cypress (a juniper), an avenue of
olive trees, loquats in bloom with a heavenly odor. Apparently any-

thing will grow here with effort. But what effort! They have what is called caliche, an impenetrable deposit, and to grow a tree the original hole has to be blasted large enough to last the growing tree roots a lifetime, else the thing dies with 'caliche blight.'

"I spent the evening with the Wehrle family and learned about all the deadly pests around here: scorpions whose sting kills a child with terrible convulsions in a few minutes; centipedes, not quite deadly but pretty bad; rattlesnakes which come out at night because they are killed by hot sun; gila monsters which usually leave you short of death but hang on like bulldogs and have to be pried off; black widow spiders which, compared to the rest, are so harmless they are kept as pets, tarantulas likewise. The Wehrles had some black widows to show me and said they had been trying to coax tarantulas to stay but they did not like the new house as well as the old. My hosts were, of course, laying it on thick to watch me squirm but they cited authentic cases and today in the laboratory I saw all these animals pickled and their habitats labeled. Dr. Mallory escorted me up the mountain to the Carnegie Desert Laboratory, where they are working on the ecology of the Sonora Desert. There I saw more rattlesnakes that had been killed *inside* their building. Verily, I'd hate to walk around Arizona on summer nights. They did say the deadliness of the venom was in direct relation to the poundage of the person so probably I would not be in much danger.

"The road this afternoon was right in the mountains. The giant cacti thrill me as stalagmites never can. Never two giants alike; I cannot fathom how a few straight sticks can ring so many changes. At Florence, I turned east a few miles to the Boyce Thompson Arboretum. Interesting, in a magnificent setting! Mr. Whitehead, the superintendent, showed me the greenhouses where he has a large collection of Mrs. Coombs' succulents, the cactus garden, and the canyon by Colonel Boyce Thompson's former residence, perched on the very top of a crag. I feel now that I have learned to recognize Mesquite and Palo Verde trees and a few cacti but I'd hate to be examined on the latter. I never knew there were so many kinds of

Opuntias. There are angular affairs of all descriptions as well as the common flat, jointed ones. Another most peculiar plant (tree?) is *Idris columnaris* which is native to one tiny region in Arizona and through Lower California. When young, a mere ten or twenty years, it looks like an inverted parsnip with green branches growing out but it becomes more columnar as it gets older.

"*Dec. 31.* El Monte, California. Well, I made it, all the way without one whimper out of the Ford. I was very proud of her; she never stalled once, made the mountains on high, never thought of tire trouble. I simply flew the 400 miles across the desert yesterday arriving here by 4:30. 'Here' is the bungalow of Elizabeth Bodger Baertschiger and her new husband Herman, where I am making headquarters. Today is bright and sunny. I am attending to the ravages to clothes and person of twenty-three days on the road.

"*New Year's Eve.* There is a mile of Christmas trees at Altadena, enormously tall deodars, lighted each year from Christmas Eve through New Year's. After viewing these we spent the rest of the evening and the small hours of the morning at Herman's mother's ranch, with a midnight buffet supper in true Swiss style. That brandy I'd been asked to get at Juárez was for this celebration.

"*January 1, 1938.* I had hurried across country to be sure and see the famous Tournament of Roses. More than a million people witnessed the long parade and everyone said it was finer this year than ever. Can you imagine five miles of floats, each made of nothing but fresh-cut flowers, interspersed with bands and gay riders on beautiful horses decked with flowers and silver saddles?

"*Jan. 2.* We drove down to Laguna Beach, having dinner in a tearoom practically on top of the ocean. I was interested in the succulents, especially *Mesembryanthemum edulis,* a coarse ground cover with creamy flowers growing thick over the sandy hillsides. Laguna is famous for its Artists' Colony and for its pottery. I tried to keep away from the latter but finally succumbed to a set of bowls. Everyone in California uses this brilliant pottery, orange, red, black, blue, green, or yellow and the sets are mixed so the blue cup is on a yellow saucer. The first time I helped Liz set the table I matched up cups and saucers but that was wrong.

"*Jan. 3.* I went out to the Bodger Seeds, Ltd. ranch and was introduced around. I never knew before how world-wide this wholesale business is. The long corridors and most of the offices are papered with foreign stamps, an amusing and breath-taking collection. Many seeds are sent to Australia because California growing conditions are nearer those of Australia than those of England.

"When I went to Pasadena for a permit to keep the Ford in the state there were feathery lanes of pepper trees with soft pink berries; gray-green acacias with yellow flowers just coming; eucalyptus with beautiful white trunks and peeling bark, white, rose or scarlet flowers. The oil in damp trees has a most delightful odor. The broad baby eucalyptus leaves are quite different from the linear leaves of the adult trees. Roses were in bloom here for the Parade but now they are being pruned back for spring. January is the proper time to plant bare-root roses.

"*Jan. 4.* Mrs. Seavey, friend of Mrs. Thorne, arranged a series of garden visits. The first was a small patio garden. The owner, Alice Riley, presented me with a copy of her *Skimming Spain* so I reciprocated with *The Plant Doctor*. She writes in a study built into the garden.

"The Reynolds had me for lunch. I adored them at first sight for they are just as cockeyed about their side of gardening as I am about mine. Mr. Reynolds raises daffodils from seed and takes you around to see each little spear sticking up and tells you the results you may get six years from now as a result of the cross. He has rigged up an old washing machine with a thermostat to treat his bulbs for nematodes. Mrs. Reynolds plays with delphinium and iris for breeding purposes, has a collection of primroses and camellias for fun, and tries anything else to see what it will do for her.

"*Jan. 5.* I planned to stay home and work but Liz telephoned the county agricultural commissioner was at the ranch so I hurried out to ask him questions the rest of the morning. I volunteered to get lunch, thought I followed directions about lighting the oven but singed hair and eyebrows in the resulting explosion. It did not do anything to the stove except put out the pilot light.

"Time off for Gay's Lion Farm, where you can see two hundred lions fed and a few being trained for the movies. Looking at one walking the tight rope, and with most evident affection for his trainer, it was difficult to realize he was a dangerous beast.

"*Jan. 6.* A photographer from International News Service arrived before 9 a.m. armed with a wire from New York, telling him to get pictures of the plant doctor spraying, treating a sick rose, working in her laboratory, doing her housework. I indignantly demanded to know how they expected to get my house and spraying equipment, not to mention Solomon, in California. They posed me for pictures for two hours, in Liz' kitchen. I was in a grand state with my hair singed.

"Then I had only fifteen minutes left to dress and get to Pasadena, ten miles away, where Mrs. Seavey was waiting to show more gardens. Her own, chiefly wooded with ferns, runs down a hillside into a canyon.

"*Jan. 7.* The trip to Riverside was through golden-fruited citrus orchards, stretching from the palm-bordered boulevards to the faraway snow-capped mountains. I made a pilgrimage to the top of Mt. Rubidoux, where they have the Easter sunrise service and lunched in the flower-filled patio of the Mission Inn before getting down to the business of the day, asking questions of the plant pathologists and entomologists at the Citrus Experiment Station.

"*Jan. 8.* Opal Scarborough, newspaper and radio garden editor, arrived for an interview. We are collaborating on an article. Went to see an insecticide firm. Mabel Myers, Cornell friend, took us out to dinner.

"*Jan. 9.* Wrote the column and business letters. Liz, Herman and I were at the Huntington Library as soon as it opened, went through the Museum in double-quick time to get to the garden, almost the high point of my trip. There are fine collections of cycads and ferns, some staghorns on trees measuring six to eight feet across, very fine palms, lovely roses and camellias, much heather, a pretty Japanese garden. The succulents and cacti kept me gasping. Imagine the flaming red and yellow of thousands of aloes blooming at once. We went to an orange ranch for supper and there was just time before dark to see a Fuller's rose beetle and the injury done by orange thrips.

"*Jan. 10.* The University of California has seven campuses. I went to the one near Los Angeles (U.C.L.A.) to talk with the entomologist and the plant pathologist appointed a year or so ago to work on diseases of ornamentals. Unfortunately, their teaching schedules have been so heavy there has been no time for research. They did have a survey which Dr. Massey had made when he was out here on Sabbatic leave from Cornell and I copied highlights from that. I had lunch with a horticultural committee, met the manager of a tree company, went home to write a paper.

"*Jan. 11.* Elizabeth and I drove to a garden district meeting at Monrovia where she was the main speaker, on new annuals. She was awfully good. See this month's *Country Home* for a thrilling account of her hybridizing work. I rated a corsage and was asked to say a few words about the book. In the afternoon we visited gardens. One had a thousand-year-old live oak; two other oaks had attained five hundred years. A paved area under one tree was large enough to seat a hundred people.

"*Jan. 12.* Dorothy Black Butler, another Wellesley classmate, drove me up to the Ojai, making sure that the first glimpse of her beautiful valley was where the red-berried toyon (California-holly) covered the mountainsides. We went to a meeting of Dorothy's garden club (where I saw ornamental kale used for arrangements for the first time) and then on to Mrs. Oakleigh Thorne's in Montecito where I am to talk to the Santa Barbara Garden Club.

"*Jan. 13.* Mrs. Thorne came in while I was finishing my breakfast tray to see what I thought about talking outdoors in the camellia garden. I hastened to approve the idea, for the camellias are in full bloom around the circular paved court. I spent an entranced hour

wandering through her shady Japanese garden with its azaleas and
soft helixine ground cover; two formal gardens with standard geraniums used like tree roses, set off by diamonds of white stone and
enclosed by Monterey cypress; the rose garden by the fountain; long
terraces of pools leading to the pavilion; a garden now being copied
from an old Italian book with a visual boxwood maze in the center
and summer houses at intervals; the desert garden featuring California natives; the fern garden with tender tree ferns; the bank of
white calla lilies; and finally the barns filled with adequate spraying
equipment and the huge compost pits. I took due note of lace bugs
on the toyon and other pests for a report to Mrs. Thorne on her
garden's health. Later that day we visited another estate with a table
made of a section of redwood, with historic dates marked on the
annual rings. The birth of Christ was a lot later than the beginning
of that tree.

"*Jan. 14.* I was out early to take pictures of the garden before we
left. When I went to say goodby to Mrs. Thorne she handed me a
check and asked if it was all right. I took one glance and protested
that it was much more than the fee I had quoted for a talk but she
said it was worth it anyway. When Dorothy's car was brought around
the nearly empty tank had been filled with gasoline. We spent the
morning at the Blakesley Botanic Garden where they are concentrating on ceanothus; at the Museum where they devote one room to
seasonal exhibits of fresh flowers from Santa Barbara gardens; the
Mission with its 'Garden of Death' planted over the Indian graves;
and the Court House, a new building with stately Spanish exterior
and colorful tiled interior. Then back to Ojai, where I tried to photograph the mountains from every angle of Dorothy's home.

"*Jan. 15.* It poured during the night but cleared early leaving clouds
below the mountain tops. We went to Pasadena to a Wellesley
luncheon and afterward they showed movies of Wellesley, including
some taken in this winter's snow; it made me a bit homesick. I asked
Dorothy to have tea with me before her drive back and we paused
before a dress shop next to the tearoom. She looked at a flowered

dress in the window and defied me to find any pests on that. I looked at the box full of geraniums in front of the window and saw a canker-worm on every leaf.

"*Jan. 16.* Listened to Opal Scarborough on the radio and wrote the column; went in to Los Angeles for a Sigma Delta Epsilon tea.

"*Jan. 17.* Another day with the Reynolds at Pasadena, this time mostly visiting nurseries, including the Coolidge Rare Plant Gardens. I returned to El Monte with three minutes left to dress for the Business and Professional Women's Club dinner. Elizabeth is president. The speaker was the Prosecuting Attorney of Los Angeles County. His figures on the tribute being paid this day to racketeers, both here and in New York, were astounding.

"*Jan. 18.* I went to the Bodger Ranch to meet Betty Ransome. Some years ago she started a commercial seed-testing business of her own and has made a great success of it. I had a chance a year or so ago to come out and work as a pathologist under her. Her laboratory now tests all the Bodger seeds and those of many other commercial growers. Sugar-beet companies have her under contract to do research for them. Lunch at Los Angeles with Mildred Fehling Davis. This Wellesley classmate has gone into the landscape business, does some nursery work, writes a newspaper column, teaches at U.C.L.A., and takes care of a husband and child. Whenever I think I'm busy I meet other people who manage twice as much as I.

"*Jan. 19.* I am down at Long Beach visiting Louise, Elizabeth's sister. While she makes a dress for me I am taking a day off—at least it is a day off compared to other days. All I have to do is work on the column, do business letters, prepare the talk for the Horticultural Institute tomorrow evening, and see a few gardens.

"*Jan. 20.* I was trembling in my boots at the thought of talking to all those professional growers at the Horticultural Institute but Maria Wilks gave an excellent introduction. She mentioned my training and experience but noted that I had come to California saying 'in a most naïve manner' that I had come to learn and not to teach.

1908: A serious child of ten.

1935: The doctor starts on her consultation rounds. (Photo: Underwood and Underwood.)

1933: Dusting in the early days, covered to the ankles.

1954: Spraying preferred, with a small duster tucked into the Ford for emergencies. (Photo: Roche.)

1956: Interviewed in Jacksonville, Fla., about materials used for lectures and classes. (Photo: courtesy of Mary Noble.)

A Rose Exhibit in the 1956 Flower Show of the Garden Club of New Jersey.

96 Essex Avenue, Glen Ridge, after the Big Snow.

Long Island Cabin.

Azalea Hall, Spring Hill, Alabama; "home" for two wonderful winters.

Azalea flower blight controlled with
Phygon (*top left*). Unsprayed bush
(*top right*). Azalea sprayed with
Dithane (*right*).

Rose Day, 1956, with E. L. D. Seymour as Honor Guest.

Hundreds of visitors stream through the garden.

The doctor and Henry in a client's garden.

These roses, belonging to Mr. and Mrs. Clayton Freeman, Glen Ridge, have survived twenty-five years of weekly ministrations by the plant doctor. (Photo: Roche.)

So then they believed such general things as I could tell them. The table decorations for the dinner were orchids, loads of them.

"*Jan. 21.* I had an appointment at Howard and Smith's (rose nursery) but when I asked about their troubles they said they never had any; they kept their plants clean. We went to see "The Drunkard" in Hollywood, now in its fifth year, with Liz attending her thirteenth performance. A most hilarious evening.

"*Jan. 22.* Mr. Rowland of Peck and Wadsworth Tree Company invited me to a private showing of some tree movies. He has two reels in color, one of moving large trees, the other of insects. I was so excited I could scarcely sit still long enough to see them; I do hope he brings them East some day. Hurried back to El Monte to dress for a tea Liz was having for me. Her centerpiece included bird-of-paradise, roses, sweet peas, stock, snapdragons, delphinium, iris, and many more.

"*Jan. 23.* Liz, Herman, and I made a farewell trip together. To the beach at Santa Monica with an unforgettable meal at Max's Swiss Chalet, to Bernheimer's Japanese Gardens, to Evans and Reeves' Nursery, and finally to Mildred Davis's for supper, where I again marveled at how she accomplishes so much.

"*Jan. 24.* Tearful farewells. I went along the coast to Santa Barbara, then inland to stay at the Santa Maria Inn, famous among gardeners for its wealth of table and window decorations. Mr. McCoy is a friend to all gardeners and on the strength of my letter from the Bodgers he reduced the bill and presented me with a book of photographs.

"*Jan. 25.* Along the coast on the new San Simeon Highway, worth crossing the continent to try. The road is sliced out of nothing and every so often there is a sign 'slide area.' Once or twice the slide was still across the road when I got there. Reached Carmel in the middle of the afternoon and the Ford put on the performance of its life in climbing the mountain to Lester Rowntree's cabin on top of the world. She wrote *Hardy Californians* and is *the* great authority on California wild flowers. She happened to be at home—usually she is off collecting—and after one look at my letter of introduction asked, 'You wrote the book?' And immediately started asking questions fast and furiously about publishers, sales, etc. She wants to come East next year on a lecture trip. She insisted on my staying overnight, a fascinating experience. We took the famous 17-mile Drive, watched the seals, and listened to them bark.

"*Jan. 26.* Drove through the redwoods to find Francis Lester* (Mrs. Rowntree's brother) who is especially interested in old rose varieties. Went on to Vetterle and Reinelt's nursery at Capitola, where Frank Reinelt and his horticulturally minded young wife introduced me to their way of growing delphiniums. They gave me a preview of Black Knight, to be released next summer, very dark with a fuzzy black bee, very high percentage of germination. The Reinelts are also getting entrancing new colors in freesias and doing interesting crosses with tuberous begonias. Arrived at Palo Alto to stay with Cornell friends.

"*Jan. 27.* Spent the morning with Beets** trying to understand some of the new genetics but it is far beyond me. He is finding out how genes work by studying the effect of hormones on eye color in Drosophila. I felt much more at home talking to Dr. Ferris about his work on scale insects. He is the only entomologist left at Leland-Stanford, once famous in that field. In the afternoon Marion took me to see gardens. At one place mealybugs were thick under the eaves of a house. We visited Elsa Uppmann who runs a school of gardening. I bought a copy of *Ferdinand,* ostensibly for young David, chiefly so I could read it myself.

"*Jan. 28.* Lunch at Berkeley with Phila Helt, the high school English teacher who told me I *must* take Botany at Wellesley. She had been

---

* Later he wrote *My Friend, the Rose.* After his death the nursery was taken over by Will Tillotson, known to most rosarians for the mouth-watering descriptions of old roses in his catalogues.

** Dr. George Beadle, now a famous geneticist, recently President of the American Association for Advancement of Science. But I knew him as a graduate student at Cornell, one of the beaus who came for Sunday waffles. Later, Marion stayed with me before their wedding which was performed on a rock beside Lake Cayuga. I threw real rose petals and they stained her dress.

teaching in Berkeley for many years. She is now on crutches from a streptococcus infection but it doesn't phase her any. I presented myself at the Plant Pathology Department at the University of California and then Dr. Thomas, another good friend from Cornell, took me to his own garden where he is working on pyracanthas resistant to fire blight.

"*Jan. 29.* A fine clear day, most unusual in the Bay region. After viewing the fine collection of rhododendrons coming into bloom at the Berkeley Botanic Garden I went in to San Francisco to meet George Brady, amateur gardener "nuts" on fuchsias. We visited Sutro Gardens with an unparalleled view of the Pacific and went to see what Victor Reiter was doing with fuchsias. We went on to gardens in Marin County over the Golden Gate Bridge, whose beautiful structure deserves a better color than that orange-red. We returned to the Presidio in time to watch the sun set into the ocean.

"*Jan. 30.* Mrs. McDuffie, another friend of Mrs. Thorne, invited me for Sunday lunch with the Sydney Mitchells. Dr. Mitchell, librarian by profession, is dean of gardening on the West Coast. Have you read *Gardening in California* and *From a Sunset Garden?* After I had sufficiently admired our hostess's triumphant hillside of azaleas in bloom, the Mitchells took me to their garden, birthplace of so many fine irises, now being disseminated by Carl Salbach, their neighbor.

"*Jan. 31.* Dr. Thomas took me to meet lots of people; to collect dozens of bulletins; to the Oakland Rose Garden, a veritable amphitheater of roses, all neatly hard-pruned for spring; to range on range of orchid houses, where they are making many new kinds including true apricot shades; to a plant pathology seminar; and home to dinner with his family.

"*Feb. 1.* After meeting Norvell Gillespie at his office, *Sunset Magazine,* he and his wife, who also does garden writing, drove me around all day. The sky cleared at intervals but every time we got out of the car it poured again. We collected Eric Walther, botanist of Golden Gate Park, to go around with us; he gave me much needed information. Norvell took a picture of the plant doctor admiring a South African Proteus. I spent the evening shopping in Chinatown.

"*Feb.* 2. While I was exploring San Francisco I bought a copy of the Sunday *Los Angeles Times* and found they had printed my article, changing the beginning and the end rather atrociously. Returned to the hotel to find that the Gillespies had invited me to stay with them in Burlingame until after my lecture near there, so I drove down. They are the nicest young couple! I fell for them hard. It was too wet to see gardens so I curled up by the Gillespie fire with Smokey the cat in my arms and read California bulletins.

"*Feb.* 3. The president of the garden club tried to show off estates despite the rain. Norvell came to hear the talk and told me that it was unusually well received, that that particular group was hard to please.

"*Feb.* 4. Started East, went through three hailstorms and saw three rainbows. The good hotels at Bakersfield were too expensive and the others too stuffy; I decided to use the last hour of daylight and go on to Mojave. The mountain road slowed me up and it got dark too soon. I skidded going around a curve and lost control of the car for a second. It plunged wildly about and I was almost scared but I managed to yank it straight and nothing happened. When I finally got to Mojave the hotel was pretty awful and just as expensive.

"*Feb.* 5. From the hot desert with its Joshua trees to clear, cold weather at Williams, with snow all around. I had to leave the Ford in a heated garage and get it fixed up with alcohol.

"*Feb.* 6. Passed the Painted Desert en route to Gallup where I paid the same price for luxury at the El Rancho as I had for squalor in Mojave.

"*Feb.* 7. A nostalgic desire to revisit Sante Fe and a conflict in route numbers between my map and the highway gave me a half day of extremely bad roads and a flat tire (until I got back on a pavement I had attributed the thumping to the road).

"*Feb.* 8. More bad roads. I was terrified when, with a nonchalant 'Bridge Out' sign, the trail led abruptly down to a wide and swift river. The Ford proved a strong swimmer but my knees were shaking when I got out to take a picture of this New Mexico highway. Then we were out of the mountains into the Texas Panhandle, with never a hill as high as your finger, where the wind howls all day and night, and there is scarcely a tree to be seen.

"*Feb. 12.* Hospitality to Texans seems to be as natural as breathing. Dallas was even more breath-taking than Houston and a lecture on pests and diseases seemed a queer return for garden visits, luncheons, and teas in profusion. Dallas is not subtropical; it has a brown winter and spring like ours but earlier. I liked best an informal garden through the woods, with lavender dog-tooth violets parting the fallen leaves. Louise Belsterling gave me her *Planting Manual for Dallas Gardens.* Nancy Richey Ranson, garden editor and poet, took me out to White Rock at sunset. This is a lake at the edge of the city; every evening myriads of blackbirds, enough to darken the sky, come to settle in the reeds for the night. The Scruggs, mother and daughter (*Gardening in the South and West*) took me under their wings for garden visiting.

"*Feb. 13.* Leaving Texas without a visit to Fort Worth's Botanic Garden, famous for its roses and its Garden Center, was unthinkable. Mrs. Will Lake, who is at the Center six days every week, gave up her free Sunday to tell me about their lectures and field trips for adults, their Saturday programs for children. Aside from sponsoring the Center, the Fort Worth Garden Club is interested in school playgrounds. The city now boasts sixty-four professionally landscaped school grounds, many of them complete even to outdoor theaters. In Mrs. Lake's Leaping Lena we visited most of the sixty-four, especially those still unfinished, where Lena leapt from crag to crag of the construction runways.

"*Feb. 14.* With every bone creaking from yesterday's tour of school yards, I headed toward Tyler. Spring came with every mile, clusters of tiny old-fashioned daffodils around every farmhouse, redbuds here and there. Mr. Watkins of Dixie Rose Nursery told me that around this little city of Tyler, two-thirds of the rose crop of our country is grown. This is planting time in Texas. I watched the bundles being prepared for shipment, learned the standards used in grading roses. I also left an order for bushes to be sent me in March for I am anxious to try Texas roses in New Jersey.

"*Feb. 17.* Memphis, set high above the Mississippi. It rained all the way up through Arkansas and is still raining. I caught glimpses of numerous city parks and visited a fine seed store, my usual custom before a lecture to get a line on apparatus and chemicals available locally. Daffodils form great yellow rivers under the trees. According to the newspaper, my first act on reaching the hotel was to buy a rose for my room, that I could not think of spending the night without a flower.

"*Feb. 18-22.* Just driving, through rain and mud and flooded roads, wondering why the Knoxville, Tennessee, newspaper had to import a picture from Illinois to show a farm under water. Through the Cumberland Mountains where the attractive stone houses of the resettlement project gave no hint about how the inhabitants were supposed to earn their living; through the Great Smokies, which must be revisited when the rhododendrons are in bloom; to Danville, Virginia, and Julian Meade, trying to persuade that gifted author to do another *Adam's Profession* about the West; to Washington, for a call on our own 'Dick' White (executive secretary of the American Association of Nurserymen) who seems to be even more useful to nurserymen keeping an eye on legislation affecting them than when he was in New Jersey doing research on their disease problems. Finally home, where the green shoots coming into view on my own hillside seem just a bit more thrilling than anything else in the world."

CHAPTER 5

PLANT DOCTOR DAYS

M<small>RS</small>. T<small>HORNE</small> sent an ebony stand for the shell container I had purchased in Santa Barbara. In thanking her I said that getting my house in order, coping with plumbers and accumulated business mail, working on a radio talk, preparing five lectures for the next ten days, doing an article for the *New York Times* and another for *American Home* would effectually keep me from idly sitting down and reflecting on my fine vacation.

That summer I had another roomer, Russell Stevens, son of Neil, our first house guest. Russell, a graduate student, had a summer job at the Dutch Elm Disease Laboratory in Morristown. It was quite a drive from Glen Ridge but his father thought he might soak up some practical plant pathology by osmosis if he were quartered with the plant doctor. It rained every day for weeks. Solomon's successor and I would hang around waiting for the plants to dry off and then just as we started to spray it would pour again. I worked off my frustration every afternoon by collecting the summer apples from under the tree and making a pie. Then I'd ask Russell for dinner (he usually got meals out), give him half the pie for dessert, the rest for his lunch next day. At that time I believed spraying did little good unless the leaves were dry enough for the spray to stick. Later I learned that it pays to spray between showers, even if you have to repeat frequently.

In 1952, when I was staying at a hotel in Houston, the telephone rang and an FBI man announced he was in the lobby to see me. My picture had been in the paper the day before but I could think of no crime I had committed. With vast relief I learned they were investigating Russell, for an important behind-the-scenes job, and were checking every place he had ever stayed. He got the job, but my poor neighbor at home, from whom the FBI had gotten my whereabouts, worried about me all winter.

In September, 1938, the Diggers came for another picnic in my garden. I refused to let them bring their own lunches—I wanted to provide New England baked beans—so they arrived bearing gifts, a gallon vacuum jug, a charcoal broiler, all sorts of outdoor utensils. But it rained and we had to have our picnic indoors. The wind seemed pretty strong so they started back to Nyack early. With time on my hands I decided to take some of the left-over beans to friends in New York. I paid little attention to underpasses full of water and signs blown down. I had no radio and it was not until the next day, when we started out to gardens and found most of the streets blocked by fallen trees, that I learned I had lived through a HURRICANE. The poor Diggers had had a sad time getting home through fallen wires.

My talk to the American Rose Society that fall, written up in the Magazine, led to a consultation job on an estate near Philadelphia. I went down once a month to check over their troubles and wrote the report in triplicate, one copy for the owner, one for the superintendent, one for my records. It has always seemed to me that the more gardeners there are on a place the harder it is to get pest control work done at the right time. There is always something else—remaking lawns, changing bedding plants, putting in vegetables—that seems more important. After a few years you feel rather silly writing the same advice over and over and charging for it. I did, however, get really excited on the estate one day because the leaves on all the roses had suddenly turned brown. I asked what spray had been used and was told 'Tri-ogen.' Starting to the telephone to tell the manufacturer that something had gone terribly wrong with his product I noticed a sheepish expression on one or two faces. With prolonged questioning I learned that a weedkiller had been used in the sprayer the day before the roses were sprayed. Each gardener thought the other one had rinsed out the sprayer.

Another time I found trouble on that estate from 2,4-D being used as a weedkiller. It had been applied to the grass as a powder, had been carried by rains down to the tree roots, and all the leaves on all the tall oaks near the lawn were malformed. I never did use 2,4-D myself; I was too busy diagnosing the queer troubles people had after that came on the market. Once a doctor telephoned to tell me of the catastrophe that had occurred to the chrysanthemums in his home greenhouse. I took one look at the twisted stems, unrecognizable foliage and said 2,4-D had been used nearby. They denied it but I found a can on the shelf. It had probably been opened there before being used on the lawn. I never put this potent material in my sprayers. One year on my travels I stopped at the University of Kentucky and they showed me a sprayer that had been used once for applying 2,4-D and then had been rinsed fourteen times with different chemicals. It still retained enough vapor so that, if put in a greenhouse where seedling tomatoes were being grown, the plants would twist and curl up.

1939

I stayed at home this winter. *Jersey Life* had folded up (perhaps its demise was hastened by my column) but a few articles for the *New York Times* kept me eating. I put on an exhibit of House Plant Pests and another of Lawn Problems at the New York Flower Show. I let myself be elected chairman of the Garden Department of the Glen Ridge Woman's Club. In a two-year regime we had what I thought were excellent meetings on a modest budget. We had Fred Rockwell, Dorothy Biddle, and other fine lecturers. We had bus trips to the Cloisters, the New York Botanical Garden, the Brooklyn Botanic Garden. I learned that everyone wants to take a trip in spring but in autumn most women think they should be home doing fall housecleaning. We had an "Information, Please" program with Mr. Seymour as one of the experts; anyone stumping the experts got a copy of his *Garden Encyclopedia.* We had a Rose Tour, ending up with tea in my garden, for the benefit of the New Jersey Arboretum and a public lecture by Lester Rowntree (here in the East with her exquisite wildflower slides) for the same cause. We had a fall Flower Show with a very practical exhibit on growing roses. I didn't mind time for Garden Department meetings or giving luncheons for the speakers but I did grudge time off from earning a living for lengthy board meetings, the chief drawback in my trying to sandwich in volunteer work. Over and over I learn that donating too many workdays means ending up the year in the red.

All during 1939 I had another book in mind, a serious affair collating known data on diseases of ornamentals. Nothing of the kind was available in America but I failed to interest a publisher. I thought the project might be attractive to the Guggenheim Foundation so I filled out numerous application blanks and wrote to Dr. B. O. Dodge for a reference. He replied that he and Dr. H. W. Rickett were just embarking on such a book [*Diseases and Pests of Ornamental Plants,* published in 1943]. With the New York Botanical Garden behind such a project there was no point in my trying to get Guggenheim money so I gave up the idea. I'm not sorry. Ten years later, when I finally did the disease book, more comprehensive than my original plan, it was on my own with no subsidy other than advance royalty on a signed contract.

1940

Spare time this year was devoted to enlarging *The Plant Doctor,* adding chapters for the things I had been learning in the Southeast and the Southwest. It was still basically sound, an encouraging conclusion from my wanderings. Troubles differ somewhat in different sections but they even up. Each section has its share but none has an undue proportion. I did some revising for the *Garden Encyclopedia* and spent a lot of time collecting and pressing material for classes. Mona Gardner wrote an article about Career Women for *Mademoiselle* and the part about the plant doctor was reprinted in *Reader's Digest.* That meant a lot more letters to answer from women who wanted to go and do likewise. They were all more concerned with ways of contacting clients and the financial remuneration to be expected than with their own qualifications for such work.

In November, Dan Walden brought the first copies of the new *Plant Doctor* as I boarded the train for Iowa. I arrived at Davenport on that fatal Armistice Day when a sudden freeze killed thousands of wild ducks, domestic turkeys, and cattle. I had asked to see gardens before talking to the Tri-City Garden Club and the women carried out their part of the bargain even with roofs being blown off houses in the gale. It had been warm up to that day; now, roses, chrysanthemums, even marigolds were quick frozen while still in full bloom. We would dash out of the car, take a quick look, then duck back out of the wind.

I had a hotel reservation but ended up staying with the Howertons, a young couple with a particularly attractive small home. At the end of the table in the dining alcove was a whole bower of blooming plants. We had a leisurely Sunday breakfast there, shared by neighbors from Cornell. Beth became another friend to go in the permanent address book, to be remembered with affection, to have a Christmas note. Some day I hope to go back.

I talked at Cedar Rapids, seeing gardens with the temperature well below zero, then visited at Wapello with Marjorie Pettis, with whom I had grown up in North Attleboro. When I spoke at the high school her children attended I was rather afraid, for teenagers are more critical than gardeners. They kept still, and evidently liked Mrs. Shirrefs' paintings. I talked at Mason City and saw the lake covered with dead birds, their tails frozen to the ice before they could take off. Iowa State College at Ames puts on an annual gala affair for gardeners, painless education. My three spots on the program included roses as well as garden enemies. I ended up at Des Moines for a visit to *Better Homes & Gardens,* and promised them an article later.

1941

Back East, I went directly to a one-room apartment on West 20th Street, New York. I had always thought it would be fun to live in New York for a winter and now I was doing it. I gave myself the usual plausible arguments. It was an easier headquarters for the courses I was to give at the Horticultural Society of New York and for the Long Island Horticultural Society in Farmingdale. The rent was less than the fuel oil bill at home. The high cost of heating my house has always been a way to have winter fun with a clear conscience. I ignore the fact that I always have a whopping big plumbing bill in spring. Not because of pipes freezing; the plumber drains those when he closes the house. It is simply because ancient pipes cannot stand idle and get to work again, so each year more old pipes are replaced with new.

The car had been put on stilts before I left for Iowa. Books and specimens were moved into New York by taxi; and I spent much of the winter putting samples of rusts, mildews, beetle injury etc. into individual packets as I had back in the materials room at Cornell. Later I evolved a much simpler, faster, and far less bulky way of handling material for class use. Without pressing or drying, a diseased leaf fresh from the garden is placed on a 3 x 5 filing card and covered with overlapping strips of Scotch tape. This can be done in any hotel room while traveling and eliminates presses and other equipment. The specimen remains soft rather than brittle and keeps its color for several years. It cannot, of course, be used for microscopic work but amateur gardeners are interested in gross symptoms.

Along with labeled material for class study I kept producing unnamed specimens for little quizzes. I would ask, "What is it?" "What do you do about it?" and, most important from a plant doctor standpoint, "*When* do you do it?" One girl was deadly serious about the course for she was starting her own garden maintenance service. For a year or two I visited some of her gardens, made suggestions on control measures, answered appeals for help over the telephone. She is still in business, doing well.

The Macmillan Company wanted a chapter for their *Gardening With The Experts*. I obliged with the usual "Garden Sanitation." All my plant doctoring days I have insisted that a paper bag was our most important garden tool. It should be carried around the garden at least once a week to collect all fading flowers, all infected leaves or infested tips.

I received prompt payment for the article prepared for *Better Homes & Gardens* but it didn't appear in the magazine. Several years later a new garden editor rummaged through their old files, found the story, decided it was still applicable. It came out under the title "Are You Your Garden's Biggest Pest?" I don't think I was clever enough to have provided that but I latched onto it, added it to the lecture list. It is rather popular and there is always new material available in this line. After I had talked on azalea problems in the South a woman remarked that I had told them what to do about everything except Willie Baxter, Willie being the handyman gardener with a hand more heavy than handy. He is doubtless the biggest problem we have, more dangerous than beetles or diseases. I say in the rose lecture that anyone can grow roses if she doesn't have a gardener.

I was home again at the end of February, poking around the back hillside. We had a very cold, windy March and everyone was worried about foliage browning on their broad-leaved evergreens. I spent hours on consultations, trying to persuade gardeners to let their shrubs alone, not to cut them back until after normal time for new growth when they could tell how much wood had actually been killed. We are always so quick to assume complete loss, so ready to chop down a plant without giving nature a chance to display her recuperative powers. I visited Long Island estates with George Van Yahres, tree expert. He was one of the first to try chemotherapy for the Dutch elm disease. Whether the injections really helped or whether treated elms merely escaped the disease I don't know.

We were working too many hours in gardens that summer. Nyack days were much too long, with three or four hours of transportation added to eight of spraying. I usually finished the day with a couple of hours devoted to spraying a large planting of delphiniums for cyclamen mite. One night going home I started to pass a long trailer truck. Not realizing in my weary state that I had plenty of room, I swerved a little to the left (it was a divided highway), hit some loose gravel and was catapulted into the truck. We weren't hurt, neither was the truck, but the Ford was pretty crumpled. I wrote the superintendent of that last garden that I would have to give up care of the delphinium; it made too hard a day. I told of the accident but said he was not to inform my client. He ignored that injunction and next day there was a check in the mail to more than cover repair bills. I tried to return it; then I tried to apply it toward the rest of the season's work. Mrs. Perry was adamant; it was her pleasure to do that for me. New Englanders don't like being indebted but I gave in to her genuine concern and affection. And I thought how lucky I was to be in a business where clients are friends!

WARTIME

The European war clouds were having their effect here. I wrote an article on "Roses in War Time" and the course I taught at home that fall was called "Garden Defense." My assistant went into the army, and a feeble old man was the only help in finishing work that fall.

December 4, 1941 the Ford developed battery trouble. I decided to buy a new car instead of a new battery, telephoning the dealers that they could tow in the present Ford and get me another at their convenience. What sixth sense made me order a new car three days before Pearl Harbor and the freezing of all sales, I don't know. By the time it was delivered, extra tires had been frozen and I had no spare, but at least I could stay in business during the war—if I could get gasoline and help.

I had been experimenting with growing vegetables for a year or two, first in my own garden then expanding into my neighbor's back yard. When Richardson Wright asked for something on vegetable troubles for *House & Garden* I had some personal experience to draw on.

The *New York Times* and the New York Botanical Garden put on a series of Victory Garden programs at Times Hall. I was scheduled for February 10th. My usual winter cold seemed unimportant and I managed to get through the afternoon speech. By dinner time my throat was on fire. The evening talk was sheer torture, for the audience as well as for me. Every word had to be torn out. I never would have made it without a microphone and afterward someone called it a triumph of mind over matter.

I negotiated the subway, the Hudson Tubes, the Erie Railroad, the walk home, and tumbled into bed. I had always believed it perfectly safe to live alone as long as there was a telephone by the bed. Next morning I learned better. Realizing I was in for a prolonged spell, I tried to order some groceries. I took down the receiver and struggled and struggled to give the number; it was no use; my mind could no longer triumph over matter. I couldn't even call to the next-door neighbors and ask them to get a doctor. I did have a stamp, so I wrote a letter, left it in the door for the postman. Twenty-four hours later the doctor telephoned, heard my grunts, said he would be right over. That laryngitis lasted a month. When I was finally able to get out I had to carry pad and pencil.

I had been appointed chairman of the Glen Ridge Victory Garden Committee and had to present preliminary plans to the Defense Council. Someone read my written report and I forced out an occasional word in answer to questions. I was hampered by being unable to use the telephone but managed to get the town organized into sections, a leader for each section. We obtained extra land, vacant lots, ash heaps (they grew fine tomatoes), playgrounds. We are terribly shady in Glen Ridge. We had not thought that we had enough sun to grow vegetables but we did. And we learned that it took less time to grow good ones than it took to stand in market to buy insipid stuff.

I had great difficulty with my own work. A neighbor started to help but got a factory job, although he was well over retirement age. His son, who had been ill several years, did such work as his health permitted. A graduate student had promised to come but changed his mind, not letting me know until he was due to show up. I ended up by spraying mornings by myself, picking up one high school boy after school for work until late supper, using another on Saturdays. One had asthma and should not have been working on plants; the other was a fledgling accountant. He kept such strict record of the minutes spent with me I had no excuse to pay him extra. Boys that trusted me in the matter of hours usually had a bonus.

With a B ration I had just gas enough to get to clients once a week or ten days; if rain interrupted, I could not return. There was no extra allowance for visiting Victory Gardens so I walked miles around town urging people to grow food. When I bought rotenone I had to swear it was for food production only; none was allowed on ornamentals. We had lots of Botrytis blight in gardens planted with the last shipment of bulbs in from abroad; and hundreds of daffodil bulbs, grown in our own Northwest, were stricken with another Botrytis disease. They rotted in the ground. I suppose that wartime had meant inadequate inspection.

I was sure we needed roses in wartime and had no patience with the Connecticut Experiment Station which sent out a press release urging us to stop growing roses so we could have insecticides for vegetables. I said let's have roses anyway and if they have to get along without a few sprays and if we have to rub off aphids and pick off beetles by hand, why not?

The second Sunday in June, 1942, my roses were officially at home to the whole town. I wanted to show how to take care of vegetables and used the roses as a "come-on." Everyone was invited to a party. I never did any black marketing, never had an extra sugar allowance, yet with the aid of honey, syrups, canned fruits etc., punch and cookies were provided for more than two hundred visitors. The variety of cookies that can be made without sugar is amazing (see the Appendix for one or two recipes). I had fun ferreting out the recipes but it was more fun getting people really interested in roses.

In addition to spraying and dusting vegetables for clients, writing a squib for *Woman's Home Companion* on "Ten Ways to Keep Victory Gardens Healthy," riding herd on our thousand Victory Gardeners, I was growing my own vegetables, 38 kinds in one summer, canning them from 10 p.m. to 2 a.m.

We put on a splendiferous Harvest Show. Anent the latter, our paper commented, "To the casual observer, just everything looked good enough to be given an award. When one thinks of Glen Ridge, as he invariably does, as a white collar community, it seems almost unbelievable that any such results could have been achieved by a group of amateur gardeners. But there it all was, right in plain sight, so luscious looking as to have been produced by the hands of the country's ablest farmers."

I was proud enough of my town to burst. We had more than a Show; we put on a Harvest Supper, making a large sum for the Nurses Scholarship Fund. Except for a few staples obtained with points allowed by the Ration Board, everything was donated, grown or baked in Glen Ridge. For the main course, the diners had a choice of chicken, home grown, or seafood which didn't take ration points, or baked beans and ham, which took the fewest points. They had to choose from nine very beautiful and succulent salads, each bowl representing a different Victory Garden section and using only edibles grown in that section. There was a prize for the group that produced the most popular salad but the guests cheated a bit and tried to taste everything; the result was a draw.

One thing is especially remembered from that year. For once, my bank, not I, made a mistake. They bounced a check when there was money to cover in the account but then wrote a generous letter of apology to the firm, hoping the plant doctor credit was not impaired. I love a bank that will admit a mistake; I make so many.

Fuel bills for the winter of 1943 were paid by working in Clara Hires' laboratory in Millburn, using rusty bacteriological techniques to transfer orchid seed. At that time Clara was starting orchids in culture for commercial growers as well as studying the growth of ferns under aseptic conditions. To save gasoline rations for spring doctoring, I went by bus and train, which meant standing on a street corner at 6 on a cold winter morning. I was glad when, at the end of February, the *Home Garden,* a new magazine that had been started by Fred Rockwell and other experts, asked me to prepare some pest control charts. It was easier working at home than commuting, also more in my own line.

In May, there was a rather strenuous week at Macy's where the New York Botanical Garden was promoting garden courses. The other lecturers came in one day a week for six weeks but the pests were concentrated into one week so that I had two half-day classes Monday through Saturday and an extra on Thursday evening.

That spring was highlighted by my being asked to work for Mrs. Charles MacArthur (Helen Hayes). She belonged to the Nyack Garden Club and was much interested in roses. My clients had been trying to get her interested in *me* for some time. Now her regular gardener was off to war and the plant doctor could help. Her place is beautifully laid out with a large rose garden on one of the seven terraces that go down to the Hudson. Working alone, it took me a whole day to prune the roses, so Miss Hayes invited me in for lunch. Most of the food had been produced on her farm.

The next spring Miss Hayes came in from a bond-selling tour while I was pruning and said she would be out to learn how as soon as she had gotten out of her last pair of nylons. She did come out, all glowing with the tributes the soldiers had paid to her daughter, Mary. Another morning, at the time she was playing in "Happy Birthday," she spent hours grubbing wild onions out of the bank. I reminded her of how stiff she would be and she ruefully agreed, especially since she had to dance in the show that night. Once she and Mary were rehearsing "Alice-Sit-By-The-Fire" in the garden when we came to spray. Mr. MacArthur was thoughtful enough to take a picture of his wife in the garden with me; it still hangs in my office. Their swimming pool was always open to neighborhood children except during polio epidemics. When my nephew Johnny was here on a visit he went swimming in the pool while I sprayed. An expert swimmer, his stunts delighted the children. Mary and Johnny, so soon to lose their lives, one to polio, the other to war in Korea!

The first time I ever saw rose midge was in this garden. The roses had been superb in June, when Miss Hayes was away on tour. When she returned in August the bushes looked thrifty but there was little color and no prospective bloom; all the tiny buds were black. I wrote to Dr. William Blauvelt at Cornell who confirmed the diagnosis and sent some of their experimental DDT, not yet on the market. I drenched ground and bushes for three weeks, got rid of the midge and had good late fall bloom. But by that time Miss Hayes was on tour again! When the war was over I was no longer needed in this garden but Miss Hayes passed me on to the Maxwell Andersons and they, in turn, to the Milton Caniffs.

CHAPTER 6

ONCE IN A LIFETIME

THROUGHOUT THE YEARS, writing for Fred Rockwell, first when he was garden editor of the *New York Times* and later when he took over the *Home Garden*, remained a challenge. I sputtered that when he decided on something he always wanted it yesterday. The day after our second Harvest Show 2000 questions were dumped on me from *Home Garden* with instructions to sort them out into 1200 for the proposed book, *Ten Thousand Garden Questions Answered,* and to return with answers in *two weeks*. I did it in six, which probably set some sort of record. The questions came from all over the country and I sent airmail letters to all forty-eight experiment stations asking for all bulletins, mimeographed circulars and the like available to gardeners in their states. I think I was supposed to make up questions to provide an over-all picture of pest problems but I didn't have to. The real questions that had come into the *Home Garden* office were varied enough, from how to control armadillos in Florida to pocket gophers in California.

I worked and I worked! I told clients they would have to shift for themselves; no more spraying that fall. I sat in my living room from before 6 in the morning to long after midnight surrounded by books and papers and my own notes. I looked longingly each day out the window at the rose garden and the lounging chairs in the October sunshine. I allowed myself a brief half-hour there each noon, while I ate a sandwich and read a story in the *Saturday Evening Post*. Soon a woman who had taken a room next door, for a brief period, came and spent that respite with me, asking all kinds of questions. It became an ordeal when I was so tired, so I gave up even that bit of the garden.

In the midst of all this I had a wire from Washington, from Dr. Samuel Emsweller, asking me to meet him in New York. I knew that Dr. Emsweller was an eminent horticulturist but he was not a plant pathologist. With my one-track mind I knew little of his brilliant researches on lilies and I felt poorly equipped to talk with him. To my utter astonishment I was offered a job, tentatively and temporarily, under that same Civil Service that had said, back in depression days, "little or no demand for female eligibles." Now they were considering females again, not because they wanted them but because men could not work on such frivolous things as diseases of *ornamental* plants in wartime. Recommended by my good friend Anna Jenkins in Washington and by Dr. Massey at Cornell, I was being offered a whack at the azalea flower spot (petal blight) problem. At least, I thought I was. When I finally got the job and was being fingerprinted in Washington I was told, "We don't really expect you to get anywhere; all we want you to do is to continue the experiments set up and keep the seat warm until the war is ended and the men can take over again." I was, however, given carte blanche to try anything I wanted and before I finished the seat got rather hot.

The appointment actually went through in record time but that fall the hours dragged while I was waiting to learn what I was going to do. The azalea disease had become economically important throughout the South. Nurserymen suffered because their clients were afraid to buy azaleas. Merchants suffered for lack of the tourist trade when the big gardens, open to the public at a fee, had to close a month or more early because of "weather" which was really blight. A special appropriation had been set up by Congress, sponsored by Senator Ellender of Louisiana and Senator Bankhead of Alabama. Dr. D. L. Gill had been stationed to work at Baton Rouge, Dr. J. F. L. Childs at Spring Hill, near Mobile, Alabama. Now Dr. Gill was in the army and Dr. Childs was being transferred to Florida for essential work on citrus diseases. Someone was needed to keep that appropriation.

I wrote to Anna Jenkins, "I think it would be a mistake to give up plant doctoring entirely. At the present time I am more useful to the country in an educational line—teaching, lecturing, writing—than I would be in a permanent research job. On the other hand, a few months in another area will increase the information I am always trying to get, and I should very much like a winter in the South. As to my qualifications for the job, I know Southern problems a little, have visited gardens there, and have tried to keep up with the literature. I have plenty of experience for control work and a vast interest in that side of the research problem. I have had enough experience with gardeners so that I can probably work with nurserymen all right. The drawbacks are that I cannot get home in time to start my spring program satisfactorily or to superintend the Victory Garden work. It would mean giving up a number of winter lecture engagements and I have never yet welshed on a date no matter how sick. It would mean turning my back on a cellar full of food and paying for room and board elsewhere. The salary would cover it but the net results might be about the same, with writing and lectures here."

By mid-November the appointment still was not definite. If I went I was to take my own car which meant getting supplementary gas coupons from the War Ration Board. These were available only if I moved "permanently" and produced a letter saying I had work. But I could not get the letter without the appointment and when that went through I was to leave immediately. I had canceled hotel reservations for an entomology meeting in Philadelphia but I went down for one day. Getting home late that night, Friday, November 19th, there was the telegram. The job was mine!

I obtained the gas coupons; gave away most of the fruits and vegetables I had canned during so many midnight hours, tried to store the rest so they would not freeze; I packed up everything I thought I would need in the line of literature, special equipment, cameras, presses, work clothes, good clothes; arranged with the bank for enough money to last until the first pay check (I thought); notified plumbers, telephone, gas, water, police; tried frantically to get a spare tire and ended up with an extra inner tube with four patches; and was off for Washington on Tuesday. All day Wednesday was spent with the U.S. Department of Agriculture at Beltsville, being fingerprinted, signing my name and history over and over, learning how to fill out the forms that would come in the future, getting the Letter of Authority which said how far I could travel, in which states, how much I could spend. I had been disturbed by the many tales of long waits for the first pay check but was assured I would get it in three weeks.

ALABAMA BOUND

That night the Ford developed a flat outside Anna's apartment house. With no spare, we had to take it off, get a cab to take it to a service station for repair, bring it back to put on. I was feeling more than worried as I started out alone to Alabama on Thanksgiving morning. Stopping at a gas station to have the tire checked, I picked up two young soldiers. I figured.I could take a chance on service men in wartime if they could take a chance on enemy guns. One was from North Carolina, only 18, going home to the "sweetest little wife you ever saw." He was taking along his buddy from Texas who had never seen our Eastern mountains. We passed the entrance to Skyline Drive. I had had no intention of taking it; it was too lonely with everything closed up; I might have more tire trouble. But the disappointed look on the Carolina boy's face made me turn around; those two could patch a tire if necessary. The day was gorgeous; the scenery was stupendous. The look of pride on that boy's face as he showed his country to his Texas buddy was marvelous to behold. We ate the few cookies and apples I had with me long before we got off the trail in late afternoon; then I provided sandwiches and ice cream in a drugstore before our routes parted. It was about the happiest Thanksgiving I had ever spent.

In planning the route to Spring Hill I had made it as straight as possible to save time and mileage and did not pay enough attention to the mountains indicated on the map. The horseshoe curves saved neither time nor gasoline and it was Sunday afternoon when I reached Mobile. Knowing how hard it would be to find accomodations near this city with its ship-building program, I had asked Dr. Childs to suggest a place to live. He persuaded the Misses McKeon at Spring Hill to take me in temporarily.

From Mobile I followed Spring Hill Avenue, thinking it a logical way to reach Spring Hill, but ended up in a remote lumber town. I retraced my way and telephoned, learned I should have taken Old Shell Road. It was dark and cold and raining when the Ford and I reached our destination. I took one look at Miss Maisie and Miss Gen, at my room filled with flowers, a fire burning brightly, and asked, "Do I *have* to leave?" It seemed pretty close to heaven and I still think so. How very, very lucky I was to have such a Southern home.

For some years "Azalea Hall" (originally Palmetto Hall, built before the Civil War, of Greek Revival architecture copied from a Charleston home) had taken in occasional guests. They were mostly parents of students at Spring Hill College, a Jesuit School. There had always been plenty of help. Now, with more permanent guests during wartime, no help was available. Miss Maisie turned out to be the world's best cook. She pampered Professor A. who taught at the College; Walter, who in civilian clothes had a hush-

hush job for the army; Thomas, who did the night shift at the Weather Bureau; and me. Especially me. The first breakfast was turkey hash on waffles, before daylight, so I could get to the laboratory long before 8 a.m.

Dr. Childs had waited over to show me the ropes, and how to drive the temperamental Chevrolet truck. First I sent in my Oath of Arrival, duly notarized at the post office. Then I learned that I had to carry my own insurance on the truck which would be cheaper if I got it through my agent back home, and until that deal went through I could not get a permit to drive the truck. Next I learned that if I intended to work in Alabama instead of being a tourist I had to get an Alabama driver's license and registration for the Ford. I learned that I personally had to pay out all expenses for the truck, including its garage, and send in an expense account. I learned that the laboratory needed practically everything and I had to pay for it all, to be reimbursed later. According to my work diary I spent all of November 30th reading regulations. The appointment started officially on December 1st. Dr. Childs left and I was on my own.

My problem was the same one Margaret Huger had been playing with when I went through Charleston in 1937. She was assisting Dr. Freeman Weiss of the U.S.D.A. who first described the disease after it appeared in the Charleston area in 1931 and named the fungus, *Ovulinia azaleae*. This was a new genus as well as a new species but it was very closely related to the genus Sclerotinia I knew so well. I used to say I crawled through Europe on my stomach; now I prepared to see Alabama in the same way, hunting for tiny apothecia on the ground. These produced the spores that caused primary infection of the flowers, then inside the petals secondary spores (conidia) were produced which spread the disease from flower to flower, by means of insects and wind, with incredible rapidity when the weather was right. At that time there was no spray that could be used on the flowers and it was thought that even if a safe, inconspicuous spray could be found it would have to be applied so often it would be entirely impractical. Hand-picking of all diseased blossoms had been recommended but was impossible. The research now was centered on ground treatments, mechanical and chemical, to inhibit the development of apothecia. I was committed to carrying these on, but I wanted to do more. After twelve years of keeping plants healthy by spraying I thought there should be some way to do it for azaleas.

I wrote to Professor Whetzel, "Thanks to the years I worked with you on Sclerotinias I am down in Alabama for the winter carrying on the azalea flower spot project. And I need help. I find myself without so many things, most of all my personal library. I packed up the 1943 copies of all periodicals but I need back files of *Phytopathology* and all kinds of separates. Could you send, as a permanent addition to the azalea project library which is practically nonexistent, separates (reprints) of any of your work on Sclerotinias or related genera and anything else you have to spare? I am awfully rusty on technique. I need help in producing apothecia from sclerotia, on culturing, everything. I brought along Dr. Weiss' material on Ovulinia but did not think, in my speed to get off, about digging out the different reprints I might need. I did pack up popular bulletins so I could carry out writing assignments for the *Home Garden*.

"Also, have you any suggestions on this problem which seems to have them stumped? I have not caught up on all the details but I gather they have trouble culturing the fungus, trouble keeping it in culture, trouble getting the sclerotia to develop, have not gotten conidia in culture, nor sclerotia to produce apothecia artificially."

Not receiving any answer to my SOS I wrote again. This time the reply came by return mail and Prof said he never wanted me to mention absent-minded professors to him again. I had headed my first letter Spring Hill, *New Jersey* (I must have been in a panic) and his secretary had so addressed the reply and all the reprints. I never did get the literature but eventually the letter found its way. "I congratulate you on getting back into scientific plant pathology. They certainly dropped you into a hole but I have no doubt you will dig yourself out eventually. I have no suggestions as to books or journals. As a matter of fact, you don't need books or journals. You have enough training and experience to solve your problems by using that training and experience with such ingenuity as you can command."

By the time I had received that excellent advice I had already learned it for myself. I had shined up rusty Cornell techniques and they were working just fine. The sclerotia were so small I couldn't find them under the leaf litter so I scraped up top sand and litter from under the bushes and brought it into the laboratory, sorting out the tiny black resting bodies under a bright light. Real hard work yielded about six sclerotia an hour. Disinfecting them with Chlorox from the grocery store, cutting them under aseptic conditions in petri dishes baked in the oven, I was making them grow on all kinds of fantastic media. Just before leaving home I had gone to a lecture given by Dr. William J. Robbins to our New York chapter of Sigma Delta Epsilon. He mentioned the necessity of vitamin B_1 for the growth of some fungi and various sources of it. I could not get wheat or lentils around Spring Hill but I tried *Ovulinia* on flasks of oatmeal and it took to it readily, producing sclerotia in culture. It also grew on bran and string-bean plugs. When I added shredded coconut the sclerotia put out fundaments like crazy.

If I was fortunate in living with the McKeons I was doubly fortunate in sharing the Field Laboratory of Dr. L. L. English, an entomologist for the Alabama Experiment Station. He had been working with satsumas (we had an orchard of that best of citrus fruits back of the laboratory) but this project was petering out. Now he was vitally interested in insects of ornamentals, especially azaleas and camellias, and was a great help. He escorted me on the first visit to Bellingrath Gardens, where we were amazed to find blight well started on Belgian azaleas in the lathhouse on December 2nd. Mid-January was the earliest it had been reported in this garden. I brought potted plants back to play with at the laboratory.

The next few days I alternated between inspecting nurseries and gardens, culturing from sclerotia collected at various locations, and RED TAPE. Even now, reading over the correspondence, I can't make much sense of all the forms that had to be filled out, complicated by wartime. The insurance company at home did not reply immediately so it was nearly a month before all the papers were signed that provided a permit to drive the truck. Meanwhile, the temperamental thing had to be run a little every day or it would not go at all.

We worked officially 48 hours a week (I usually put in more than 70) with no holidays off except Christmas. Every day had to be accounted for. I spent a day in bed with a cold and debated whether I had to put in for sick leave. I had spent those 14 hours reading literature about the project and planning work. I continued to ask questions of Washington. How do I get alcohol, tax exemption certificates, approval to give lectures?

For Christmas, various service men descended on Miss Maisie. We all went to midnight mass and I provided Christmas trees, made out of the huge cones of my favorite long-leaved pines, for each breakfast tray. Maisie cooked a big Christmas dinner but she was out on her feet with flu. I got it soon after and spent more sick leave than was due me for the short time I had worked. Then I did not know how to handle that on my reports. The first expense account was a nightmare. I did it over and over and it still was not right. So I didn't get reimbursed for all the money I had been forking out for the government. Because of the delay in getting the truck permit and because someone in Washington forgot to send me something vital to sign I had received no salary when I was scheduled to go off to New Orleans and Baton Rouge. By that time my own money was used up and Miss Maisie was letting me eat on credit. Two of the house guests, whose salary checks were coming in regularly, advanced the money for my official trip for the government. I was horrified at the idea, my only borrowing had been from a bank, but there wasn't much else to do.

Harry Daunoy and Camilla Bradley did the honors in New Orleans, arranged for me to see gardens and parks, to meet the right officials, make the right connections to get materials for the mulch experiments. At Baton Rouge I learned what had already been done there on the azalea problem, worked in the library, talked at a seminar. When I returned to Spring Hill on January 21st *three* salary checks were waiting for me.

I came to more grief in expense accounts. I forgot to get a receipt for taxi fare. Once I rode a short way coach when my ticket allowed pullman. I bought some goods in a Mobile store and the bill was $2.54. But the dealer had not added it right; it should have been $2.64. I did not notice the error until the voucher went to Washington. The government said that if the mistake had been the other way around we could ignore it, but if we owed ten cents we had to pay it. I sent forms to the dealer. He ignored the letter; he couldn't be bothered to spend a dollar's worth of time to get back a dime. Still, I couldn't have any of my own expenses reimbursed until I paid that dime. Eventually I took a half day off, took a bus to Mobile (didn't have enough gasoline to take the truck), paid the money and got the forms signed. I figured it cost us taxpayers about ten dollars to be honest about ten cents.

Many are the days in the work diary marked simply RED TAPE. In every mail would come reminders about not wasting paper and in every mail would come huge expensive catalogues from the purchasing department offering me all kinds of medical supplies that had nothing to do with plant pathology. The second year I was there they sent a letter saying New Year's Day could be taken off if the position entailed no service to the public on that day. A few days later they changed their minds and sent another notice; no one would be allowed to take New Year's as a holiday.

Except for the filling out of forms, everything else was smooth.

I had requested and received permission to talk to garden clubs provided each date was cleared separately and I filled out an affidavit that there would be no expense to the U.S.D.A. Clubs were allowed to pay travel expenses but I could accept no other remuneration. I was allowed to continue writing assignments (on Sundays) and could receive remuneration for those—a special favor, because government agents are not supposed to have outside work. I was allowed to plan and carry out any experiments I wished.

I talked to the Birmingham Federated Garden Clubs, the Spring Hill and Mobile Garden Clubs, on the need for general cooperation and individual work in getting rid of azalea blight. I wrote an article for *Hortensia,* organ of the Garden Club of Alabama. In sending it to Dr. Emsweller for clearance I wrote, "It seems to me the most important thing to say is that control will take *work* on the part of the individual. As near as I can find out they are all sitting around waiting for a miracle and wondering why the government does not provide it."

When I was asked to speak to the Garden Study Club in New Orleans I wanted to go by truck so as to survey azaleas en route. Regulations said I could not take it more than ninety miles from home base so I drove it as far as I could. It was enough; I had studied plenty of azaleas on that bumpy ride to Bay St. Louis, and was glad to rest my sore limbs overnight. Next morning the station master gave me permission to park the truck at the railroad station but I worried. Regulations said it had to be under cover at night and there was no cover in all of Bay St. Louis. I kept thinking of the extra tire strapped underneath and expecting it to be stolen. I did have gasoline stolen once in those rationed days, but this time everything was intact on my return. Meanwhile I had been seeing a city well blighted, weather conditions having made the disease appear a week earlier in New Orleans than in Mobile. I arranged for various experiments to be carried out there the next winter, directed by Mr. Daunoy.

I had not been idle at Spring Hill between jaunts. I was working on many potted azaleas, donated by nurseries, on the laboratory grounds and I had put all of the McKeon azaleas into one huge experiment to see if ground treatments would reduce the disease. Some of the large bushes were mulched with bagasse (sugar-cane pulp), others with ginned moss, asphalt paper, pine needles, alfalfa meal. Most of the mulches inhibited apothecial development but the azaleas all came down with blight by March 13th, after a rain on March 11th.

The ground around other azaleas was treated chemically—with Elgetol; Dinitro C; calcium cyanamid granules. Under two big bushes I quartered the ground, using the three chemicals, leaving the fourth quarter untreated as a check. Again I spent days flat on my stomach, looking for and counting the tiny apothecia. The chemical treatments also prevented their development, compared to the numerous fruiting bodies in the check plots, but did not delay blight more than a day.

I was also spraying azaleas, every other day to keep up with opening flowers, using a knapsack sprayer on my back, rinsing it very thoroughly between chemicals. In Washington I had been given a sample of U.S. Rubber Company 604. Soon after arrival at Spring Hill I had read a release from the Connecticut Experiment Station about a valuable new fungicide, disodium ethylene bisdithiocarbamate. Applied as a liquid this forms an invisible protective film over a plant and it was suggested that the new chemical might be good for onions and other hard-to-wet tissues. I needed something invisible and azalea petals were difficult to wet; it was worth a try.

I wrote asking Dr. James Horsfall, whom I had known at Cornell before he went to Connecticut, where I could get a sample. He immediately sent some of the HE 175 that had been supplied him by Rohm & Haas, the manufacturers. At the time I had little idea that spraying outdoor azaleas would be really practical. I did think that perhaps it would help with potted azaleas like the Belgian varieties at Bellingrath Gardens. These tender varieties became diseased as they wintered in the greenhouse and carried early infection to the outdoor plantings.

I was also trying various other chemicals—mercury and copper sprays, fermate dusts. The azaleas were not the low shrubs we have in New Jersey. They were the big Indian varieties, much taller than I was. Spraying was arduous but I enjoyed every single minute of those days. I kept remembering the chapter, in Elizabeth Lawrence's book on Southern gardening, titled "Spring Comes in February." It surely does in Alabama and I was overflowing with the excitement of everything coming out at once. Yellow jessamine flowered on all the fences and through the woods, cherokee roses along the roads, wisteria in the treetops. Camellias were spectacular that year. When the Men's Camellia Society put on a show for the public someone remarked that the line at the door was even longer than the lines at the liquor stores. Everyone was slightly balmy over camellias, mortgaging their futures to get some new, enormous-flowered variety. I loved best the old bushes, covered with thousands of flowers, that went past the second-story windows at the McKeons.

Father Yancey brought his biology students to the laboratory and I went over to Spring Hill College to talk at a biology fraternity meeting. I tried to tell the boys how much fun it was finding out things but they were pretty skeptical. They allowed as how it might be fun when you got to the teaching stage but not much in the student stage.

Always obsessed with my idea of teaching, educating the public, I invited all gardeners and nurserymen to a public demonstration of the experiments in the McKeon garden. Everything was labeled and each guest was given a mimeographed sheet giving the story of the disease, the fungus causing it, the ground treatments and sprays being tested. We also fed the public, as I always did at home on Rose Day. Maisie made her very special spiced tea and I did the cookies.

The results of the spray tests were only beginning to show up the day of the demonstration but soon we had another rain and the differences were immediately striking. Every flower on the un-sprayed bushes collapsed into a slimy mush, as did all those with only mulches or chemical ground treatments. Bushes sprayed with HE 175 or US 604 were full of color, with scarcely a single bloom blighted. There was slight phytotoxicity (plant injury) with the 604, none that I noted with the HE 175.

On March 22nd I wrote to James Horsfall, "You can chalk one up for your HE 175. It has just put on a spectacular performance here at Spring Hill and more than justifies further experimentation and wider demonstration another year."

Thus it was that a routine progress report from an experiment station, that I read by chance, a sentence about an onion, and a good friend, plus a little back-breaking work by me, meant the control of azalea petal blight.

Dr. English helped me take pictures to prove the unbelievable results, using his color-film adapter on my Zeiss Ikon with its good lens. A half-and-half bush showed up very well, every flower on the unsprayed side blighted, every flower on the sprayed side perfect. Later the sprayed half dropped its petals normally while blighted flowers on the other half dried and hung on the bush as an eyesore for months. This was characteristic of the disease; you had blighted flowers during the season and then an unsightly bush long after-wards. Sprayed flowers dropped quickly and cleanly at the end of their long period of bloom.

In thanking Dr. Massey for some ferbam-sulfur dust he had sent for testing, I wrote, "I often think of the awful mess I made of my oral examinations and the way you kept insisting I was doctorate material. I hope I have justified your optimism. At any rate, I have been offered a full-time position, starting with a P-3 rating, which with base pay and overtime is a fair salary for a woman. I turned it down in favor of plant doctoring on my own but I do want to come back next winter and try out protective spraying on a larger scale."

I thanked Professor Whetzel for his training. He replied, "You have certainly been most fortunate in your work down there this winter. It is with a good deal of pride that I learn that one of my old students and assistants has put it over the boys who have heretofore worked on the azalea blight. The Cornell training does show up, doesn't it? Your personal experience as a practical plant pathologist has also greatly contributed to your success on this problem. It is not enough to solve a problem of this kind. You have the spirit and technique for getting your solution before the public; that is quite as important as the research work itself."

Of course I had not really "put it over the boys." I had merely been lucky in having a new chemical to work with that had been developed for wartime needs. I was, however, very glad that as a woman I was able to do a little more than "keep the seat warm." After returning home I made a special trip to Cornell, sleeper up one night, back the next, just to tell Professor Whetzel in person what he had done for me and to show him the azalea pictures. I've been so grateful that I did this, for Prof died, of the cancer he had fought so valiantly and so long, just as I returned to Alabama the next autumn.

I wrote up a very cautious statement of the results of the spray tests, cleared it in Washington, and sent it to Camilla Bradley as a scoop for *Home Gardening for the South*. She had started this publication, so very useful to all Southern gardeners, in 1940 and I had been promoting it wherever possible for it reached the very people I wanted to educate in plant doctor lines. I called the article, "New Hope for Azalea Lovers" but I offered no false hope. I merely told the readers to keep their fingers crossed and that "maybe, just maybe, after the war when you can take time from rolling bandages to spray azaleas, there will be materials for you to use."

I started back to New Jersey the first of April, after filling out the numerous forms of departure and telling the Mobile Ration Board I needed gas coupons to move "permanently" again. I was supposed to visit azalea gardens and nurseries all the way but the gas allowance ran short; some detours had to be omitted. I did stop at a nursery in Georgia. The owner said he'd certainly like to see this disease everyone was talking about. I asked, "What do you think is the matter with those azaleas along your walk?"

"Oh, that's just weather, happens every time we get a rain."

I decided a powerful lot of public education was needed if a nurseryman did not recognize azalea flower spot when his plants were completely blighted.

INTERLUDE AT HOME

April 8th, when I reached home, was a little late to pick up the threads of plant doctoring. I had help from various high school boys, sharing them with baseball, until late May when Lacelle came into my life, an unadulterated blessing. He was not quite fifteen but strong. Because his father was ill in the hospital and the family income had to be augmented I had no compunctions about his age. He had to work for someone and it might as well be me. Lacelle was intelligent and he also had common sense, a rare commodity. He knew what I wanted or needed before I did; he was calm and cheerful. At last I could relax and let someone take care of me instead of always trying to please a helper enough to keep him. Pumping a sprayer is an art. Lacelle had an effortless rhythm that was a joy to see. He had a photographic memory and made sure that we never left pails, measuring spoons or cups, dusters, sprayers, pruning shears, lopping shears, dusts or liquids behind us in gardens.

There is also an art in packing and unpacking the Ford ten or twenty times a day. Most reporters talk about my station wagon but I have never wanted one. As long as they were manufactured I operated with a business coupe. They were easy to get before World War II and not too expensive although corrosion from the various plant doctor chemicals made the trade-in value almost nil. I remember once, when I had to be towed in because of gear trouble, I simply had them transfer all the apparatus to a new coupe. That was cheaper than holding up spraying while repairs were made.

Now I have to buy a Tudor. On special order to the factory it comes through without the rear seat and the dealer revamps it for me, raising the floor to make a shelf in the rear-seat space and opening through under this by removing the partition in the trunk. We can store everything away far more easily than in a station wagon, the apparatus doesn't jounce around, the chemicals don't spill on the good part of the car, and I can always take off for a lecture without unpacking or having visible equipment. On work days the shelf is used to carry the bushel baskets in which we bring home diseased material for burning.

Lacelle was interested in photography and we spent rainy days building up a collection of pest pictures. He was also not above washing the kitchen floor on rainy days. I do loathe cleaning and could do little in that line myself because all the spare time was going into bug stories. The *Home Garden* was having Eva Melady do a series of exquisite color pictures of insect pests and I had to dig out life histories and control measures to match. Eventually they would go into a book.

SOUTH AGAIN

It took many months to unwind the red tape and get an appropriation for a return to Alabama but finally the way was cleared and I left on November 8, 1944. I couldn't see myself persuading the Ration Board that I was again moving "permanently" so I went by train, sending many, many boxes of books and reference materials ahead on government bill of lading. This time I was not going to be stuck without a library. I had also ordered new sprayers and had maneuvered a 30 (working) -day appointment for Lacelle to come and help when it was time to spray. I told the high school that the trip would be an education for him and I told Washington I would not be able to do the experiments with the kind of help available at Spring Hill.

On arrival at Spring Hill I learned I had to get a release from myself as a plant doctor through the War Manpower Commission before I was free to work for the U.S.D.A. and then I had to release Lacelle from me before he could work.

The gasoline situation was terrible. I had only seven government coupons to last until January, which meant less than seventy-five miles a week. One round trip to Bellingrath Gardens was fifty-five miles and I needed to go out at least three times a week. I also needed lots of gasoline to keep the truck running. If it was idle more than a day Dr. English had to tow it around with his state truck before it would start. The government grudgingly coughed up a few extra coupons but in the interim I took advantage of Mr. Bellingrath's hospitality and stayed overnight when I had two days' work in succession.

His home was a show place; he took visitors through it a dozen times a day; every room was filled with museum pieces. I slept in what he called the Marie Antoinette room, surrounded by all sorts of fragile china figurines. I was petrified for fear of breaking something; I never dared open a fountain pen for fear of spilling ink. It was always good to get back to Miss Maisie's where I could be my sloppy self but Mr. Bell was a grand person and I did enjoy visiting him.

I asked Mr. Bellingrath and Mr. Hunt (the superintendent who had first talked azalea blight with me back in 1937) to sign a release stating that they would not hold me, or the government, responsible for any injury from spraying experiments. They thought it very strange. Why should I want to injure their plants? It was well I was cautious because the chemical, now named Dithane, that had seemed so safe and effective in 1943 wasn't at all safe now that the manufacturers had changed from laboratory mixing to large-scale production. Everything I tried was injurious. Rohm & Haas kept sending different batches of Dithane as wettable powders and finally sent liquids. I was treating 360 azaleas in the greenhouse and 300 in the lathhouse and was worried sick. Every time some new injury showed up I wept on Mr. Hunt's shoulder before he could protest what I was doing. Then he had to cheer me up and forgot about scolding.

After a good bit of trial and error I evolved a method of testing phytotoxicity on separate blossoms floated in water that seemed to check with the results obtained by spraying whole plants in the greenhouse. Now I could work in the laboratory and stop injuring so many valuable azaleas.

I tested at least thirty chemicals, most of them in many different strengths. The blossoms were sprayed, then inoculated by placing a block of agar, on which the fungus was growing vigorously, on a petal. Chemical injury showed up in minutes or days, according to the material used; blight started in a very few hours.

I was working against time, trying to get something safe before blight started in outdoor gardens. I heard that they were using liquid Dithane on potatoes but making it safe with zinc sulfate and lime. I tried all combinations. The potato spray was too strong for azaleas. I reduced the amount, added 25% zinc sulfate instead of the usual 35% and thought maybe I had something.

The help out at Bellingrath's numbered about fifty. Some of the men had done quite a bit of work in connection with the experiments; all had been courteous and cooperative.

I wondered what to do about Christmas. I couldn't single out one or two, nor could I buy fifty gifts. Cookies again to the rescue. I baked batch after batch evenings in Miss Maisie's oven, whose door had to be propped shut with a broom handle just as the trunk-lid of my Ford had to be propped up with an All-purpose Hoe all through the war years when replacements were not available.

Soon after Christmas the New Orleans Trail Association invited me to come there to show the slides of last winter's work and to plan a spraying program for their parks for this winter. I had to go by bus, standing most of the way. We had checked their projector but the bulb burned out as I started to speak and we could procure no spare. I had no way of proving spraying could be effective.

The lame speech completed, I was invited to the French Quarter for a drink. Before I had one, and walking between two stalwart men, I tripped on the uneven pavement and fell flat, injuring my wrist. When I couldn't sleep I took too many aspirins and then overslept my appointment with the Daunoys. There was no time for even a cup of coffee before a morning of seeing park superintendents and arranging tests. Then the long hours by bus back to Mobile, another bus to Spring Hill, a walk in the dark on our dirt road. We had no street lights, no sidewalk, and there was a ditch along one side. One night Professor A. fell in the ditch coming home from the College and grumbled that they had better roads than that even in Russia. I liked our dirt road but you could break a spring if you drove a car through after a rain before the road scraper filled up the pot-holes.

It took a month for the sprained wrist to get back into working order; meanwhile I drove the truck with one hand. I had divided all of Bellingrath's many acres into replicated plots, with Coca-Cola tags painted different colors to show what was to be sprayed with which chemical and what was to be left as a check. I was spending most of my time on the damp ground checking on apothecia. Because the season in New Orleans was so much earlier than Mobile it had been arranged for Lacelle and me to start the work there as soon as he arrived from the North. I met his train, waiting hours in a cold station; next day was in bed with grippe. Our reservations were canceled but as soon as I could move I wired for rooms and we started. I should have known that it is impossible to get a place to lay your head in New Orleans in February. After trying for hours I telephoned Camilla and she took us in.

As we helped the park people get started spraying, we learned something very important. The Dithane mixture had to be continuously agitated to remain safe. One of the city sprayers had an agitator that only went part-way down. Spray from the bottom of the tank, below the agitator, caused injury that was apparent by the next day. We returned to our own spraying, carrying a 50-gallon barrel of water and a 12-gallon Paragon sprayer around on the truck. With the aid of Lacelle's strong right arm we sprayed, *three times a week,* every other Elegans azalea at Lyons Park (they were as tall as the lamp posts), leaving the alternate bushes unsprayed as checks. We treated the Pride of Mobile azaleas in Memorial Park, cutting the park in half from the flagpole to the monument, spraying all the bushes on one side, leaving the others untouched. In a private Mobile garden we sprayed the Formosas on one side of the walk, left those on the other side as checks. We did one block of the neutral ground (central parkway) in Spring Hill Avenue and every other azalea along the main avenue of Spring Hill College. In the Long garden in Spring Hill, with its hundreds of azaleas of many varieties, we divided the bushes into blocks, spraying some with Dithane, some with U.S. Rubber Company 604 (later named Phygon), leaving some as checks.

The Braswell garden had huge bushes, brought from France more than a hundred years before. Some we sprayed, holding our breath for fear of injury; others we left untreated. At the Van Antwerp's we divided big bushes right down the middle, spraying one half, not the other. With small bushes we were able to follow the complete outline of a bush with the spray rod and yet keep the chemical away from the bush touching it.

We had an elaborate setup at the McKeon's. Before leaving the previous spring I had put 2-foot square frames under the bushes and these were filled with fallen flowers. On February 24, 1945, a frame under the half of an azalea that had been sprayed in 1944 had only one apothecium, while the frame under the unsprayed half had 184 apothecia that had developed from sclerotia formed in the old blighted petals. Under another unsprayed bush 317 apothecia were present on the ground inside a 2-foot frame while there were only 2 under the next bush that had been sprayed.

This proved that spraying during one season reduced the amount of inoculum (infective material) for the next year almost to zero.

To further test the efficacy of spraying I had switched bushes for the 1945 treatments, spraying those left as checks the year before, leaving untreated those sprayed the year before.

Meanwhile the men at Bellingrath Gardens were spraying the azaleas there with a 300-gallon power sprayer. It took two days to complete one round and then they started over again. As the winter wore on and they were getting no injury, as well as no blight, they started spraying all the blocks I had tagged for no treatment. Having a beautiful garden was more important to them than a scientific experiment. I understood that but I argued that they owed it to their many visitors to leave some example, some place, where people could tell whether or not spraying was effective. They promised faithfully to leave half of the round bed of azaleas near the house untouched. They did, for a while. Then, on the day Postmaster-General Farley was due to visit, they noticed a little blight on the unsprayed half and they reneged. That big sprayer was brought up in a hurry to spray those few untreated azaleas. So I had no demonstration there for the public, no test to *prove* spraying was effective.

For a long time it looked as if we couldn't prove anything around Mobile. It was unusually dry that winter and early spring. The azaleas remained fine and everyone said, "The disease is past; we don't have to spray."

Celle and I kept doggedly spraying every three days, trying to keep opening petal surfaces of all those hundreds of bushes protected. Remembering the injury in New Orleans we kept a stick in the tank to supplement the regular agitator. When we seemed to be getting slight injury because plants were too dry, we tried desperately to get the bushes watered. The Formosa azaleas wilted completely from drought. When we implored the owner to let the hose run under his bushes he refused, said he had the blight which came every year and watering wouldn't help. I persisted, he reluctantly agreed, and next day the flowers were back to normal.

THRILL OF A LIFETIME

It was almost time for Lacelle to go home and the azaleas were still healthy. We would have to stop spraying still without proving anything. Then, about 5 o'clock on the morning of March 15th, we had .04 inch of rain and some drippy fog. It was enough. In a few hours white spots appeared all over the petals, by noon the next day nearly all the flowers on every azalea around Mobile and Spring Hill were collapsed with the brown, slimy, limp blight. EXCEPT, those we had sprayed. We drove around town with increasing and incredulous astonishment and joy. It couldn't be true! No scientific experiment ever had such clear-cut and marvelous results. No statistics would be needed, no involved mathematics working out probable errors. All we had to do was to take pictures.

Dr. English did the Kodachromes for us with my camera and his adapter; Celle and I did the black and whites. Every flower on every bush in the unsprayed half of Memorial Park was brown, every flower on the sprayed half was pink and turgid. The sprayed Formosas that had wilted from drought were wonderful, those across the path a slimy horror. The sprayed block of the neutral ground had the only color in all of Spring Hill Avenue.

"They" had said that spraying would never be practical unless the whole town did it, yet here was Pride of Mobile with every flower perfect and touching it an untreated bush with every flower gone. The line of demarcation between sprayed and unsprayed halves of bushes was as sharp as if drawn with a paintbrush.

They had said that the disease could not be controlled without everyone cooperating on sanitary measures, destroying infected flowers, mulching or otherwise treating the ground to prevent development of apothecia. Yet in the McKeon garden the sprayed bushes remained blight-free despite the hundreds of apothecia under them in spring, while those with no infective material under them but left unsprayed in 1945 were a hundred per cent blighted.

They had said that spraying would injure the flowers or leave an unsightly residue. Yet we had applied up to 12 sprays per bush and the only residue was a very faint white spotting unnoticeable at a distance. The only injury with Dithane had come when it was applied while the flowers were wilting from drought. With Phygon there was a faint white stippling of the petals and a slight blackening of the foliage but this, too, could not be seen from a distance. The over-all effect was of glowingly healthy plants.

They had said that nobody could be persuaded to spray three times a week nor could afford it but at Bellingrath Gardens spraying had prolonged the season about six weeks and for the first time in ten years they had had a good display of the tender Belgian azaleas. With 5000 paid admissions on a single Sunday the entire cost of spraying was covered many times over. (Two years later, when I stopped at Cypress Gardens in Florida and introduced myself to Mr. Pope, he said that a spraying program had saved them $25,000 the first season.)

Lacelle took the train back to school and I had no time to sit around and gloat. I had had to wait to run spore germination tests until the widespread secondary infection provided conidia to work with. Now I did them for all the chemicals, but Dithane and Phygon remained the only possibilities. The various mercury compounds were too injurious to azaleas at effective concentrations, copper did not inhibit spore germination, ferbam was too unsightly and so on.

The assignment was completed. I could go home to my own work. I packed up books and data, arranged for the well-being of the truck, tried to leave all shipshape for my successor when the war was over, and left on March 24th.

It was the earliest spring on record in New Jersey. Daffodils, forsythia, crocuses, scilla, grape hyacinths were all in bloom, the temperature like Alabama. We hastily applied a dormant oil spray to lilacs but the tops were so far out I only dared do the trunks. The ground was right for planting. I put in onion sets, broccoli, cabbage, and lettuce in my own garden the first day, then tried to prune all my clients' roses at once, before they came into full leaf. I was committed to a lot of lectures and articles, as well as spraying, but the most important thing to squeeze in was getting the azalea work down on paper.

SPREADING THE GOSPEL

To my mind, the problem was only half done when an effective control was found for azalea petal blight. The other half was public education. In the normal course of events, a technical article is prepared for a scientific journal such as *Phytopathology*. This is published in the next year or two or three as space permits and then maybe, if anyone is interested, a résumé may appear in a popular publication. I was far too impatient for this. I wanted Southern nurserymen and gardeners to have the facts immediately. I wanted chemical companies to have their products on dealer's shelves in small package form for home use before the next spraying season. And I wanted, as a private citizen no longer employed by the U.S. Department of Agriculture, to go around the country lecturing on azalea blight and showing people how to use the chemicals properly. All my wants came true.

Camilla Bradley and I hoped the results could be published in the July-August issue of *Home Gardening* when there would be enough paper for a full treatment and early enough for a public demand for chemicals for the next season. Rather surprisingly, this was allowed. I had a vague feeling at one time that the results might be soft-pedaled because I was a woman and because they were in rather direct opposition to previously published statements but the article was cleared in time for publication. I was very grateful.

After publication, I was free to use the data personally and I wrote a booklet on the azalea blight with specific instructions for using the liquid Dithane D-14 safely. Rohm & Haas distributed this to their dealers, some of whom made up, for home gardeners, special azalea kits, containing a bottle of Dithane, the right amount of zinc sulfate, lime and spreader to go with it, and the instruction booklet. (Later a wettable powder, zineb, was produced. This was the zinc salt formed when zinc sulfate was added to disodium ethylene bisdiothiocarbamate [Dithane D-14]. Zineb is now sold under the trade names of Dithane Z-78 or Parzate and is easier for home gardeners than the complicated mixing.)

I wrote a reminder article for January *Home Gardening* asking Southern gardeners, "Are You Going to Control Azalea Blight?" National magazines helped in the cause; almost all those with gardening pages mentioned the encouraging results. My good friend E. L. D. Seymour came to Glen Ridge to write a human interest story on it, "They Said It Couldn't Be Done." I wrote an article for the *Home Garden* and provided two very striking color pictures of the azaleas in Memorial Park, one blighted and brown, the other true watermelon-pink. But when the story appeared in print the blighted side was pink, too. I demanded to know why and learned that the printer thought it looked so awful he touched it up. So you can't even believe a picture!

Nor what you read in print! Various people in Mobile sent clippings from the local paper of an interview with the head of the parks system, concluding that the U.S.D.A. hoped to control azalea blight with *DDT*. That was the year DDT was getting all the ballyhoo but no claims were made for it as a fungicide.

It was a whirlwind lecture trip that next winter, with most of the dates arranged by Camilla and *Home Gardening*. People were really excited at the prospects of azaleas again and it was fun to be regarded as something of a heroine. (That didn't last too long; after a year or two many home gardeners decided it was too much trouble to spray; the public gardens, dependent on tourists, have continued.) The war was over; there was gasoline for travel.

At Wilmington, North Carolina, the Sprunts, father and son, came in from Orton Plantation bearing a tray of gorgeous camellias. The next morning, missing the right road to Orton, the Ford and I floundered through miles of almost cart paths until a man in a cabin in the wilderness headed us in the right direction. "Of course," he drawled, "there's one bridge you'll have to hit rather lightly but the mailman usually makes it that way." The Ford lightly leaped from hole to hole and the beauty of Orton more than made up for a few more gray hairs.

Route 17 passed Brookgreen Gardens. Here enormous old moss-hung oaks, a fine collection of correctly labeled vines, shrubs and trees, and a magnificent outdoor sculpture collection, mostly animals, make a most unusual garden. It is free to the public, protected only by the words, "These gardens are entrusted to the courtesy of the visitors."

Arriving at Charleston, I found that C. Norwood Hastie, Jr., was in bed with virus pneumonia but that did not prevent our discussing azaleas all evening. The next morning Mr. Hastie, Sr., substituting for his son, presided at the meeting of growers called at Magnolia Gardens. Nearly every show place and nursery around Charleston was represented and all agreed they would have to spray azaleas to keep in business. I was delighted at their response to the Kodachrome slides of the U.S.D.A. work.

Afterwards I spent nearly two hours in the garden with Mr. Hastie who kept asserting, "Now, I'm not going to walk you to death," only to think of some other camellia or vista lovelier than the last. The Pringle Smiths bore me off for another two hours of camellia-viewing at Middleton Place and Sunday dinner, featuring home-grown turkey, ending with flaming crepes suzette.

Cocktails were at Pierates Cruze, with the Dana Osgoods, who turned out to have made their first home at my grandfather's house in Hopedale, Massachusetts, after he died. First Mrs. Osgood, then Mr. Osgood, took me around and introduced me to each camellia. Then there was supper in the entrancing sea room, two sides glass down to the floor, with sunset and moonrise over Charleston Harbor.

I lingered too long in Savannah, meeting John Cope of the Reliance Fertilizer Company, Elbridge Freeborn of H. G. Hastings Company, who just happened to be in Mr. Cope's office, and Bill

Robertson of the Park Commission. I did not arrive at Jacksonville until after seven. My room was a bower of azaleas from the Federated Garden Circles (there were over seventy at that time just in Jacksonville) and Mrs. Halle Cohen, the president, was on the telephone asking if I wanted to hear the First Piano Quartet or go to a lecture on camellias. I chose the concert, feeling that I had all the camellias I could take for a while.

A spraying demonstration next morning, with my trusty 12-gallon Paragon brought along in the back of the Ford, drew a large crowd. Had I had an agency for sprayers I think I could have sold fifty right on the spot. The Martin Seed Company telephoned back to my own dealer, Andrew Wilson, Inc., of Springfield, N. J. and ordered every one they had in stock.

Eva Noble, garden editor of the *Florida-Times Union,* associate editor of *Home Gardening for the South* (a post later filled by daughter Mary) gave a luncheon and there was a strenuous afternoon of garden visiting before the evening lecture.

A talk in Tallahassee, arranged on 24 hours' notice, drew a surprising number of hardy souls despite a cloudburst which made the streets almost impassable.

There was a glorious sunshiny day along the blue Gulf before I went inland to Laurel, Mississippi, old in wealth from lumber, newly rich from oil. An evening with the Thomas M. Gibbons, publishers of the *Laurel Leader-Call* sponsoring my two lectures, and a look at local gardens in Kodachrome preceded real visits the next morning. I was especially intrigued by the garden house of Mrs. William Mason, where the fig vine made entrancing designs on white brick walls.

With my usual propensity for figuring out wrong roads the Ford and I slithered around on a lot of gravel and saw a lot of tung-oil trees before reaching Lydia Frotscher's charming house in the Pines at Covington, Louisiana. Minna Koch, Cornell friend, was waiting there to welcome me. I was fascinated by the myriads of white violets and the crawfish mounds over the lawn. I wanted to dig down after crawfish but was assured they would stay below my reach. Southern spoon bread for supper was consolation.

After a Sunday morning visit to the notable camellia collection of Mr. and Mrs. Sigmund Katz, who also go in for Audubon prints and china, I had a leisurely (for once) drive to New Orleans. As usual, the Bradleys made me feel that I had come home. Harry and Marie Daunoy came over to talk azaleas all evening. I was skeptical when Harry said blight was already well started but he proved it next morning. Just before the lecture at the high school, in walked Irene Dobroscky Van de Water. She and Vandee, on their way home from Mexico, had read in the paper about my coming and had stayed over. The Daunoys took us all to dinner at Arnauds for the traditional shrimps remoulade, pompano, and crepes suzette, served with the usual rites.

In Lafayette I learned that they have even more azaleas than Mobile and that Professor Riley had started a splendid demonstration spray program both in the town and on the campus of Southwestern Louisiana Institute.

Entering the lecture hall that evening I was waylaid by Mr. and Mrs. Lutcher Stark, of Orange, Texas, who informed me I was lecturing there the next night. I demurred but Institute officials took me aside, told me Mr. Stark was one of the richest men in eastern Texas, might be of great help in the azalea program.

So next morning I was on my way to the Stark's incredible Shangri-La, a garden encircling a lake and enclosed by a bayou, where, as you drink coffee on a houseboat, you see wild ducks by the hundreds, blink your eyes at white squirrels and equally at camellias planted with "skyhooks." Camellias and azaleas had never done well in this low country until Mr. Stark conceived the idea of planting them *on top* of the ground, building a large plateau of soil around each root ball.

That Mr. Stark could influence gardeners was attested by the number who came from Beaumont and Port Arthur as well as Orange to the talk that evening. I was offered a house and laboratory if I would return to Shangri-La to work on camellia diseases but

I declined with thanks. It had been a lot of fun, however, this glimpse into another world where wishes are granted as if you had rubbed Aladdin's lamp. I begged for an orchid, from the big greenhouse full of them, to take along with me but I was not allowed to wear it as a lecture corsage; it was too commonplace. For the lecture, it was a Victor Emmanuel camellia. I also started back with a case of Stark figs, a Jensen silver corsage pin, to say nothing of lecture fee and expenses.

The little side trip to Texas meant a long day's drive back East to Pascagoula and Longfellow House, guest house of the Ingalls Shipbuilding Corporation which was sponsoring my talk there. I wondered if the big room I slept in was where Longfellow wrote "The Ship." Legend says it was in that house.

I had planned ten days of relaxing in the sun at beloved Spring Hill. Did I get it? No, not one hour of sun-sitting. I went around to gardens with Dr. D. L. Gill, back working on azaleas at the Field Laboratory and starting much needed research on camellia dieback. We went out to Bellingrath Gardens, more unbelievably lovely than ever after a year's absence, and straightened out a little spraying trouble. I stood around for hours while gardeners tried to start their gasoline engines so I could show them the proper way to spray (and decided my hand-pumped sprayer had much to be said for it). I put on two public spraying demonstrations, talked to the Mobile Azalea Trail Association at a luncheon, showed slides to the Mayor and Commissioners, and to Father Yancey's biology class.

Back in New Orleans once more, Camilla took me to my first Carnival Ball and Parade, to gardens where they were really getting results spraying azaleas. In a small garden the owner, a woman, was doing her own spraying and her azaleas were beautiful. Next door the azaleas were well blighted, despite spraying. Here they were being done by the handyman and every time he started to spray he had to stop to act as chauffeur or was sent on an errand. The two gardens showed very clearly the necessity for regularity in treatments.

We went to Natchez, house guests of Miss Myra Smith at historic D'Evereux. Through Camilla as a member of the press, we were also guests of the Pilgrimage Garden Club for two days of visiting the glorious old houses, most of them with original furnishings intact, ending with the very beautiful Confederate Ball. The Natchez pilgrimage is well worth a journey halfway across the continent.

Camilla and I were invited across the Mississippi River to Ferriday, Louisiana, to spend the night with the U. B. Evanses at Haphazard Plantation. This was way off the traveled routes, 12 miles from a telephone at that time. Haphazard carried on in the old way, growing cattle and cotton, providing milk, vegetables and meat for the Negro families on the place. We had fish for supper, caught just outside the door. High water had completely submerged Mrs. Evans' garden the year before but she was starting again, more enthusiastically than ever. Later she was president of the Louisiana Garden Club Federation and in 1956 given a national award as the woman who had done most for horticulture in 1955.

In the morning, before five, Peg, the peg-leg darky, rang the plantation bell, built up the bedroom fire and brought a big cup of coffee and hot milk to the bedside. I left Camilla sleeping and started North, though still westward. They were picking cotton in Arkansas and everywhere Japanese quince and golden narcissus were in bloom. At a highway intersection the local garden club had planted a big triangle thickly with bulbs.

Pine Bluff was urban again, on the border between South and North. It was growing peonies and lilacs as well as camellias. They had sold tickets for both an afternoon and an evening lecture and I was relieved when most of the people in the audience came up to say they had had their money's worth.

Three days of hard driving, over the mountains and through Kentucky's bluegrass and horse country, marveling at huge distilleries and warehouses surrounded by cornfields, brought me to Mary Seckman at Clarksburg, West Virginia. She writes about all kinds of garden plants, with details gained from personal experience, but I can only vouch for her skill with house plants. It was too dark to see her garden when I arrived and I started out the next morning, on the last lap home, in a blizzard.

CHAPTER 7

FOR FINGERTIP
REFERENCE

BETWEEN LEAVING the South in the spring of 1945 and returning there the next February to spread the gospel, I wrote a book. It did not start in as anything too serious, merely adding to the series of articles I had been doing to go with Miss Melady's color paintings of insects for the *Home Garden*. Dorothy Biddle once told me, when she visited overnight after lecturing near Glen Ridge, that finishing any book was a chore. I learned the bitter truth of that statement with *The Gardener's Bug Book*.

Against my better judgment, I signed a contract agreeing to do the work for a flat sum and no royalty. I had held out for the latter but could not get it and the payment seemed reasonably adequate for writing that would have to be sandwiched in between spraying, lecturing, and articles already promised. The first task was a literature survey and when I realized the enormity of that I hired another boy to go out with Lacelle to spray most of the time so I could stay home and work. I went broke buying reference books.

A BOOK ON BUGS

I finally decided to scratch all the articles already published and start over. There had been no unified plan. The color plates had been done in groups with no particular relation to each other. They were not all according to host plants or types of insects. They had been painted two pests to a page according to the topics the *Home Garden* had wanted covered that particular month. If I discussed the insects under Host Plants, as is so often done in texts, there would be a vast amount of repetition or else vast quantities of "see page —." I finally decided to do a dictionary with the 1000 "Bugs," which now included all sorts of animal pests, in alphabetical order by their approved common names under groups: Ants, Beetles etc., also in alphabetical order. The last third of the book would be an alphabetical check list of about 500 plants common in home gardens, including trees, shrubs, vines, lawns, flowers and vegetables, with the pests known to attack them.

It was October before I had worked out this plan, figured the approximate length of the book, and realized that I'd have to grind out at least 2000 words every single day, including Sundays, until the end of January. I paid Lacelle and a friend of his to come in after school, when they were not playing football, and make a card catalogue of all the hosts mentioned under each insect as I finished treating it for the first part of the book. There was a lot of drudgery involved because some insects go on dozens of plants. I could never have finished on time without this extra help.

In late October an artist friend came to stay while she did the black-and-white drawings for the book. Her work was exquisite but slow. Instead of two or three weeks it was taking two or three months and I was spending time every day finding specimens or photographs or making sketches to show what I wanted. I can finish a job under pressure only if I am alone. There is some queer quirk in me that demands solitude; I become frantic with someone else always around. For the second time in my life, the first being when I took that oral doctor's examination, I thought I was losing my mind. Soon there was only a month left and most of the book unfinished. I called a halt on illustrations, promised to take care of any financial loss if only I could have my house to myself.

I don't know whether this work requirement is pure selfishness or orneriness or laziness. I can work wonderfully shut up in a small hotel room, with strangers making noises all around, but in my own home I cannot concentrate with either a guest or a cleaning woman on deck, or even a man to oversee in the yard. Maybe it is because I hate to be caught bluffing. I talk about working from 6 a.m. to 1 a.m. but I stop and walk around or read a story or make coffee. In the interim I don't want my thoughts distracted. Despite a many-faceted life, I like to concentrate on one thing at a time. I don't want to be asked out to dinner for I don't like to stop at any prearranged time; I need the feeling of complete, uninterrupted leisure. I am not proud of my hermit propensities but it is the only way I can finish books. And I do love to have friends come to visit when I can stop long enough to enjoy them.

The daily stint had grown to 3000 words when New Year's brought the luxury of an empty house. My Waterloo comes at 9 p.m. I am desperately sleepy then, completely exhausted; I'd give anything to go to bed. But once I fight through that slump, I can, faced with a deadline, make a fairly good comeback, go on for several more hours. Without the deadline, and my signature on a contract, I'll slump in the big chair, turn on the radio, open a magazine, stay half asleep.

The Gardener's Bug Book did get done, more than 150,000 words of it. I took the last of the copy in to New York on Monday, January 30, 1946, packed on Tuesday, left for the South on Wednesday.

All the way home from the South I kept contrasting in my mind the beautiful houses I had seen in Natchez and the shabbiness of my own house. The last payment due on the Bug Book, the only part not already spent for reference books and extra help or given to the Internal Revenue Service, went for painting and papering.

Spare time that spring went into reading proof. Many corrections had to be made in galley proof because I had been given no chance to see the manuscript after editing. Now I have a definite understanding with publishers that a book does not go to press before I have checked editorial changes.

Reviewers sometimes compliment my indexes. They ought to; I nearly die doing them. For this one I was allowed only three scorching summer days. At the end of that period I took a huge suitcase of index cards in to *Home Garden* and the secretaries there divided them up, typed them onto pages for the printer. I had no time to check their copying, for the book, with a 50-page double column Index, came out almost immediately. I could only hope the mistakes were few.

The reviews were quite favorable. Apparently the book did provide, for gardeners, nurserymen, dealers, tree experts, the fingertip reference volume I had envisioned. It was even used a bit in colleges. One scientist wrote that he had found only one *Lapsus calami*. That was a bad one, however. I had written, from very second-hand information, that porcupines are not much as garden pests. The scientist, and one or two gardeners, informed me that in some areas they are tremendously damaging.

A BOOK ON DISEASES

The Home Garden and American Garden Guild planned a book on plant diseases as a companion volume to the Bug Book but I was not going to start writing it until I had explored the country more at first hand. No more boners like the porcupines for me! We planned color photographs taken of diseases as I met them in the field. Lacelle and I spent a lot of time, and $100 for film, on this project.

A little teaching that fall provided a lot of material for photographs. George Van Yahres, the Long Island tree expert I had known for some years, was starting an Arborists School for war veterans under the GI bill, with headquarters on the Whitney Estate. I went over Saturdays to teach diseases and pests in the classroom (one of the stables) and then out in the field, wandering through neighboring estates. That was the year 2,4-D first came into wide use, before all its drawbacks had been charted. One Saturday we found rhododendrons, next to a lawn that had been treated with the weedkiller, with their leaves peculiarly twisted and rolled. I was sure this must be 2,4-D injury although it was reported to have little or no effect on broad-leaved evergreens. After class I started out to my cabin for the weekend, stopping at an Inn for a belated lunch. At the next table was Dr. A. M. S. Pridham from Cornell. He had done most of the original research with 2,4-D and was somewhat incredulous when I described its effect on rhododendrons, but after going back to the estate to see for himself, agreed with me. That was a black-and-white picture that eventually went into the disease book.

October meant a glorious trip to Asheville at flaming foliage time and more ammunition for the book. The Southern Shade Tree Conference had asked me to show the azalea blight slides. It was flattering to have a group of men ask a woman to come and talk to them and it was fun to go along on their field trips.

I saw a power-saw in action for the first time and a nursery where the boxwood was all bronzy. I did not know the answer then but think now it must have been due to meadow nematodes. I saw the famous gardens of the Biltmore Estate, with their magnificent azaleas and rhododendrons (and somewhat neglected roses).

I found a species of Sphaceloma on English ivy and sent specimens to Anna Jenkins, who has spent her life with that genus. Dr. Bitancourt, also a specialist in this field, just happened to be in New York from Brazil the day I returned home and came out to dinner. He and Anna wrote a brief paper based on leaves that I had tucked in my pocket while waiting in front of a hotel.

On November 20, 1946, the Ford, now with 38,000 miles on it since Pearl Harbor, started out on a tortuous route to California, more up and down the map than across it. Thanks to the azalea work there were enough lecture dates to pay for gasoline and motels on this trip to learn enough to write another book.

The first stop was Baltimore to hear papers at an entomology meeting, then Beltsville, to learn the latest on nematodes from the U.S.D.A. After autographing Bug Books and visiting the Nobles in Jacksonville there were two talks at Winter Park, staying with the Trismens in their lakeside home, surrounded with orange trees and all kinds of subtropical plants, and a rose garden, too. Mrs. Trismen took me to see many gardens, told me names of many plants I had never met before but which went into the book.

I went to see vegetable gardens around Fort Lauderdale and to the Fairchild Tropical Gardens below Miami, then up the west coast of Florida to Bradenton, center of work on gladiolus as well as vegetables. I lectured at Tampa, then raced north to talk at Macon, Georgia, staying at Merriewood, charming home of Marie, author and lecturer on flower arrangement, and George Wood, camellia expert.

At Montgomery, Alabama, the Stokes had a buffet supper before the public lecture. The Governor was there, Big Bill Folsom. Contrary to legend he was wearing shoes and I did not see him kissing any girls. The Commissioner of Agriculture was there; Camilla came from New Orleans and the Wilbys from Atlanta.

I talked azalea blight in a hotel in Pensacola, right across from the bar where a juke box was blaring wildly all evening. I yelled as loud as I could but I don't know how much the audience heard.

There was an all-too-brief visit at Spring Hill, Christmas with Cornell friends in Birmingham, and then Natchez, where Miss Myra had again asked me to stay at D'Evereux while waiting to talk to the Garden Club after New Year's.

The first afternoon was beautifully warm and we visited many gardens with camellias in bloom. In one garden the azaleas had a sort of dieback and I diagnosed it as a result of frost injury a year or two before. The owner haughtily assured me that Natchez NEVER had frost like that.

The very next morning, before starting off to Haphazard Plantation, I worked for two hours scraping enough frost off the windshield to see to drive. At the Plantation the bawling cattle were huddled against the fences, backs to the wind. Inside, the fireplace, which covered almost the whole side of the living room, blazed all day long but a few feet away it was freezing. The cardinals came to the window sill in droves looking for food that was not encased in ice.

When I returned to my room in D'Evereux I worked in bed to keep warm. One gas grate makes little impression in a 20-foot bedroom with a 12-foot ceiling. The next day at Stanton Hall they had the fires going all day in preparation for the evening talk but the supposedly liquid chemicals I had with me for demonstration remained frozen solid. A few hardy souls arrived that night, huddling together in fur coats, but my lecture was not exactly a success. (Lest these remarks deter anyone from making the Natchez Pilgrimage, let me say that January often does have surprises in the South; spring comes in February and March is almost always wonderful.)

I went on to talk azaleas in Beaumont and in Houston, under auspices of the Blume System Tree Experts. Houston is so big and sprawly it seems to have about doubled in size every time I go there, but I like it.

For some months I had been writing an occasional article for *Sun-Up,* a home and garden magazine of the Southwest published in San Antonio. They had arranged for me to see a lot of gardens and I was spending a week there. I was taken to a few, the first morning, in a drizzle. Then it started to pour and kept it up day after day without ceasing. For all that week I sat in the motel and wrote articles (they pay for gasoline, too). I could hear the lions roar but it was too wet even to go to the zoo.

Came time to go on West and Route 90, the most southern highway in the United States, was closed to traffic on account of SNOW.

It opened up the next day and I drove as far as Alpine, so well-named. I had to find my galoshes before getting out of the car. According to my records I had 21 consecutive days that winter without seeing the sun. In El Paso, the children were throwing snowballs, making snowmen in the gardens.

I meant to stay in Tucson, to visit the University again. It had become my habit, in planning a trip through tourist infested country in my less venturesome middle age, to write for rooms in advance, sending a check to insure prompt reply. I left home before receiving either confirmation or returned check from Tucson. I reached there before noon, sure that I could find some place to lay my head before night. I was wrong. From the car licenses it looked as if all of California as well as most of the East had moved into Arizona. I headed for Phoenix and it seemed as if motels were lined up solid the entire route, every one with a "No Vacancy" sign. It was late evening when I made my last try at a Phoenix hotel. They already had 150 travelers spending the night in the lobby; I could join them if I wished. The smoke was too thick. I returned to the Ford, parked it on a back street, went to a movie, staying until everyone was ejected. Then I locked the car doors, huddled down under a robe. In early morning, as I freshened up at a gas station, the attendant told me they had been arresting people staying in their cars all night, I was very lucky to have escaped. I had breakfast at an all-night restaurant, drove out on the desert to watch the sun rise behind the giant cacti.

I already had a place to stay near Phoenix, two days hence. I was visiting more Cornell friends. Dr. A. L. Harrison was at the Vegetable Laboratory in the Salt River Valley where they raise dates and citrus as well as winter vegetables. But I did not know how to reach the Laboratory in the dark and I hated to arrive unannounced late at night, so far ahead of my invitation. They were surprised enough to see me next day.

For the return trip I planned a more northern route, less popular with winter visitors, and I made a reservation at Flagstaff. I underestimated the mountain driving by nearly a hundred miles, forgot that I would lose an hour with change of time, neglected to allow for officialdom. I stopped for inspection at the Arizona border and they said my license plates were too old. New Jersey had changed its yearly system, now operated from March to March, rather than from January to January. They didn't believe me, kept me waiting while the luggage of a long line of cars was inspected, then found a book of regulations and decided I was legal after all. I say that I don't drive after dark, especially in mountains; I do, at times like this.

One good thing about this trip. They no longer looked askance at a woman driving alone. On my previous tour through the West it had been seriously suggested to me that I should, for safety, acquire a dummy to ride beside me.

I was visiting Mabel Myers, still another Cornell friend, in San Diego. I found her street, found the right number, but there was no one home. I waited and waited; finally I learned from a passerby that the street I thought I was on had turned a corner without notice. Mabel had asked guests for dinner and they were waiting and waiting for me. The next day we went down into Mexico, to Ensenada, for the weekend. There was the sun and I finally got warmed up.

But not for long! My next destination was Santa Monica where I had a week's reservation at a motel. It was raining when I arrived and stayed damp and chilly. Because so many people in California motels had asphyxiated themselves with unvented gas grates, the bathroom window was nailed wide open to provide oxygen.

I suspect that that part of California would have seemed cheerless to me then no matter how bright the sun shone, for Elizabeth Bodger was not there. She had died some years before, a few days after her son was born. I had chosen Santa Monica because it was convenient for extracting information from UCLA. I also received help from many nurseries and private gardens.

Santa Barbara was a sunny interlude. Mrs. Oakleigh Thorne had moved to a new house with a very modernistic garden. She invited the garden club to hear me as a sort of housewarming.

I went to the University of California at Berkeley to pay my re-

spects to Dr. E. O. Essig, whose work and writings in entomology I
had so long admired and used. He invited me to the graduate students' seminar and I was immeasurably puffed up at being introduced as the person who had written the most useful book in entomology in recent years. I was inordinately pleased to learn that I,
who had been entirely self-taught in this field, from gardens and
books, had done well enough to be recognized by a real, and very
great, entomologist. I went to the plant pathology department for
information on rusts and mildews, blights and nematodes.

Returning I studied more Texas gardens, talking at Fort Worth
and Waco. Leaving Dallas, I stopped to scrape frozen snow off the
windshield just in time; there was a ditch and a barricade across
the road. I stopped at Tyler, where Eldon Lyle, plant pathologist for
the Texas Rose Foundation, took me to various wholesale houses.

I talked at McGehee, Arkansas, at Paducah, and Lexington, Kentucky. I left Lexington at 6 a.m. for Louisville, where I visited seed
stores to see how they cared for their dormant roses, gave a talk on
the radio (the garden club thought it would drum up trade for my
lecture that evening, which was to be on roses, not azaleas). There
was a luncheon but before I could get a bite to eat a reporter arrived
for an interview.

It was still dark when I departed for Columbus the next morning.
I scarcely realized the ground was covered with sleet until I started
to use brakes going down a hill. I had not been going fast but I
ended up about two blocks away, faced in the other direction, next
to a ditch and a barbed-wired fence. Some Providence watches over
me; no one else was foolish enough to be out on that four-lane highway, so nothing at all happened except a scare. I returned to Glen
Ridge, having gone 12,000 miles without even a puncture.

Now I had the background for the book. It would take at least
two more winters at a desk, abstracting and writing, plus going to
as many meetings as I could scrape up cash for. In December an
article written for *Household* almost paid expenses to the AAAS
meetings in Chicago. There wan't time to go home to New England

for Christmas with my brother as usual so I left for Chicago a little early, on Christmas Day. I was traveling coach to save money and going early would give me a chance to catch up on sleep after arrival. How lucky I was! That was the famous holiday snowstorm and the eastern scientists who left that night via pullman were 24 hours late. After hearing, but perhaps not digesting, nearly 150 papers I returned home just three hours ahead of our worst New Jersey ice-storm. The trees suffered terribly; 200,000 families around here were without electricity and heat for days. My luck still held; my utilities kept functioning; I kept right on working.

I was abstracting thousands of articles, buying dozens of books, paying more than $20 a week just to keep part of the house reasonably warm. I was confidently expecting an advance on the book to keep me going and then, suddenly, I was out of luck. *Home Garden* decided not to do the book after all. It would be too technical, would not sell to enough thousands of gardeners, the cost of color reproduction was now too high. They did authorize one general article on diseases for the magazine, using a few of the black-and-white pictures, but that paid only a small portion of the fuel bill.

I was pretty discouraged. Plant doctoring did not pay enough during the growing season to keep me the whole year. The Bug Book was selling very well but I wasn't getting any of it. Should I give up my independence and try to get a regular job? And if so, what? What was I really fitted for?

I went to a meeting of the Montclair Garden Club in March. It was in a private home and crowded. I arrived late, along with Gertrude Smith, landscape architect and writer. We sat on the stairs, far from the lecturer, and I told her how the plans for the disease book had fallen through. She thought Van Nostrand might be interested; they wanted to get into the garden book field. Gertrude wrote to Malcolm Johnson about me and he seemed decidedly interested. My name might be a wedge into the amateur gardening line and they were so used to doing textbooks the technical angle of my disease book was no barrier. By June I had a contract and an advance! Life looked a lot brighter, I wasn't yet washed up; somebody thought I was still useful.

There was another winter tied to a desk at home, paying more fuel bills, but the manuscript, 200,000 words this time, was finished in the summer of 1949. It still had to go through the press but I was planning on being South again the next winter, making a few lecture engagements there. I did galley proof at home, then there was a short respite while I lectured and visited cousins in Virginia. Page proof caught up with me in Columbia, where I was talking to the Garden Club of South Carolina, and continued to arrive like clockwork after I reached my favorite working place, the Hotel Thomas at Gainesville, Florida. It is comfortable, very inexpensive compared to southern Florida, and is set in acres of lawn and gardens. It is also close to the University where I can ask for help when I need it.

I settled down there for three weeks, but there was a three-day break while I journeyed to talk at Tallahassee, De Funiak Springs and Panama City. Returning late and tired, I did not bother to take much out of the Ford, leaving it locked in its usual niche in front of the hotel. About noon the next day, in the midst of proofreading, I suddenly remembered the cameras and scurried out to look. The side of the car that I had seen from the dining room window at breakfast was still locked; the other door had been forced open. My hats were strewn over the ground as useless but both cameras were gone— my good Zeiss Ikon and a Kodak. They had taken the extra pair of glasses from the glove compartment, a knitting bag, which contained the only sweater I had ever attempted for myself, all completed except the last cuff. Luckily, they had not found the projector behind the seat and had paid no attention to the priceless portfolio of water colors.

That marked the end of photography for me. After I got home I did buy another secondhand Zeiss Ikon but it was much too big, not fitting into my stand for taking pictures in the office, and the film cost too much. I also purchased an inexpensive Argus and later was given a very good Kodak but I never seem to have time to use them or even to get acquainted enough with them to know how to use them.

Whenever I do a book, and particularly an Index, I think of that old definition of genius as being the "ability to apply the seat of your pants to the seat of your chair." It is always hard to make myself sit at a desk from dawn to midnight with no breaks except for meals. It was especially hard there in Florida with flowers and sunshine just outside. I indexed as fast as page proof came in, getting almost through one batch by 4 p.m. when the next arrived by Special Delivery. The format of the Disease Book was the same as the Bug Book, a description of the diseases in alphabetical order according to types, followed by a check list under hosts.

To make it easier for the reader I had asked to have a running head of the types, Anthracnose, Black Spot, Blights, Blotch Diseases etc., and had carefully marked the manuscript. Through some mix-up, the running head that actually came through on the page proof used the scientific names under the types, so that we went from *Asterina* to *Stigmatea* in a couple of pages, then from *Alternaria* to *Volutella* in the next few. This system provided 35 different alphabets and no possible way for the book to be used for fingertip reference. The first batch of proof showing this mistake arrived in Florida late Friday afternoon, after the New York office was closed. It was too late to telephone to expostulate so I wrote to explain matters.

They evidently thought I was a finicky author and that changing at this late date would cost too much. The headings continued to arrive in that impossible fashion. I have always tried to be cooperative but this time I became a mule. I dared not let anything like that go out under my name. The only way I could prevent it was to hold up everything, refuse to finish the Index, but I felt mean as the devil; I don't ordinarily act that way. They had to capitulate and they did not charge the cost of changing all those plates to the author, which I had rather expected. We ended up with a book we were both proud of.

REVISING

The trouble with my books is that they get out-of-date too fast. Science marches on, inexorably. I have to march too, if I want to be sold. *The Plant Doctor,* now published by J. B. Lippincott Company, who had bought out Stokes Company, needed to be entirely re-written. In return for an advance, I had promised the publishers not to accept any more lecture dates that winter, other than those already signed up, and to spend my time on revision. I did stipulate that seeing the *Plant Disease Handbook* through the press had to come first and that took much more time than I had anticipated. There was no chance to even start the other book before leaving Florida. I journeyed across country again to talk in Monroe, Louisiana, then back to Dublin, Georgia, where I had a "free" week before the next lecture. Waiting in the mail was proof of the Index for the big book. I started to check it with the manuscript, decided to do it back to page proof, despite those unwieldy sheets. I found a mistake, a little later another. I kept on until I had used up that whole week just in check-ing. In the end, I had caught only one or two more errors but I felt I had at least done my duty. My other publishers had a different idea; they thought I was double-crossing them.

Finally, at Charleston, I tried to cram a winter's work on *The Plant Doctor* into six days. I was at the St. John again, in the old section, and I looked at gardens through the gates as I walked out for lunch and again for dinner. The rest of the time I typed madly. I stopped on the way home to talk at a dinner meeting of the Roanoke Rose Society and to the Garden Club of Virginia in Richmond. I finished the book at home, before the spraying season, now with 45 clients, got into full swing. The *Plant Disease Handbook* made its debut March 20th at the New York Flower Show, and I autographed copies at the Van Nostrand booth.

The Gardener's Bug Book came out just as DDT was starting a flood of new chemicals. It was costing more than a million dollars to get each new pesticide up to market stage, not counting the cost of actual manufacture, yet they flooded the market. The control measures in the Bug Book were old-fashioned long before the big printing was exhausted. There was no point in reprinting the original edition and so Clara Claasen approached me about doing it over completely. With the demise of the *Home Garden,* Doubleday had acquired all rights to the book and was in a position to offer the usual royalty. They offered also a generous advance but they paid it so promptly, in May, it was spent before I could start the work the next winter. So again it was a struggle to keep fuel bills paid for I had purposely cut down on lecture engagements to have working time.

I had one lecture date in St. Louis of long-standing. All January I cut down on the food bill (the only way I know to economize, professional dues and books being necessities in my scheme of things) because most of my cash was tied up in a round-trip to St. Louis. Then when I got that back and paid for fuel with the lecture fee, I still couldn't eat for I had invested in a ticket to Charleston, West Virginia, for my other date. In the fall I had agreed to do a magazine article to have a little eating money in the winter. Some magazines pay on acceptance, some on publication. This one apparently did neither. About a month after publication I telephoned to see what had happened. "Don't worry, you'll get your money." I did, late in the spring when I no longer needed it.

I was due to leave for Charleston on March 2nd. I had the ticket but no cash to travel with. I had expected a royalty check from Van Nostrand on March 1st, not much, but possibly enough to keep going until spring spraying. Nothing happened. The mail came at noon on the 2nd and still no check. The bank, my last chance of borrowing money, closed in two hours. I telephoned over, to see if by chance the check had been sent directly there, as had been done once when I was traveling.

"Oh yes, it came in two days ago; didn't we send you a notice about it?"

There was more than a thousand dollars waiting for me while I had been wondering how to pay for a taxi to the station or for porters and meals on the train.

Both those trips were worth the preliminary anguish. Dr. Edgar Anderson, head of the Missouri Botanical Garden, met my train in St. Louis. A couple of years before I had been excited by Dr. Anderson's *Plants, Man, and Life* and much pleased to learn that he was to be the banquet speaker at the American Horticultural Congress in Philadelphia. When my turn came to be introduced at the cocktail party in his honor I told him how glad I was to meet him. He said, "I'm awfully glad to see you *again*."

Horrified at having forgotten meeting this celebrity I asked where it had been. "At Harpenden." My New England accent had made such an impression on him that summer in old England he had remembered my name for a quarter of a century. I blushed at my own untrustworthy memory. And now in St. Louis Dr. Anderson was being kind again, showing me the city (my first visit), Shaw's Garden, the site where National Council is to have its permanent home, and making a particularly graceful introduction. He told the audience that I had much to give them because I learned things through working in many, many gardens whereas most people could speak of experience in but a single garden.

That evening Wellesley graduates in the vicinity of St. Louis had a get-together and Eleanor McClure, garden writer and landscaper, showed the pictures she had taken of some of my gardens while following me around spraying one day the previous summer. They were much more beautiful than I see them with my plant-doctor eye looking for trouble. The next morning I had a chance to see some of the research work of Monsanto Chemical Company before taking the noon train back.

The West Virginia trip was highlighted by seeing the garden where Dr. O. M. Harper grows his prize roses, lunching in a dining room filled with his trophies.

I went back to reading and writing for the Bug Book. If I stopped to keep up with all the literature I could get no writing done, but if I ceased reading, the book would be out-of-date before it went to the printer instead of after. The manuscript seemed to weigh a ton when I took it in and laid it on Miss Claasen's desk. She wanted to know where the other copy was. I looked blank and she mildly reminded me that the contract I had signed said I was to deliver *two* copies. I thought I had read it carefully the year before but I had missed that. It had not been required for other books.

Another copy meant more work but also a chance for more revision. Publication had now been deferred until spring (1956) which meant it would not go to press until fall. Six more months for new chemicals to be included. And new names!

Scientific names are simply impossible. Everyone is at work learning things that change the names of insects. For the first edition of the Bug Book my guide was the official "Common Names of Insects," published by the American Association of Economic Entomologists (now combined with the Entomological Society of America). Immediately after the book was published, a new list of Common Names appeared, with a lot of changes in the scientific names. When we planned the new Bug Book we thought it would be clear sailing, because another official list was due late in 1954. It still had not appeared when I finished the first revision and started on the rerevision. Dr. Reece I. Sailer, head of the committee preparing the list, was most helpful. I sent him the list of the thousand-odd names I was using and he parceled them out for comment by specialists in different groups. I kept changing names in the manuscript. When the second typing was nearly completed I spent a very hot day in Washington going over Dr. Sailer's file, trying to get the latest corrections. The official list was not yet published when my book went to press but I had done the best I could.

It had been a nasty summer, terribly hot and sticky. I sprayed all day and one of the new sprays I was trying out made blisters over my arms. Then I'd try to type on the porch all evening but the gnats and other midgets that came through the screen settled on the blisters and I'd have to move indoors. Along with redoing the Bug Book I was spending nearly forty hours a week as president of the North Jersey Rose Society, with meetings, board meetings, getting ready for our first Rose Show, getting advertisers for a Rose Directory to pay for printing schedules for the Show. I decided it paid to get older. You really did not need so much sleep.

I took my whole summer's vacation one evening. I had driven up along the Hudson to lecture to the Kinderhook Garden Club and should have returned that night. But I remembered what had happened the summer before when I had tried to drive home from the Catskills after a talk. Stopping to get a cup of coffee to avoid an accident I had precipitated one (property damage only). So now I was splurging and staying overnight at the Rhinebeck Arms. I treated myself to a very good dinner and read a detective story. It was wonderful! Of course, I left soon after 5 a.m. to get home in time to spray the next day but for once that summer I had a leisurely evening and a good meal.

All that hard work paid off. The new Bug Book had as many and as lengthy reviews as if it were a first edition and they were even more favorable, for those who had used the first edition were sure they would need the second. The Davey Tree Expert Company, impatiently waiting for the book for their classes, warned me never to let it get out of print again without giving them a chance to stock up.

And now everyone wants to know when there will be a new *Plant Disease Handbook*. I'm beginning, but it will take at least three years, two winters for reading and writing, another to get through the press. There is a lot of new material on antibiotics and nematodes as well as new names and chemicals to be assimilated. I no longer dare use trade names. They were a feature of earlier books, a help to the gardener trying to purchase the right chemical. Now there are too many, about 32,000 registered with the U.S. Department of Agriculture when I was finishing the Bug Book,

and I have learned through rather sad experience that the manufacturer is apt to change the ingredients in a proprietary compound
while retaining the old name.

COMPROMISES DON'T ALWAYS PAY

Garden Enemies, published in 1953, was a compromise. We thought
it might appeal to the gardener in Levittown who would not be
interested in, and could not afford, the larger reference books. To
keep the price down we omitted photographs and I provided diagrammatic sketches for help in diagnosing the different types of
diseases and pests, as well as lists of the common enemies and control
measures. The reviews were excellent but it does not continue to
sell the way the big books do. Apparently people want all or nothing.
The book came out with a photograph of a garden forming the
cover, rather than with a dust jacket. I thought it a clever new idea
(it was not mine) but the bookstores disagreed. A bright orange
jacket has now been provided and we wait to see if it helps. But
I doubt that I'll have to slave on a revision of this book. As a matter
of fact, it is still reasonably modern, for the flood of new chemicals
slowed to a trickle when the Miller Amendment was passed regulating residues. The only thing really dating this smaller book is
"malathon." Right after publication the powers that be put an i in
the word and it is now "malathion."

CHAPTER 8

THE LIMELIGHT

LATE IN THE SPRING of 1947 I sent Lacelle to the Internal Revenue Office to get some information. He came back and said they wanted to see me; they thought I was trying to gyp the Government. For ten years I had been reading everything *Florists Exchange* and other trade papers said about Social Security. It seemed to me my business was growing things, even if for other people, and that my new service would surely be horticultural or agricultural. The officials argued about it among themselves but finally decided I was not agricultural, that I should have been deducting Social Security from everyone who had ever worked for me, even for an hour, for the past ten years. I put all my accounts in order and an agent came and spent one entire day in June going over them, giving me the impossible task of getting Social Security numbers for all my past fleeting helpers. He said that since it was an honest mistake and that my new kind of business was subject to different interpretations he would ask that the penalty be waived and that I have to pay only the sixty per cent interest. Washington didn't agree. I finally had to pay both sixty per cent interest and sixty percent penalty for the years I had not been deducting from my helpers.

DOCTOR, SAVE MY ROSES

On that hectic day we spent on my books, a photographer arrived from *This Week* magazine. She had to have a picture of me to go with an article they had accepted from Stephen Booke, who had come out to interview me the summer before. At least he actually had come out, though he did not go to gardens and see me in action. Heretofore the plant doctor and her "station wagon" had been mostly written up by people who had not even met me.

The photographer perched me up and she perched me down, with pruning shears and without. She tried pictures from a stepladder looking down at me and others looking up. Between poses I dashed back inside to explain to the Revenue man that, "Once I did pay two dollars to the girl next door to do some typing. She moved away; I don't have any idea what her address is or if she ever had a Social Security number." "Yes, I got an old man to help me out one morning when my helper was sick. He was a friend of a gardener. I paid cash and I never was sure of his name."

The *This Week* article, called "Doctor, Save my Roses" with a pretty awful picture, came out on July 19th. I never before knew that *This Week* went out with so many Sunday newspapers all over the country. On July 29th I wrote to my San Diego friend:

"Dear Mabel,

Thank you for the clippings (of that article). Your brief note sounded as if I had not yet answered any of the pleasant notes I have had from you since leaving California. Maybe I haven't, though I have meant to and have thought of you often. I feel as if my life were lived under a ton of bricks and if I ever get unloaded so I can breathe easily or take a minute to write to a friend I get smashed flat again.

"This spring I was listed as Consulting Rosarian for the American Rose Society, since when people have called for help from the U.S.D.A., Mexico, Austria, and way stations. The Austrian casually suggested that I send him all my books. And then that darned article came out in *This Week* from some interview I gave casually more than a year ago. The author promised to let me censor any article he wrote, which he never did, and promised to make it plain I could not answer letters, whereupon I have been snowed under—to date, 21 states and Washington D.C., everybody wanting free advice and more than half not even sending postage. I went in to *This Week* to see if I could sell them an article myself which would take up some of the more important needs of these people but they were decidedly cool to that.

"So Stephen Booke gets the money and I get the headaches. I answered forty letters this weekend, together with getting my nephew Tommy married over in Bronxville and having a woman from Portugal out for supper. She said she simply had to see me, to get the latest spray information, but all she wanted to do was to tell me what a wonderful pathologist she had been in Lisbon before the War. (True.)

"And last Tuesday I got supper ready for a professor from Minnesota and his wife. He telephoned he had to consult with me and I am only home for meals. Half an hour after they were due they telephoned from New York they had gotten too weary from their day's doings and were not coming. Me, I'm too poor with all this donated time to even buy meat for myself but I bought lamb chops for them. Was I mad!

"*This Week*'s headaches include a free radio talk over the New York City station in September, a request from the Laurel, Mississippi, Chamber of Commerce to help plan their garden and parks program, apparently free, the usual requests to test chemicals, a diagram from a woman of everything in her back yard to ask if she had bird lice on her clothes, a request from a woman 79 years old for quick help before she dies (her state experiment station is too slow), a request to find an uncle for a woman whose mother's name was Westcott and a few dozen others.

"I got the final bills this week from the Government, for all the Social Security interest and penalties due, just after I had bought Tommy's wedding present and a dress for the wedding. The Government waits not at all to collect its money and some of my clients are away with their bills unpaid, so, after I paid Lacelle his salary this morning, I had to borrow back from him enough to buy stamps for this bunch of fan mail. If I ever give another interview it will only be after I have gone insane. I can't afford publicity!

Love, Cynthia"

That letter to Mabel is the only record I have of that queer collection of letters. The *New Yorker* magazine took most of them and never did return them. I do remember one from a woman in Denver. Her son was a newsboy and she was sitting out in the yard looking at my picture. I seemed to be kind; maybe I could help her.

A PROFILE

With this experience behind me I was decidedly unreceptive when Eugene Kinkead asked if he could trail me around occasionally for the next few months. He was on the staff of the *New Yorker,* had a Profile in mind. I said, "No." I dreaded another flock of letters. Then I began to fear that all three of my publishers would cheerfully murder me if I passed up such an opportunity to plug books, so I reluctantly agreed. The *New Yorker* is thorough. It does not do profiles at long distance but I wanted neither my clients nor my spraying schedule upset. I arranged to meet Mr. Kinkead that first day at a garden in Palisades, New York, and told him how to reach it. His office, however, sent him to a ferry that no longer existed and he had to telephone to say he was delayed. My client, who was unwell and had difficulty walking, had to come way out where I was working to give me the message. That upset me so much I went off and left behind a bottle of tetraethyl pyrophosphate, a deadly poison.

We met Mr. Kinkead along the road, parked his car at a gas station, and took him along for the rest of the day at Nyack, West Nyack, New City, and Nanuet. When he wanted to stop and write things down I kept on walking and spraying. He was exhausted by mid-afternoon but we had to finish our jobs before I could return him to his car on our way home. I simply did not have minutes to spare, even for the *New Yorker*. I was surprised, when the Profile finally appeared two years later, to find the treatment more sympathetic than I deserved. He only made fun of my driving; and most people, knowing of my coast-to-coast jaunts, did not take that too seriously. One club did. They were considering having me down in Virginia and thought it much safer if I came by train.

Mr. Kinkead continued to come around occasionally. He went on a few more spraying trips but near-home, half-day affairs. He came after work to look at every book in the library, every rose in the garden. He talked to most of my friends and if he found any enemies to pump I did not hear about it. He listened to a lecture and wrote that I closed my eyes when I started to speak. I still don't know if that is true; it seems to me that I always have a very wide-awake view of the audience. He took due note of my assistant. Lacelle was no longer with me; he had gone into banking, and was putting himself through college at night. My high school helper that summer was a banker's son, investing wisely all he earned from me, baby-sitting at night for his fun money.

On those after-work interviews I served sherry, the only alcoholic beverage I can afford to keep on hand, and Weary Willie Cake. Both were mentioned in the Profile and one of the fan letters was a curt request for the cake recipe. A couple of years after the Profile finally appeared I lectured down on the Eastern Shore of Virginia and was most cordially entertained. We were gathered for drinks before a buffet supper and on being asked my choice said Bourbon. There was a stunned silence for a minute. Going home my overnight hostess chuckled and said that after reading the *New Yorker* everyone that thought they would have a chance to entertain me had laid in some sherry. They almost never drank it themselves.

Late on Saturday night before my Rose Sunday in 1952 my refrigerator was full of fruit juices ready for the punch, ice in all the trays, when it suddenly ceased operations for good. I salvaged most of the punch ingredients and my neighbor went out for buckets of ice next day but we could not quite keep up with the 700 who came. We had expected 500 at most. For the first time in Rose Day history the punch ran out.

As soon as the stores opened on Monday I telephoned to order a refrigerator, any make, just so it could be installed immediately. I was waiting at home for it when a man arrived from the *New Yorker*. The Profile was finally scheduled and the "checking department" had to see that every picture, every rose bush, every book mentioned in the article was correct. By this time my summer assistant had changed from the slim banker's son to Lacelle's brother, of different appearance, so changes were duly made in the manuscript. I was not allowed to see what had been written but tantalizing parts of sentences were read to me so I could comment on their scientific accuracy.

On July 15th, I was just leaving to put a letter in the corner mailbox for the 5:45 p.m. collection when the telephone rang. The *New Yorker* was checking again. As he was about to hang up, at 6:50, the man remarked that he would call me again the next night. I said he couldn't, I was lecturing in Katonah the next day, driving on from there to Lake George. He wanted to know where I was going to spend the night so I gave him the name of a motel near Albany but said I could not possibly reach there before 8 or 9. When I arrived the next evening they told me New York had called at 6, would call again later. The only telephone was in the manager's office so I stayed dressed until midnight, waiting. They never did call back and I was never quite sure the thing was really going to be published when planned, if at all.

The next week, talking to the Mountain Lakes Garden Club, I started to discuss peony Botrytis blight and was reminded of a question by the checking department which I had not been able to answer fully because he would not read me enough of what had been written. I mentioned this and said that I did not know if they would see a Profile of me that week or not. Someone excitedly jumped up and said, "It's already out; I brought my copy along!"

PROFILE AFTERMATH

Although the inquiries that came in after publication were written on monogrammed notepaper rather than in pencil on ruled paper the proportion that enclosed postage was less, if anything, than after the *This Week* article. I was again spending hours and hours answering letters and I don't really know whether or not the Profile increased the sale of books. It did, however, bring me a number of very enjoyable lecture engagements.

The Cosmopolitan Club in Philadelphia wanted me—an interesting change from garden clubs. There were only three states I had not been in, Washington, Oregon, and Oklahoma. The Profile remedied that but I had to wait to work these in. When Iowa State College invited me to talk Roses there in October, 1953, paying expenses halfway across the continent, it seemed the logical time to take in the Northwest.

I arrived in Seattle on Saturday and was put up at the Sunset Club, a woman's club teeming with activity during the week, quiet on weekends. The afternoon was devoted to roses, in private gardens and in beautiful Woodland Park. I had seen the huge roses of the West in shows; this was my first sight of them growing. I felt as if I still had everything to learn about roses.

It was hard work to hold myself in bed the next morning until the breakfast tray arrived. I was more than ready to see gardens in this area which grows most of the tender things of the South, has most of our Eastern plants, specializes in the English rhododendrons that we cannot have in the East, has all kinds of broad-leaved ever-greens of its own, and the lushest lawns ever produced. I was collecting specimens as we went and was delighted to finally see the earwig I had been writing about in books (two years later I saw it in Glen Ridge). I was also interested to see that many of our eastern pests were present, especially tent caterpillars.

The Wellesley Club had a tea that afternoon and Mrs. Henry Isaacson, with whom I had been corresponding, had a Sunday supper, so-called. It was really dinner and the food was superelegant. I forgot all my good resolves to watch calories.

Monday morning the Sunset Club was quiet as a ghost and the telephone switchboard not yet working when I started to take a bath. Already in the tub, I found it too hot and turned on the cold water full force. Then I couldn't turn it off! I pulled the plug but the water was running out of the faucet far faster than out of the tub. Visioning immediate floods I grabbed towel and bathrobe and ran shrieking down the stairs, looking for the kitchen. The furnace-man had just arrived; he coped with the situation.

I was scheduled for two talks in Seattle. The first was for the benefit of the Arboretum Fund, to be held at the University of Washington. They had sold a lot of tickets but did not want to overlook any chances so they had me interviewed on a couple of radio programs. In between, I visited the Arboretum, met its efficient Director, Brian Mulligan, and prepared specimens for demonstration. I thought it especially important in talking so far from home that I *prove* to the audience that I was discussing their own pests.

About five minutes before the lecture was to start and surrounded by a dozen people asking questions, I was introduced to the dignitary who was to introduce me. I never did get his name and he knew no more about me. When he asked for information all I could do in the confusion was to thrust my lecture leaflet at him, which has a couple of paragraphs giving my life history. Instead of selecting a couple of sentences from those he started reading the whole darn leaflet, beginning with the list of lecture subjects and my fees. Everyone in the audience had bought a ticket because they knew who I was. The newspapers and the radio had been full of the Plant Doctor. So everyone sat and squirmed and I sat humiliated for about ten minutes. It was scarcely an auspicious beginning for a talk across the continent but the audience was so sorry for me it paid rapt attention. I ended up by enjoying the evening and loving everyone there. I was especially pleased when "Aunt Emmy" Hale, who with her husband owns and edits *Pacific Gardens and Homes,* came up to speak.

After talking to the Seattle Garden Club and their guests the next afternoon I visited the Chrysanthemum Show in town, seeing arrangements made by real Japanese artists instead of arrangements in the Japanese style done by Americans. On Wednesday the manufacturer of Carco-X, a pesticide popular in the West, drove me to Puyallup to see some of their tests, then turned me over to Wellesley classmate Martha Robbins Myers for lunch in her new home.

At the Western Washington Experiment Station at Puyallup the man I wanted to see was Dr. C. J. Gould, specialist in bulb diseases. I needed information for myself but I also extracted a promise of an article for the Brooklyn Botanic Garden. I had been commissioned to edit for them a "Handbook on Plant Pests and Diseases" and was trying to get the very best authors I could, from all over the country, though I hated to ask professional people to donate so much time.

Portland was altogether delightful. I saw the wonderful International Rose Test Gardens as well as innumerable estates. I was a guest on Dean Collins' television program, gave my own talk to a capacity audience. I behaved with reasonable propriety and nothing untoward had happened, like the bathtub episode in Seattle, until I was packing to leave Saturday morning. Luggage on such a trip is a problem. Lecture equipment, in the form of two large, heavy leather portfolios, is all I can carry in one hand and a good-sized suitcase is all I can manage with the other. I had purchased a hat-bag, with a long handle to go over my arm, for train use. Gradually it had been stuffed with mementos and that morning the zipper, which went clear around the thing, refused to zip. It wouldn't work even when the bag was empty. There was no time to go to a luggage shop and all the porter at the Club could do was to provide rope to wind round and round. I hoped too many things would not fall out as I made my undignified exit from the swank Town Club to the waiting station wagon. A garden club member was giving up a whole day to drive me to Oregon Agricultural College, at Corvallis.

There we bought a suitcase; I was through with zippers. Then we lunched with the McWhorters. Dr. Frank McWhorter had been working on viruses way back in Cornell days. He was still doing so and had also become an expert photographer, making his own apparatus to take high-speed pictures of live insects as well as photomicrographs of diseased material. I put in an urgent plea, later gratified, for some of his pictures for the Handbook.

My chauffeur drove me to her charming ranch home for the night, and next morning others took me up to lunch at the Lodge on Mt. Hood, returning just in time for the train East. It had been a marvelous trip, thanks to the *New Yorker*.

The Oklahoma visit was by Ford near the end of another prolonged period of wandering, with all kinds of weather. Fog all the first day, so thick you could not see a truck right in front of you, then a mild sunny day to talk in Chevy Chase. The next day I managed only sixty miles in snow before having to give up, but the fourth day I made it to Raleigh. The big trailer trucks, the highway department trucks, many of the wreckers, were stuck along the road. Most of the light cars were getting through. One by one the links in my chains snapped. Most gas stations were not dug out enough so you could drive in. None could supply chains or links or repairs. Clanking louder and louder and louder I ended up with a terrific cacophony down the main street of Raleigh.

I went to the Camellia Society meeting in Charleston, talked in Summerville, Jacksonville, visited at Winter Park and Spring Hill, then spent a fabulous two days at Holly-Bluff-on-the-Jordan with the Crumps. Now I could really take in this garden of hollies and azaleas I had seen so briefly before. It was cold and a photographer was there from *Holiday* magazine, taking pictures of a pretty girl in a bathing suit. He had imported the girl, plus chaperone, from nearby Gulfport College. He had brought bathing suits with him for his pictorial progress along the Gulf and was choosing girls to fit. This day the chaperone hugged the fire. The poor girl posed on the bridge by the water, with some azalea branches broken off and thrust in the stream to make it colorful (never believe what you see in a picture). She posed in the boat, by the camellias, hours and hours in a bathing suit when I was wearing a winter coat. I saw the pictures in June *Holiday* but I never did learn if the girl got pneumonia.

A day in New Orleans, another in Baton Rouge, and then I was in Houston for a weekend with Marguerite Palmer, garden editor of the *Houston Press,* and a Monday morning lecture to the Houston Judges Council. I drove to Corpus Christi that afternoon. All the hotels had their names in lights, except the best one where I was to be housed. I went round and round that city in the dark trying to find my hotel. Eventually checked in, I learned we were to go out to a Mexican dinner, then to see roses by flashlight.

I collected specimens in gardens all the next morning, taught a class all afternoon, gave a public lecture that evening, taught another class until noon the next day, packed up, drove 200 miles to Austin, and was just thinking of a few minutes to rest before the evening talk, perhaps milk toast in my room, when the telephone rang. I was invited out for another Mexican dinner. I couldn't face that but I gave up the nap, went downstairs to visit while they ate dinner.

The meeting was in a beautiful new medical building and the audience sat around in comfortable armchairs. Unfortunately, from my standpoint, there was no ventilation except the air-conditioning and in my exhausted state I could not yell loud enough over the hum. At long last, I persuaded them to turn it off and then, using half as much energy, I managed to finish. It was not one of my best efforts and I should have known better than to cram so much into so few days.

I drove up to Oklahoma, still tired, but in Tulsa my understanding and delightful hosts, the Cunninghams, provided rest as well as entertainment. I had to see the municipal rose garden Friday afternoon, before talking at the dinner of the Men's Rose Club that night, but Saturday and Sunday were leisurely.

When I arrived, there was the tantalizing smell of nut bread baking but I had to wait until Sunday to taste it. About forty gardeners came in for supper. Then we had nut-bread sandwiches, creamed tuna fish on Fritos, a jellied salad, dessert and coffee—simple but so good, and a lot of people fed with very little fuss. I love to see women entertain with no apparent effort. I can't quite manage it myself. I am always doing too many things at the last minute as guests are arriving.

Monday I visited Mrs. Spillers, past president of National Council, listened in on the garden club meeting with Mrs. Cunningham presiding. George Cunningham was president of the Garden Center, sponsoring my talk that evening, and all excited about acquiring a permanent home for the Center, which later materialized.

Tuesday I saw gardens and the University at Norman, talked to the Rose Society. Driving East on Wednesday I could not see the Ozarks for duststorms but I felt better with each mile of solitude. With more than usual luck I got through the Smokies near Asheville a day ahead of the snowstorm that closed the route to traffic and arrived at Winston-Salem ready to enjoy the entertainment that went with the lecture and Plant Clinic there. The last talk was to the Durham Rose Society. I had a chance to see the fine small animal clinic my cousins have established in Durham and to see gardens with R. S. Witherspoon who plants and cares for roses in that area about the way I do in New Jersey.

CHAPTER 9

BLOSSOMS AND
BLIGHTS

As if I did not have enough to do that summer I was answering all those *This Week* letters, I let Helen Hull, then president of National Council of State Garden Clubs, persuade me to accept a new position on the board, chairman of Garden Enemies. I said I could not attend many meetings but I did go to one in Montreal in September. After driving 400 miles I stood in line two hours for my room but some of the women had been waiting all day for their reservations, since their sleeper arrived in the morning. For years I thought that perhaps Canadians did things at a slower pace but I have just returned from a meeting in this country where I entered the coffee shop for dinner at 6:30 and by 8 still had not been served. So I mentally apologize to Canada.

QUARANTINE HEARING

In November I represented National Council in Washington at a Quarantine Hearing, arguing that there was no reason to put on a

quarantine against Dutch bulbs. We already had in this country all
the bulb diseases apt to occur in Holland and I testified that, in
my limited experience, more disease had come into gardens from
bulbs grown in our own country that are not inspected, than from
those imported from abroad under rigid inspection. The bulbs were
not quarantined and later they worked out a better inspection
service. Now, instead of breaking open and repacking crates in
Hoboken, men from our own Department of Agriculture go to
Holland during the shipping season and inspect the bulbs there.

I had a very personal interest in the Dutch bulb situation. I had
spent that delightful three months at the Bulb Laboratory in Lisse in
1930 and now that the war was over Professor van Slogteren was
sending me each fall a big crate of bulbs to try in my own garden,
reporting to him later on their general state of health. Some were
planted in the garden for spring, some buried in pots to be brought
in through the winter. The "prepared" hyacinths were started in the
cellar, in water or soil, to be given away to friends for Christmas. I
learned that the latter did better in soil (a mixture of sand, garden
loam and peat moss) than in the regular hyacinth glasses. The trick
is to keep them in the dark long enough, until the flower buds are
well developed.

Forced bulbs are the easiest possible house plants, about the only
kind I can have when I go away so frequently. Many early tulips
and daffodils force beautifully. If I am home all winter I start in
January to bring in pots, but if I am away they can stay safely in
the ground until March, then are brought in to flower for Easter.
Brilliant Star, an early red tulip, forces well and so does orange-red
Prince of Austria and bright orange General de Wet. I love to have
the double pink tulip, Peachblossom, on the window sill or the
double yellow van der Hoef. Every day they are in bloom I send
grateful thoughts across the water.

Speaking of forcing, have you ever tried evergreen azaleas? I
prune my *hinodegiri* in February, putting the branches in a blue

bowl. Instead of their usual outdoor magenta, the flowers come out a pleasing peach-pink.

For years I planted tulips on the back hillside and for years the children would come and break them off. I never could make a child understand that was part of my garden and not an empty lot. So I went to the other extreme. I planted masses of the early Red Emperor surrounded by the various varieties of waterlily tulips in front of the house, in the strip between the sidewalk and the gutter, where I have never been able to make grass grow because of the tree roots. Not one child has ever broken off a tulip there or run over one with a tricycle. The little ones sometimes bend down and sniff to see if those blooms are fragrant, people driving by stop their cars to admire, but the blossoms are left for all to love, an advertisement, I hope, for bulbs.

CAMELLIA FLOWER BLIGHT

A couple of years later I was on the other side of a quarantine argument. This one was domestic and I thought it long overdue. Again I had a personal interest.

After the azalea flower spot appeared in South Carolina in 1931 it spread like wildfire throughout the South to California. By the time that nurserymen knew it was spread long distance by means of sclerotia in the soil around balled and burlapped or container-grown plants or in old flowers clinging to the plants, it was too late for quarantines.

A similar disease, caused by a related fungus from Japan (*Sclerotinia camelliae*) appeared on camellia flowers in California in 1938. The facts were quickly made known by Drs. H. N. Hansen and H. E. Thomas at the University of California and the disease might have been confined to that state, possibly even eradicated there, had the knowledge been widely applied.

The disease starts with brownish specks on the petals, often darkened veins, sometimes a browning of the center, but soon the whole flower is brown and a very large compound sclerotium is formed at the center. If diseased flowers are not removed before they rot, the sclerotia are left on the ground to send up apothecia in spring. One sclerotium may produce up to 20 apothecia in a spring (they are ½ to 1 inch across, much larger than the azalea apothecia), and of course they release millions of spores to infect buds showing color or open blossoms overhead. One sclerotium may continue active for at least three years.

Unlike the azalea blight, there is no secondary spore stage for the camellia fungus, no conidia to carry the disease from flower to flower. Theoretically the camellia disease was easy to control. All that was necessary was to clean up fallen flowers, take care in shipment. It was recommended that camellias be taken out of containers, all soil washed off, the roots rewrapped in peat moss, and all flower buds showing color removed (apparently the fungus cannot penetrate a tight bud without color). But most growers honestly believed the disease was of little consequence; they thought the camellias would die if bare-rooted, and customers wanted flower buds left on. They continued to ship as before.

While I was working in Alabama there had been rumors that the camellia blight had appeared in Atlanta, in a private greenhouse, but there was no official confirmation. Later, when I was on my way West to get material for the disease book, the Wilbys, owners of the greenhouse, came from Atlanta to the buffet supper in Montgomery to urge me to go back with them to investigate. I could not change my schedule and it would not have been exactly the thing to do. Dr. Gill was now working for the U.S.D.A. on camellia diseases. Besides, from their descriptions, I did not really think they had the disease. I was wrong, horribly wrong.

When I reached California and met camellia flower blight I knew the Wilbys had been right and this was later confirmed by Dr. Gill. There in a lathhouse near Pasadena I saw the large, soft, brown mushroomlike apothecia thick as a carpet and overhead the camellia blooms were in every stage of blight. I did not dare take specimens, except a few sclerotia and apothecia safely pickled in alcohol, but I took lots of pictures.

As soon as I had time after reaching home I wrote an article warning Southern gardeners about camellia blight, urging them to purchase their plants from the West Coast bare-rooted, with flower buds removed. The story was not used, for fear of losing vital advertising. I had not thought of that angle and had been under the delusion that my photographs, taken on the spot, would be welcome. Unwarned, camellia enthusiasts continued to buy plants in cans.

By 1949 the disease was well established in Oregon and that summer Southern states took action. Alabama, Florida, Georgia, Louisiana, Mississippi, North Carolina, South Carolina and Tennessee adopted quarantines regulating the movement of camellia plants with soil and flowers.

I never could understand why the Western growers were so furious, for California had always been terribly fussy about plants coming into the state. When I was at the Field Laboratory, Alabama nurserymen brought their camellias there to be fumigated in methyl bromide before they could be shipped west.

One grower wrote that camellia blight was no more a problem than rose mildew, but that was an unfortunate comparison for rose mildew is a terrific problem along the West Coast. Another wrote that the disease was unknown to 99.9 per cent of Californians but not so long after that a gardener admitted that they had had flower blight appearing in all the shows, with blossoms thrown out by the hundreds.

In 1950 the disease appeared at a camellia show in Shreveport, Louisiana. A survey of gardens was instituted and blight was found on camellias that had come into the state by way of Texas, which did not impose a quarantine. The Men's Camellia Club waged a rigorous clean-up campaign, combined with a lot of publicity and public education, and apparently their efforts were successful.

My next personal brush with camellia blight was in 1951 when Harry Daunoy took me to a New Orleans garden with suspicious symptoms. As we parted the mulch under the camellias the spores were puffed up in clouds. I collected 1000 apothecia under a single bush. We reported to the proper authorities and I showed the specimens on television, together with enlargements of the pictures taken in California. There was insufficient public interest and funds. Besides, many thought the blight should be discussed in whispers, as we formerly did with cancer. When I returned in 1956 the blight had spread from the original garden over two square miles of the most beautiful part of the city. They were ready to shout about blight, to clamor for help. Funds are still low but the State is spraying the ground, hoping to inhibit apothecial development, and they are trying to educate the citizens to clean up all fallen blossoms, at least once a week, put them in a special bag provided for collection in a special garbage truck routed directly to the incinerator.

Meanwhile camellia blight had become widespread in Virginia, had appeared in several counties in North Carolina. When it showed up in Augusta the State of Georgia took drastic measures. They quarantined the infected properties and 130 surrounding gardens immediately. In the 17 gardens where blight had appeared they removed, for two years, every flower bud from every bush and sprayed the soil monthly from January through April. The camellias are being allowed to bloom in 1957 but each property owner has signed an agreement to remove every old flower, on the ground or on the plant, at least once a week.

It was a little sad that Augusta, the first city to sponsor a camellia show, should be the first to cancel one because of disease. I have had interesting times in that lovely city. My first appearance brought out the fire department, at least they had to be called while I was checking a projector in preparation for a lecture in the Old Medical Center. The fire turned out to have started from a cigarette in the waste basket in the Ladies Room and not from any short circuit.

Next day, before my morning talk in North Augusta, I was taken to see the wondrous camellias Judge Henry Hammond grows under tall pines. Each year he puts an advertisement in the paper inviting all his "friends and enemies" to visit the camellias. Guarded by swans they are safe from snippers even when the Judge and Bud, his man Friday, are not at home.

Some years later I was staying a few days in Augusta, drawing local pests for an article on "Southern Garden Enemies." Bessie Baird, author of *Roses for Southern Gardens,* had a big Sunday night supper party. I learned later that she had canceled a trip to Atlanta and the Sadlers' Wells ballet for this event and I felt truly guilty when, later in my travels, I was taken to see that ballet in Orlando.

Gentle Judge Hammond, then well over 80, came to supper. He refused cocktails and it was about 9 p.m. when we sat down to an ambrosial seafood casserole. The Judge took one taste and then, with a most beatific smile, said, "And I only had two bananas for lunch!" (Bud, his cook as well as gardener, had had the day off to go to a funeral.)

It is hard to say whether he or I enjoyed that supper more. I was on a gastronomic holiday. Having read that you die earlier if overweight I decided that was just fine. Plant Doctoring was never going to provide for an inactive old age so I might just as well have fun and die in harness. For once, I was going to accept entertainment offered without worrying over calories.

I did just that. There was a steak dinner at the Augusta National Golf Club, where President Eisenhower plays. There was the Cloister's famous fish fry on Sea Island. There was a big Southern breakfast of grapefruit and orange juice, bacon and eggs, grits and waffles provided by Mrs. Bradley Morrah, soon to be president of National Council. There were oysters eaten at a bar in New Orleans, where you paid according to the number of shells laid up in front of you, and the marvelous seafood of Biloxi, where National Council was having its annual meeting. There it was that I learned I had become legend. A woman from Texas, giving her report, said how glad she was to be there, she had actually *touched* the plant doctor.

I kept away from scales until I was back in Glen Ridge. Then I learned that my holiday had added ten pounds. I also developed a kink in my thigh; I could move only with the most excruciating pain. The doctor said it might be a twisted muscle or it might be the small calcium deposit revealed by X-ray but one thing was certain: I was going to take off that extra ten pounds, and twenty more for good measure, pronto. Gone was my pleasant theory about "eat, drink, and be merry for tomorrow we die." I had not thought about having to die by inches. This time I cooperated on a diet with great enthusiasm; getting rid of pain was a lot more incentive than slimming for good looks.

I pruned roses more by crawling than walking, then let my helper go alone for fertilizing while I sat in the sun and enjoyed the bulbs, about the first time I had stayed home in daylight to see how beautiful the hyacinths and daffodils and early tulips really were. By June I had lost the thirty pounds *and* the pain, though I have a sneaking suspicion that diathermy treatments helped more than losing weight. I was ready again to make hundreds of cookies for Rose Day (without tasting them). One year I had been incapacitated with a sprained ankle just before Rose Day. I dared not stand up to make cookies and ordered many expensive and delicious little cakes. The guests merely looked at them and wailed, *"Where* are your homemade cookies?"

My last visit to Augusta was just before another Rose Day, in 1956, for a meeting of the Georgia and South Carolina nurserymen. I arrived about 9 a.m., gave two lectures, took a train back soon after 3 p.m. The engagement was of long standing but in the interim camellia flower blight had shown up in Summerville, dangerously near the famous Charleston gardens. My words had added meaning.

I am still shouting about this disease, still trying to wake people up to do something about it before it is too late. I started another magazine article, thinking it of national importance despite being Southern in distribution. My telephone rang and a client asked a question about heating her new greenhouse. I did not know the answer but Mary Noble's new *Gardening in a Small Greenhouse* had just arrived and was well-arranged for fingertip reference. My client said she had just received her camellias from California; they were in a container with a little of the soil removed from the top. I didn't consider that sufficient to prevent transportation of sclerotia and realized that maybe Northern gardeners needed education as well. With polyethylene on the market, bare-rooting is quite feasible and works no great hardship on the shipper of small plants.

A few years ago a horticultural chairman preparing a paper wrote asking me to name the best method for controlling plant disease. I had to say there was no best method and mentioned azalea and camellia flower blights, two similar diseases caused by similar fungi, yet they have to be controlled by diametrically opposed methods. I have spent more than ten years telling people they *must not* rely on sanitation for the control of azalea petal blight; it is entirely impractical and there has to be protective spraying. And now I have spent nearly that long telling gardeners that they *must* practice sanitation for camellia flower blight.

CHAPTER 10

ROSES

D<small>R. J. H</small>ORACE McF<small>ARLAND</small>, that eminent rosarian, once wrote to me that for a long time he thought I loved only rose bugs and diseases but had finally decided I loved roses too. I do love roses, quite apart from their pests. Around these parts they are more apt to call me the "rose lady" than the "Bug doctor." Once during World War II, when I telephoned the U.S. Employment Service in the forlorn hope of getting any kind of help, very young or very old, I was surprised to have the man at the other end of the line identify me as the lady who specializes in roses. A plant doctor meant nothing to him; roses did.

The more I sprayed gardens the more I realized that roses were the easiest possible plants to keep healthy. A little *regular* spraying was sufficient and they did not die even if the regular spraying was omitted. When Dr. McFarland wrote to inquire about the possibility of promoting roses via radio, I answered that I had just been interviewed by Nancy Craig on her "Woman of Tomorrow" program and had spent the time plugging roses. I also wrote him:

"I want to write a cheap rose book for the veriest amateur, not so much from what I have learned spraying roses in fine rose gardens but from what I have learned growing roses without time, without much space, and with very little money in my own back yard. I want to talk about living with roses, about the row of Else Poulsen which brightens my life for six months each year, blooming in the same narrow border with pink Briarcliff and blue pansies and forget-me-nots, then with Pallida iris, with pink snapdragon and blue ageratum, later with blue eupatorium. I want to talk about using Kirsten Poulsen in a low bowl with dark purple pansies, about Vanguard, which makes such an odd and lovely color combination with Dr. Huey and has such fine foliage, untouched by Japanese beetles even if left unsprayed.

"I want to talk about diseases and pests, of course, but the emphasis would be on how easy it is, and how little time it takes to care for pests, the right use of floribundas so those midsummer doldrums can be minimized. The other day a circular came to my desk, 'Roses are fussy—they must have special food.' I want to shout to the world, 'Roses are not fussy, try them and see; try them especially in wartime when Victory Gardens take so much energy there is little left for the flowers we need as desperately as food.'"

My first lectures, and my first article for the *New York Times* had been titled, "Keeping Roses Healthy." Now I switched the emphasis and called my lecture "Anyone Can Grow Roses." Many people asked me then, some even wrote, to do a book like *The Plant Doctor* but just on roses. Lippincott had the refusal of the next book but did not want to do it in wartime, nor without expensive color plates. Even The McFarland Press turned me down. I had to wait.

There was another war when the book was finally started. My nephew John was an expendable second lieutenant leading his men at the Chosin Reservoir, Korea. Now I knew we needed roses, for courage, for memorials.

I had more evidence of their inherent toughness. As I wrote the first pages we had our big hurricane of November 1950. I thought I was getting off lightly; the glass window on the porch was shattered but the electricity stayed on and the trees near by seemed safe. Next morning I discovered that power-saws had been going all night cutting up the three trees that had blown across the road from my back hill, blocking traffic, cutting off lights for others. In all the wind, not one of my 500 roses had been disturbed to the slightest degree.

A LITTLE ROSE BOOK

With the big, technical, and expensive disease book launched, Van Nostrand had been receptive to the idea of a small, inexpensive book for the masses. They were somewhat dubious about a rose book. There were lots of rose books already. How could we sell another without color pictures? I argued that anyone could get a catalogue full of color for a three-cent stamp; I wanted a book everyone could afford to buy, that anyone could understand. I offered to do it without a contract, without an advance, just to have a chance to set down what had been for so long in my heart.

I financed it with more Southern lectures, writing in hotel rooms. I had a lovely time in Houston. My dates there were nearly three weeks apart so I could settle down comfortably in the Hotel Warwick, a wide view of the city from my window, a park to roam in across the street. It turned out to be perfect weather for writing and I wasted little time in the park. We had an ice storm, not just an ordinary affair but a real humdinger. Believe it or not, my Ford was solidly covered with ice, there in that subtropical city, from dawn on Monday to noon on Saturday. I managed to get the door open and I ran the engine once or twice but I dared not move the Ford in the hotel driveway for fear of breaking the tree branches frozen down on top of it.

The newspaper had a columnist who wrote somewhat in the style of Will Rogers. He complimented the "furriners" from Maine and

New York who knew enough to stay holed up in motels, or if they did venture out, had enough respect for the ice to creep around corners. He scolded his fellow citizens, "he-man Texans" who went · boldly around corners, ending up in the ditch.

I was scheduled to talk in Tyler that week and wondered how I'd make it with the roads practically closed, planes grounded, almost no trains. I need not have worried. Tyler telephoned they could not get their cars out to come to a lecture; it was postponed to the next Monday. I changed my hotel reservation and drove up on Sunday. There was some snow but the roads were quite passable. When I asked why the hotel garage was so overflowing with automobiles I was told all the traveling salesmen had been stuck there for a week; they had not dared to drive on. I thought they ought to get back to work; if a woman driver could get through, a man should be able to make it.

Back in Houston the weather moderated and I went to a Garden Extravaganza and Tea at the Hotel Shamrock. It was a fashion show but the models and costumes had been flown up from the Rio Grande Valley. Everything worn was some part of a valley plant and the costumes were in two classes, perishable and nonperishable.

In the latter class the bridal costume that took first prize had overshirt and bodice of green corn, split grapefruit seeds for pearls ornamenting the yoke, grapefruit membrane forming the bridal veil and train. A perishable ball gown was made of lavender bachelor-button petals. The sweepstakes winner had a champagne-colored gown of hegira, gloves, shoes and handbag to match, jewelry from radishes, green peppers, grapefruit seeds, pomegranate seeds sprinkled with glitter.

The details of these costumes were not remembered, I am copying them from a souvenir booklet saved from the occasion. But the descriptions do not convey any idea of the really incredible beauty of the creations. I have a vivid recollection of the over-all effect.

It was hot the week I spent in New Orleans, teaching a class, lecturing, writing. A woman in the front row fainted at the Rose

Society meeting. She remained on the floor in front of me as I talked until they could get medical advice about moving her. It turned out to be nothing serious but it was hard to keep the audience paying attention to rose pests.

I had talked in Knoxville on the way through Tennessee and had thought the Arnold Hotel a most comfortable and wonderfully inexpensive place to write. I hustled back there from New Orleans, nearly finishing the book before having to retrace steps to Chattanooga the first of March. It was hot there, too, at least in the hotel. With the air-conditioning on, I couldn't make them hear; with it off, we all expected to pass out. We alternated all evening as we talked roses.

After returning home I made several quick trips by train to plead the cause of roses. I talked in Rochester, New York; went down to Charlotte, North Carolina, for Easter Monday, having to repeat my descent from the sleeper for the benefit of a photographer. Cora Harris, garden editor of the *Charlotte News,* gave a luncheon and there was tea with Elizabeth Lawrence, who writes so charmingly of Southern gardens. I went to Washington for a dinner meeting of the Potomac Rose Society and they asked for a repeat performance one hot Sunday in July. Going down and back the same day by train I was truly grateful for air-conditioning.

Advance copies of *Anyone Can Grow Roses* came out in January just before I started South again. I was awfully pleased with it. Because of the lack of pictures, the only illustrations being my own charts for the identification of pests, diagrams of planting and pruning, the publishers had gone to great trouble to give it a distinguished style and jacket. I was presenting a copy to each of my clients, because they had helped me so much while I was learning about roses in their gardens.

Due to depart for the winter on Tuesday, I spent all Saturday morning delivering books, leaving the house a shambles of packing for the trip, books being wrapped for mailing. Returning soon after noon, with just time to grab a sandwich, dress and drive to the

New York Botanical Garden to give an afternoon talk on Roses, I found the house cold, pipes drained, electricity and water turned off. The plumber had mixed up my return date of March *19* with my leaving date of January 22. Today was only January 19 and being Saturday all offices had closed at 12.

I finally got an emergency message through, washed up next door, started for the Bronx. The plumber was still here working on the slow process of warming up the house again when I returned in the evening. I asked how he thought I could have gone for the winter with all that packing left around but I suppose my place is always in such confusion a little more was scarcely noticeable.

My hunch had been right. People did want to read my personal kind of rose book. The reviews were almost uniformly kind. I bristled a bit when Milton Carleton thought I had bitten off more territory than I could handle and that while roses might be easy to grow in New Jersey they were harder around Chicago. I reminded Milt that I had not said that anyone can grow roses *easily* and that I had written that rose book in Texas and in Louisiana and in Tennessee, not New Jersey. I had seen roses growing in practically every state and had letters from enthusiastic rosarians in the rest.

So many people wrote to me from the hard states. Like the woman from Minnesota who wrote to thank me for doing the book. She said she, and her mother before her, had grown well the hybrid teas not supposed to thrive in a location with such cold winters.

One reviewer said the pages "glow." Why not? I was writing about roses. I love to give rose bushes for Christmas, for birthdays. I have even given a pair of pruning shears as a wedding present. I was surprised at the number of brides who used the book, for gardening used to be taken up by women after their families were grown. Now they grow children and roses together. They grow roses as foundation plantings around the new ranch houses, as hedges, over fences, shrubs in the background, groups in the perennial border.

Of course I think everyone should join the American Rose Society and I have made much use of my Members' Handbook in answering inquiries. If someone in a town in California wants to know what varieties are best there I look up A.R.S. members living in that town and send their names and addresses. Their on-the-spot advice will be better than mine.

I was very much pleased with Victor P. Hass' fine review in the *Omaha World-Herald* but rather overwhelmed when he entered a contest in the American Rose Magazine on "My Favorite Books on Roses." Winner of the first award, his article began:

"Actually, that title should refer to only one book for though I have many books on roses, some of them very beautiful, my heart rests with a single volume—Dr. Cynthia Westcott's *Anyone Can Grow Roses.*"

He went on to say that after reviewing the book he had gone out and bought roses, lots of roses, and shifted the perennials to a single bed. He had "sold" more copies of the book than the local bookstore by singing its praises to his friends. He had "wooed one ardent raiser of potatoes, squash, corn and similar stuff from them to roses. Now he is buying those mundane things fresh frozen and fighting to keep his roses from freezing. He is a happy man."

For this book the sales kept up with the reviews. There were more printings, soon there had to be a second edition. I didn't rewrite it all. I couldn't change my enthusiasm for roses but I did put in some new varieties, new chemicals, wrote a new chapter on showing roses. I combined getting information from the American Rose Society for that new chapter with a lecture in Columbus, Ohio, under auspices of the Wellesley Club. They had sold tickets for benefit of the scholarship fund and I wanted everything to be just right. I spent a long time with the hotel electrician getting the lights adjusted to show up the water-color paintings of pests. Just as I started to speak the lights went off in a thunderstorm. They came on again as I reached the last sentence of the hour's talk.

Leaving the hotel the handle of that suitcase I had purchased so hastily in Oregon came off. I asked the taxi man to take me to a luggage shop; it had closed but he knew the proprietor. The shop was opened, the handle replaced, and I still made the train.

In addition to lecturing on roses, I was giving practical courses in growing roses and starting a rose garden in Montclair.

The latter was quite a project. Through the vision and determination of its then president, Mrs. Robert E. McNeill, Jr., the Garden Club of Montclair was starting a Garden Center at the new Social Agencies Building, taking over the planting and care of the grounds. Avis Campbell, our landscape architect, planned a Wheel of Life Garden with pie-shaped sectors radiating out from a central fountain and walk. There was a sector for chrysanthemums, one for herbs, one for iris and daylilies, one for annuals. The two central sectors were for roses.

It did not seem too difficult. The money collected from the course on roses I gave to the garden club members was almost enough to buy 200 roses at wholesale prices with a few being donated by nurseries. I thought I could donate a couple of days of Henry's time for digging beds. I knew that the land was partly subsoil from the excavation for the huge new building but I thought I could make it suitable for roses with enough manure, real and dehydrated, lots of peat moss, and all the compost from my own garden I could transport in the Ford.

I did not know, until we started digging, that the long spell of dry weather had turned that subsoil into cement which had to be chipped out inch by inch, taking weeks instead of days. I did not know that down underneath other rubble were foundations of an ancient greenhouse that had to be extracted and hauled away. I did not know that when the rains finally came, and the melting snow, all the excess from the eaves and downspouts of that big building would rush to the rose beds in the north sector and keep the roots standing in water all winter. (Better drainage was provided the next year and many of the roses proved tough enough to survive a winter of submersion.) I did not know that I was letting myself in for so much time spent through the growing season that I'd have to forego two or three paying clients, nor that the roses would bloom so well, even in that impossible soil, that I'd spend every other evening there in early June, cutting off dead blossoms to keep that garden looking neat, rather than staying home to slick up my own garden for Rose Day. (And one Sunday I went to church and coming out a member of the congregation mentioned the Garden Center and asked, "Why don't they ever cut off the dead roses?")

But I also did not know how much that garden would mean to so many people. To apartment dwellers who have no garden of their own and sit there evenings. To the staffs of the many social agencies centered in that building and to the people who come to consult them about their problems. To all who come to the Public Library next door. Writer Dorothy Waugh, who works there, spends every coffee break in the garden; she says the roses stimulate her far more than caffeine. And of course to all the gardeners who are thinking of starting a few roses of their own.

I planned the garden to demonstrate roses that do well in New Jersey, of different heights, 1 to 5 feet, and types, with lots of floribundas as well as hybrid teas, and in pleasing color combinations. When Eugene Boerner of Jackson and Perkins sent 50 plants of floribunda Spartan to try at the Garden Center, a year before it went on the market, I did not put that orange-red color in with the other roses but massed it along the drive, in front of the dogwoods, between the barberries, where, with its excellent foliage, reddish when young, it makes an unforgettable picture from April to Christmas. It is just as Spartan as its name, paying no attention to cold or heat or drought.

A ROSE SOCIETY

Although commercial rose growing in America had started in New Jersey we had never had a Rose Society in this state. I had realized this lack vaguely for some time. When the Garden Club of Montclair became an associate member of the American Rose Society

I thought that by getting some of their members together with Fred Glaes, Director of the Penn-Jersey District of the A.R.S., for pep talks at my annual Rose Day in 1953 perhaps something could be started without my having to run it. I was too selfish to give up the necessary time from earning a living. The interest was there, and many signed up as wanting to join a New Jersey rose society, but no leader developed.

In September, the first Convention of the Penn-Jersey District was held at Cape May. Florence McNeill went down, representing the Garden Club of Montclair, and invited the group to have their 1954 Convention at our Garden Center. We needed a rose society to cooperate but I was still holding back, afraid of more work. Florence then invited all American Rose Society members in our area interested in a local society to meet at her house. The response was wholehearted. We chose a steering committee and temporary officers and I breathed a sigh of relief. Next day the tentative president got cold feet and backed out. Not willing to let the interest evaporate I agreed to serve, protecting myself somewhat with the By-Laws. Officers could not be re-elected after their two-year term of office. I wanted the North Jersey Rose Society to stand on its own feet and not be the plant doctor's rose society. It has done so, magnificently.

The first formal meeting of the North Jersey Rose Society was held January 16, 1954, at the Montclair Garden Center. It was such a very snowy day and my driveway was so difficult I went over by taxi. To our great surprise more than sixty people, some from more than forty miles away, turned up in the snow to be charter members. We decided the lure of roses must be strong to have such enthusiasm and that the new Society could not possibly fail. Before long we numbered two hundred and were quite ready to help with the Penn-Jersey Convention in the fall.

Mrs. McNeill ran the Rose Show and the meetings at the Garden Center; I ran the rose tours: Friday afternoon, with tea at my house, Saturday morning for those not putting in exhibits, all day Sunday by bus.

I could never have managed without Henry. I have not talked about him before but he has been my mainstay for some years. The first season Lacelle went into banking I alternated for help between the banker's son, who was excellent but so young and slight I worried about his lifting the sprayer, and a boy from the Brooklyn Botanic Garden whose hands did not quite seem to know what to do with the tools of his trade. I wanted a man, preferably colored, to work full-time the next season.

Arriving home from the South on a March Saturday I bought up all the local papers to look at advertisements. Henry was the first applicant I called; he came to see me Sunday and has been around more or less ever since. The adjustment was not too easy. As an employer I persist in the delusion that I have a right to say what I want done, when I want it done, and how it is to be done and of course any employee is sure he knows a better way and time to do it. Henry found it harder than others because he had been his own boss, running a catering service among many other things. He stipulated that he have an occasional day off to cook a church supper and time off in the summer, when I could get high-school help, to cook at a Boy Scout Camp. I stipulated that he not smoke while working for me for smoke really does bother me.

Far from being lazy, Henry does a job in half the time I expect and then goes on to something else I may not have authorized. I like my climbing roses kind of sprawling. Henry, if he has to trim the hedge in back of them, wants those roses all neatly cut back and he gets it done while I am inside typing, thinking he still has a lot to do on the first job. We argue sometimes, and occasionally get real mad, but fundamentally we like and respect each other. And when Henry gets tired of pumping a sprayer I may give up the active day-laborer side of plant doctoring. We are both on the far side of middle age.

Going back to that Sunday bus trip for the Convention. Henry provided the box lunches, for about one hundred, that we ate at Mrs. Averett's beautiful estate in Chatham. He had cooked the turkeys for sandwiches and had made apple pies, expertly seasoned, from Mrs. Averett's apples.

All the gardens we visited were those of my clients—in Short Hills, Springfield, Summit and Chatham. I could not resist swaggering a little as a plant doctor. I told the assembled rosarians that I would give a dollar to anyone who could find a single leaf with blackspot on it in any garden. They looked hard but I did not have to pay up (I did not confess that there were one or two gardens not on the tour where they might have seen a little blackspot). The roses that day were really gorgeous, at their peak of fall bloom, with healthy, luxuriant foliage down to the ground, an excellent demonstration of the effect of regular spraying.

The North Jersey Rose Society had its own Rose Show the next autumn in East Orange, at the Colonial Life Insurance Company Building. Colonial Life had a rose garden, which I had been tending for some years, and had joined our Rose Society. Looking at their enormous main floor one day, with its attractive pale green walls and efficient lighting, I thought what a wonderful place for a Show. It took only the slightest hint to receive a warm invitation. They did better than that; they agreed to cover the desks with plywood, making long tables and to keep their maintenance men on duty at no cost to us. They provided a big, big sign, floodlighted, advertising our first annual Rose Show.

All summer I had worried about staging, what to use to cover the tables. I tried samples of burlap, various plastics. Everything was too expensive, nothing looked quite right. Mrs. Thomas came up with a bright idea. She knew a salesman to florists; we could get paper wholesale. The right side of the florist's paper was shiny with a white design of gardenias but the wrong side was a soft green, perfect for that room. Our covering problem was solved at little cost. We wanted to have a permanent trophy but had no funds. Mr. Robinson sent out such a persuasive letter scads of money came in from our members for this cause.

Our theme was LIVING WITH ROSES in Colonial and Modern

Times. In addition to the regular specimen and arrangement classes, we invited garden clubs to do early American arrangements as a Colonial Welcome in the entrance foyer. They did supper tables, "Candlelight and Roses, 1655," and dinner tables, "Candlelight and Roses, 1955." We asked commercial florists to "Say It With Roses" in special competitive classes: "Best Wishes on Your Anniversary"; "Congratulations on the New Baby"; "Thanks for a Lovely Weekend." Most of the florists donated their containers so the arrangements were auctioned off at the end of the Show for the benefit of the American Rose Foundation.

Future Farmers of America, boys from Central High School, Paterson, prepared a model of the real rose garden they had planted in their park. We provided "Roses To Take Home" in the form of corsages, potpourri, handmade aprons spattered with roses, rose cards, books. We made a lot of money, thanks to very hard work by many people (and Colonial Life), and the treasury of the North Jersey Rose Society was in a very healthy condition when I stepped down from the presidency. I thought, rather wryly, "At least I can keep an organization going, even if I can't keep myself solvent."

Always our Rose Society has been plagued by bad weather, starting with the snow when we organized. It snowed again for our first birthday luncheon; it poured the day of our Show; we had a sleet storm when we planned a pruning demonstration the end of March. We decided to have our second annual meeting and luncheon in November when the weather would be good. Guess what? It snowed! Most of us came, with our roses. I had enough salvaged from my own yard so each member could have one to wear. I put Orange Triumph on every window sill of the club, gay contrast to the snow outside. Centerpieces were a contest, end-of-the-season arrangements from our own gardens, featuring roses.

I received the past-president's pin from our members and put the Society into the very capable hands of Kay Signiago. I was well rewarded for all the extra hours of the past two years. Lots of work, yes, but lots of fun, and many, many new rose friends.

Instead of being president of a local rose society I was now director at large of the American Rose Society. I had given advance notice that I probably could not leave my client's roses long enough to attend spring meetings but I promised to attend fall meetings. The money due on completion of the manuscript for the new Bug Book went for a plane ticket to Texas.

The night before leaving I went in to New York to have dinner with Professor van Slogteren, just arrived from Holland, and Dr. Emsweller, up from Washington to do the honors for him. The Professor insisted on going to Music Hall at Rockefeller Center. He and I had done it the last time he was in America, twenty years before; he wanted a repeat performance. With my wretched memory I had not the vaguest recollection of what we had seen. The Professor knew and could recount the whole story. So here we were on a Saturday night in New York standing in line for a movie. I barely got to sleep before it was time to return to New York en route to Idlewild.

It took longer to get there from Glen Ridge on Sunday morning than it did to reach Dallas from the New York airport. There were some hours to wait before the plane for Tyler, so Mrs. Belsterling met me and drove us around the new Dallas suburbs. I had retained a mental picture of the South as being slightly down at the heels, with trash piled on back verandas because there were no cellars. The Dallas I saw that Sunday was very different. The rear yards were as neat as the front and beautifully planted. The houses were modern but not aggressively so. The North could learn a lot from some of the new South.

Unloading a coffin-like box of roses from the plane at Tyler was Charles Garner. I had stayed at his home when I talked to the Virginia Peninsula Rose Society, marveled at his roses. He had made them even better by putting in an underground watering system. The next year, at the Potomac Rose Society Show, I saw his Frau Karl Druschki win Queen of Show. Now, here in the rose capitol of the world, Virginia roses again won top honors.

Tyler weather changed from boiling hot to frost, my influence I presume. At the outdoor barbecue we jumped up and down to keep warm, hurried back to the hotel to look at rose gardens via Kodachrome. Next day we saw thousands of acres of roses growing in the field. Hundreds of roses, perhaps thousands, were massed indoors for the banquets. One dinner featured Pink Frost, the other Lemon Chiffon, the "yellow rose of Texas."

I flew to Washington for the American Horticultural Congress already in session. Professor van Slogteren had come to America at this time to receive a citation for his outstanding work in providing healthy bulbs for American use. I received a citation, too, and felt particularly honored to have it then when they were paying tribute to my old friend, Professor Dr. Egbert van Slogteren.

My citation read:

The
American Horticultural Council
through its Board of Directors
presents this
CITATION
to you,
Cynthia Westcott
of New Jersey

for outstanding accomplishment in the
SCIENCE AND PRACTICE OF PLANT PATHOLOGY

Healer of plants; helper of all who grow them; practical scientist and scientific practioner; teacher by word of mouth, by printed page, and in gardens—despite self-effacing modesty, you have been conspicuously successful as an apostle of proper cultural methods and intelligent plant protection. Courageous, conscientious, untiring, uncompromising, you are held in high esteem and deep affection by clients, colleagues, and fellow gardeners. Their number, already great, is growing steadily as the realm of horticulture expands, in which you occupy so honored and so merited a place.

October 28, 1955.

E. L. D. Seymour was chairman of the awards committee and I know that he personally must have written those fine words. He could have been much less complimentary. Instead of uncompromising he could, remembering our battles over words, have said stubborn. Foolhardy could have been substituted for courageous. I am not as untiring as I make out to be and I must have forgotten modesty to quote this tribute. To be even less modest, I admit that increasingly of late years I have been feeling that wave of affection as I meet rose lovers and other gardeners.

Apparently I have encouraged some of them, as well as discouraging them with talk of ever-present pests. Instead of dedicating the Bug Book to anyone I quoted a little poem I had seen:

> *"The rose-bug on the rose*
> *Is evil—so are those*
> *Who see the rose-bug*
> *Not the rose."*

If I have helped people to continue to see the rose, while eliminating the rose-bug, I have accomplished all that I set out to do.

Before returning to Holland, Professor van Slogteren visited here for a couple of days. I invited in the neighbors and friends with whom I had shared his bulbs. It was an evening to treasure. By word of mouth and Kodachromes we made him know how much his good-will gesture had meant to so many and he brought us pictures of the Dutch bulb fields.

Next morning I tried to drive Dr. van Slogteren to Hoboken, to the Plant Quarantine Station. To make sure we did not get lost I took with us a man who works there and lives in this vicinity. He commuted by train ordinarily and proved to know less about getting to Hoboken than I did. We got hopelessly snarled in traffic and the morning was far advanced when I deposited the professor in front of the right building. There, on the sidewalk, he opened up his suitcase and gave me a parting memento—a photograph taken on his birthday, as he lunched with his Queen, Juliana of the Netherlands. And I remembered when I had seen Juliana as a young princess, attending a flower show at Aalsmeer.

More royalty from the new Bug Book paid for the American Rose Society meeting at Louisville the next autumn. This time I went first class, the weather was fine, the roses marvelous. I flew home and there were only five hours between leaving the hotel and walking in my front door. Quite a contrast to the previous trip. Then, to help finance entomology meetings in Cincinnati, I talked in Louisville under auspices of the *Courier-Journal* and the Nurserymen's Association. Nature chose that day to put on a wonderful display of ice, sleet, and snow. Cissy Gregg, food and garden editor for the paper, took me slithering around gardens, falling down as much as walking. It was good to get back inside the warm Courier building to watch cakes being photographed for Christmas pages a year hence.

My train, due to leave at noon, was hours late coming in from the South, and of course missed connections in Cincinnati. The next train from there, due to leave at 11 p.m. finally got off about 3 a.m. Normally due in Pittsburgh very early in the morning, it had no diner. It was nearly noon when we stopped at a small town and took aboard supplies. Then the conductor came through and announced that coffee and buns were in the next car "on the house." I changed again in Pittsburgh, reached Newark about 11 p.m. (17 hours late because I was traveling coach to save money). I took the trolley to Glen Ridge, lugged heavy suitcase and lecture stuff to the station for a cab. None was there. The Glen Ridge Cab Company had gone on strike in my absence. I stood on the corner for half an hour, with the temperature zero, before one finally came from Montclair. At least, my trips are not monotonous.

ROSE DAY

The second Sunday in June, the roses at 96 Essex Avenue, Glen Ridge are At Home from 2 until dark. June, 1956, marked the 16th such annual event. I send postcards each year to those who signed the guest book the year before (I don't dare go back farther than that), send a notice to the papers that all are welcome, label up the spray tests and rose varieties, start baking cookies, nights, after 10 p.m. If I start much earlier in the evening they burn while I answer the telephone.

With the numbers increasing, now usually 500 to 700 from more than a hundred towns in nine or ten states, I thought that perhaps there should be something more than the guinea-pig roses and instituted brief talks under the apple tree. Mary Noble was here for Rose Day right after her book, *Corsage Craft,* was published and demonstrated making rose corsages all afternoon. She was a great success.

Fred Glaes came to talk as Director of the Penn-Jersey district. It would be hard to say whether he or Edwin DeT. Bechtel, honor guest the next year with Mrs. Bechtel (for many years children's book editor of the *New York Herald Tribune*) has more infectious enthusiasm for roses.

On Rose Day, 1955, Phil and Ruth Alampi and their three sons were the star attraction. It was their wedding anniversary so we had a big cake with roses on it in addition to having cookies. I don't know how many people came because of their radio and TV fame but we had a crowd. Most of us rejoiced for them, mourned for ourselves, when our Phil became dignified Phillip Alampi, Secretary of Agriculture for New Jersey.

I had an unexpected guest the day before while making preparations. A squirrel, evidently a nursing mother, was climbing all over my back screen door. I thought perhaps her babies were trapped in the attic so I invited her in. She accepted the invitation without much hesitation but she only wanted company and food. All day she was around underfoot, eating walnuts, cadging peanuts to bury. She didn't like peanut butter and other squirrel delicacies. I named her Minnie the Moocher and she is still around the neighborhood sponging on other weak-minded folk, delighting visitors. She is afraid of nothing, will even chase the big cat from next door when he comes to my garden for refuge from the boys in his family. Almost always when I have supper on a tray near the roses she comes and sits on my knee. I don't think she has ever dug up one of the thousands of peanuts she has planted round about but she is indefatigable about putting them away, the only limit being my pocketbook.

Along with Minnie for the next Rose Day, 1956, we had a cardinal on her nest, right beside the walk where the hordes had to pass to get to tea and the back garden. I only discovered her the day before, on cutting back the Betty Prior she had placed her confidence in. I hastily stopped pruning, said a little prayer for her safety. She stuck it out in position until the crowds got too great, returned for two days right after they left. But she must have let the eggs stay cold too long; she departed without hatching anything.

The invited honor guests that day were my first garden editor, E. L. D. Seymour, to whom I had owed so much for so long, and my latest, Clara Claasen, who was helping to celebrate the successful launching of new Bug Book. I was brash enough to plan a buffet luncheon on the porch for Clara and Ned. George Brady just happened to be visiting from San Francisco, Eleanor McClure from St. Louis. Betty Merriam, president of the Garden Club of New Jersey was here, and representatives from various rival pesticide companies. I love to let each one speak for a few moments on Rose Day, reminder to gardeners that there is no one best material. After lunch, local friends took our out-of-state visitors to see the roses at the Garden Center while I cleaned up the debris (easy because I had used mostly throw-away plastic) and got the kitchen ready for the boys who would keep punch flowing all afternoon. I always make up enough for 500 guests in advance and have all kinds of additives on hand.

The boys cope as best they can while I stay out in the garden.

We are almost always lucky in weather but if it does rain there is always a display of cut roses, named, on the porch, punch in the living room. The guests come with umbrellas and go out in the garden anyway.

When I moved to New Jersey people said roses were too much trouble; our summers were too hot. More and more visitors go away from Rose Day determined to try and then their neighbors start. I like to believe that the few guinea-pig roses on Essex Avenue have resulted in a million more in dooryards. One young man told me he used to come for the cookies; after he was married, he came to learn about roses.

SLOWING DOWN

On Friday, August 3, 1956, I had a letter from E. L. D. Seymour. He wanted to confer with me about revising the *Garden Enemies* for the proposed new edition of his *Garden Encyclopedia*. I was at the typewriter on Sunday, preparing to answer the letter, when Helen Hull telephoned to ask a question. As she was hanging up, and almost as an afterthought, she said, "I suppose you have heard about Ned Seymour."

I had not seen Saturday's *New York Times*. It was a terrific shock to learn of his fatal heart attack. I imagine that not since the death of Liberty Hyde Bailey have so many gardeners felt such a personal loss in the going forward of a garden writer, editor, counselor, and friend. I had always thought of him as of another generation yet according to the paper he was only ten years older than I. It was time for me to slow down, to stop trying to be a three-ring circus.

As a matter of fact, the summer of 1956 had been a lot easier than 1955. I was no longer president of the Rose Society, I was not retyping the Bug Book every night and, for the first time in the seven years he had worked for me, Henry, instead of a teen-ager, had been my assistant all summer. I have enjoyed the boys who have helped me out through the years, have seen no trace of the much publicized juvenile deliquency. But some of them, as is natural for their age group, are given to unpredictable moods and sometimes take it out on the apparatus. In October, Henry remarked that we hadn't had to buy a new sprayer all season. That was true. He had nursed our last year's model along, handled it with care. He had not kicked it when he got mad, nor pumped it so violently it burst.

One year I had a boy who worked fine the first day, poked the rest of the week. The next week, as he started a slow-down strike on the day he wanted to be through early, I reminded him that if he pumped a little faster we could be through a lot sooner. He didn't believe me but tried it out. We finished a whole hour ahead of schedule. So then he tried pumping feverishly whenever he had a date in the offing but that didn't work. The spray came over me instead of the plants and that made me blow up instead of the sprayer.

When it came time for our Second Annual Rose Show I sort of forgot good resolutions about overdoing. With someone else to stage it, I volunteered to be hospitality chairman, to provide luncheon for the judges and important guests, to keep coffee and cookies going all day for the workers, sandwiches noon and night. I went on a cooking spree the day before, a holiday from spraying. I made orange bread, oatmeal bread, butterscotch rolls, brownies, Highland toffee, butterscotch bars, ginger, chocolate and almond cookies and Henry made his famous apple pies. I made mountains of chicken salad, potato salad, roast beef, ham and set up the tables over at the Colonial Life cafeteria with roses everywhere. That was a lot more fun, for me, than working on entries or classification but I must admit that the day after the Show my knees didn't work very well.

I have no sense whatever about cooking. It is nearly Christmas as I write this section. I saw a new recipe for fruit cake, tried it out, and liked it so much I made two more batches, ending up with fifteen small loaves. I had to buy tins, find wrapping material, to send these to friends and relatives and I expect each recipient is barred from sweets as much as I. It would have been far easier, and no more expensive, to have ordered a rose bush for each name on the list, but it would not have satisfied that compulsive urge to cook at holiday time.

Another gesture toward slowing down was to inform the remaining clients in the Nyack area that I would not be back another season. It took several hours each time for transportation and I was getting awfully tired of competing with trucks in rush hours. If it rained before I finished all the gardens, other clients had to be postponed while I took a day off to return. My clients were understanding but sad, especially the Milton Caniffs. They do not have many roses and these can be kept reasonably healthy with about ten minutes of dusting a week but, because I made roses bloom on a mountainside where none had been before, they attribute magic powers to the plant doctor.

Planting the roses there had been somewhat of a challenge. There was little soil on top of the rock ledges. The bushes had to go in small groups wherever we could dig down far enough. They had to be kept away from all walls because of copperheads but we only saw two snakes in our years of spraying. One was curled in the sunshine on the steps leading from the terrace down to the roses, so thereafter I took the long way around. The soil dried out fast in periods of drought but no water could be spared from household uses. And yet those roses flourished, one more reminder that roses are tough and that anyone who loves roses can grow them anywhere.

At the third annual luncheon of the North Jersey Rose Society there was a clever skit about growing roses with songs written by our members, Janice and Charles Jensen. The finale was a song named for my Rose Book: the words of which are included here by permission of the authors.

ANYONE CAN GROW ROSES

"Life's no bed of roses, in each some rain must fall;
A scorching sun or wintry wind can blast the hopes of all;
But through the seasons' challenges, life richer, sweeter grows
If we will learn this lesson from the lovely, sturdy rose:

Anyone can grow roses
The secret all may share;
A plot of earth, some sun and rain,
And tender, loving care.

Anyone can grow roses,
It's not a mystery;
They like some simple comforts
The same as you and me.

Just dig and plant, then water well,
And mulch and feed and spray;
For half a year the rose gives back
A wealth of blossoms gay.

Everyone who grows roses
Has happiness to share;
So why don't you grow roses too
If you have love to spare?"

CHAPTER 11

THE PLANT DOCTOR
GOES AROUND IN
CIRCLES

SEVERAL YEARS AGO, when the American Association for the Advancement of Science met in New York, our local chapter of Sigma Delta Epsilon tried to show what some of our women scientists were doing. We were caricatured by Dr. Mary Rogick, clever artist as well as biologist. Her cartoon of the plant doctor depicted me working at a book on the typewriter, swinging through the tops of trees with pruning shears, going after sunflowers with a dust gun, prescribing for a line of plant patients in the doctor's office. I called my exhibit "The Plant Doctor Goes Around in Circles" and I presented a diagram, with attached specimens in the form of photographs, articles etc., of the interwoven cycles in my career. There were six circles, with a small arc of black ink in three—doctoring, writing and lecturing.

The fact that I am still afloat after all these years shows that the black ink has retained a small lead over the red but the problem of keeping plant doctoring going by itself without the support of writing and lecturing has not been solved. Nor do I know anyone else who has been able to maintain a service program without additional props. The work is too seasonal and too dependent on weather during the growing season, with days suitable for spraying not averaging more than four a week. The tree experts, whose work is most closely akin to mine, depend for their props on acts of God like hurricanes and icestorms, line clearance for utility companies, clearing ponds of weeds, estimating losses for income-tax deductions. I have a friend who is a pest control operator in Florida. You would think that in a land where indoor and outdoor bugs flourish the year around, sidelines might not be necessary; yet this man has branched out into a Garden Supply Shop. His customers are lucky because they have a trained person to advise them.

It may be that much of the plant doctoring in the future will have to be done through such garden shops. The man in Levittown certainly cannot afford regular weekly service for his shrubs and flowers and not too many estates can either. The do-it-yourself gardener needs advice, first in diagnosing his problems, second in choosing the right chemical from all the thousands presented with high-pressure advertising on the radio or in the Sunday newspaper.

This problem was recognized, but by no means solved, in a panel discussion I participated in recently. The entomologists there assembled were considering the plight of the home gardener who needs immediate help on his personal problems. The experiment stations are not geared to give it to him speedily, perhaps not at all. One of the representatives present wondered if it was legitimate to take time away from problems of the farmer and the commercial grower to answer individual homeowners who number in the millions. About the best they can do is to send out bulletins, answer an occasional question when they have time. It was pointed out that a single question on a brown area in a lawn might belong in the province of a plant pathologist, a nematologist, a plant physiologist, a microbiologist, or an entomologist.

All admitted that plant doctors were sadly needed but if it were possible to train a man with all these different qualifications how would he get paid? Someone suggested he could be stationed in the Garden Supply Store and subsidized by chemical companies but I doubt if many of us want that kind of commercial tie-in.

As for myself, I started as a plant pathologist, I have become somewhat of an entomologist but there has been no time to learn the other things. Nematodes are much in the news these days. I have spent the past two years reading up on them, asking questions of experts, but I have done little work with them personally. When I was asked to do a tape-recorded interview to be published as an article in a magazine I had to refuse. They wanted something on pests in general but with emphasis on nematodes. I might have written something, surrounded by notes and papers. I did not dare ad lib off the top of my mind. There isn't enough in it yet about nematodes; I couldn't even tell a saprophytic from a parasitic nema under a microscope. So this book ends up with an account of what I do and not as the record of an ideal plant doctor.

DOCTORING

This is basic. All other activities are merely offshoots of trying to keep plants healthy, learning to diagnose their troubles, trying to find a preventive measure (only rarely can we "cure") that does not bring more problems with it. I think there has not been a day in all the years that I have been working in gardens when plants have not taught me something.

Some of my high school assistants have wanted to put spraying on a mass-production basis, to go out themselves and take on as much as they could cram into a day. It wouldn't work. They forget that the hardest part of the work comes in the spring while they are still in school. They do not figure in the rainy days. Besides, the few times I have stayed at home to meet a deadline and have let two boys carry on temporarily, blackspot has started on the roses, other problems have gone beyond incipient stages. The value to the client of a plant doctor is that a *trained* eye is around every week. Even I miss things. You can glance at a garden and think it all right; when you actually spray every bush you notice unsuspected wrongs.

One day a client asked me to talk with her just as we started to spray her main rose garden. When I came out of the house I found that Henry, who can't bear to stand idle, had finished spraying the roses in that section. I maintain that it takes two people to spray properly but Henry insisted he had gotten good coverage. He had used so much spray I did not dare go over the bushes again. The next week I discovered that rose midge had gotten a head start; all the little buds had turned black, there would be little or no fall bloom. I applied a copious dose of DDT but I was beginning much too late. If I had sprayed those roses myself the previous week I would have caught the first few black buds before the problem became acute. It was the first time midge had appeared in this garden in twenty years of spraying but that did not excuse me.

My clients are wonderful—and human. I am sometimes blamed for things that are in no way my fault and, more often, given credit for success due more to the Lord than to my ministrations. Most thank me effusively for the joy their roses have given them. One comes to the garden to rejoice in her roses, and to thank me, but she keeps just ahead of the spray rod; I keep having to tell her to move so she will not get drenched. One woman worries over each individual bush as if it were a baby, another fears that every slight defect on a leaf is injury from my spray. One client objects when I praise her gardener, she thinks it will spoil him, yet she cheerfully pays extra for the long hours required and has always paid my bill on the day received, so there are other ways of expressing appreciation. One client hates to spend a stamp. She makes out the check when the bill arrives, then holds it until she happens to see me, which may not be until I have put a "statement rendered" on the next bill.

I do everything in my power to get sprays on regularly but it is not easy to juggle fifty gardens a week around rainy days, days when a shower comes up on the last job and you have to repeat thirty to a hundred miles the next day, lecture dates, days when Henry has to cook (and they never coincide with my lecture dates), and days when a client is having a meeting of the garden club or her garden open for a tour. I do succeed fairly well, as I learn when a client decides she can get along without me. I agree wholeheartedly and give complete instructions. The gardener and the owner struggle along for a couple of years, then, when their roses are completely defoliated by midsummer with little prospect of fall bloom, I am called in again.

I speak as if I were doing nothing but caring for roses. In the beginning I tried to do practically everything, including feeding shade trees, spraying fruit trees. I had few clients and could stay long hours on one place. I was paying 40 cents an hour for help in 1933, only $600 for a Ford. Now, with help and transportation four times the 1933 level, but with most clients not able to pay much more, I service a lot more gardens and spend the minimum amount of time in each one. A plant doctor is a luxury, not a necessity like an M.D., and one that people with fixed incomes could afford better in depression days than at present.

Now I concentrate on things that will provide the most return for the money spent. That means I want the client to have roses to insure a weekly visit. In return for that the client receives six months or more of rose bloom and a weekly inspection of her peonies, chrysanthemums and other perennials and some shrubs, with any outstanding problems being taken care of.

I no longer try to do anything about trees for we have plenty of certified tree experts in New Jersey. The tree man, however, seldom gets on a place more than two or three times a year and on my weekly rose visits I can catch sawflies hatching on mugho pines before they chew off all the needles, or lace bugs on Andromeda before the leaves all turn white. This past October when I was spraying roses I found a late brood of lace bugs just hatching on Andromeda. I had added DDT to the rose spray to control leafhoppers;

it would also control lace bugs. I could spray the shrubs in passing at no extra cost but if the client had had to call in a tree expert for a special spray on a few shrubs it would have been quite expensive.

My basic rose spray is Tri-ogen but I use this like a basic cake recipe, adding to and subtracting as occasion demands. I don't like the miticide presently included well enough for all-season use so I ask the manufacturer to make me up special batches without it. Because I use six to eight of the large $30 Estate Kits a month this is not too much of a favor even considering the wholesale discount. Then I add Aramite for red spiders (mites) every other week until mid-August when they are no longer serious. The alternate weeks I add Ra-Pid-Gro as a foliar food. This is in addition to more than a ton of 5-10-5 fertilizer I have applied to the soil (a trowelful around each rose bush) right after pruning. In June I may add lindane for thrips, in late summer Mildex for powdery mildew, and in late fall DDT for leafhoppers. After the Japanese beetle season is over I often cut down on the amount of Number 1, the lead arsenate, in the three-in-one mixture, to reduce the amount of conspicuous residue.

I am hipped on the subject of keeping ornamentals ornamental, free from spray injury or unsightly residue. I get furious with the tree men who come in to spray shade trees and give the roses a swipe while they are there. The awful, unsightly white coating scarcely wears off all summer.

In the beginning I figured roughly that out of gross income from doctoring 25% went for wages, 25% for transportation and office overhead, 25% for chemicals, apparatus and incidentals, and 25% was left for me as profit or salary. My own percentage is much less now with costs going up a lot faster than I dare increase fees. I figure it takes most of the working days each month just to keep going; if it happens to rain on the last few days my share nearly evaporates.

The same thing is true if we have a delayed season. I usually plan on ten days of dormant spraying and rose pruning at the end of

March to help pay Henry's salary through April. In 1956, a very heavy snow around March 20th meant no work whatever that month. My last bills had gone out November 1st, I could send no more until May 1st. That is too long a spell to survive without other means of support.

I don't dare apply my regular rose spray when the temperature is below 55° F. but it is safe for roses in very hot weather, which is one reason why I do not change to something which might be a somewhat more efficient fungicide. Day after day we keep on spraying in summer sun, even when it is over 100° F. in the shade and some astronomical figure where we are working in the sun.

I'll have to admit that in really hot weather it is easier to be out in the sun spraying than home with your fingers sticking to typewriter keys. But some of the work is rather back-breaking, especially in spring when around 12,000 roses have to be pruned all at once. I learned in plant physiology about incipient wilting, when you could revive a plant by giving it a drink of water; and permanent wilting, when it would no longer resume turgidity given a drink. Most nights I am in the stage of incipient wilting, completely exhausted but able to revive with a few hours in bed. Sometimes I seem almost to reach permanent wilting, going around too tired to move for weeks.

But I do move! I alienated a rose friend once by being brutally frank when I went to see her roses. I had never seen such a collection of rose-slugs, aphids, leafhoppers, curculios, mildew, and blackspot in one garden and I wanted to know why on earth she didn't do something about it. I thought she could spend a little energy dusting roses even if spraying was too hard. But she looked at me wistfully and said how nice it was to have robust health; hers would not allow her to do such things.

A lot of people are allergic to the work entailed in keeping their roses healthy and sometimes a real allergy gives them a legitimate excuse. A woman called me up the other day and asked if it was possible to have an allergy to flower dusts. The answer is "Yes" but sometimes I don't know how much is real and how much is imagined. For years I have been spraying a garden next door to a man who has asthma. For years his wife insisted that spraying my client's roses made her husband ill unless I gave them warning so they could close all their windows, take the washing off the line. Eventually she decided it might not be necessary to close all her windows if I sprayed early in the day, while her husband was off at work. Then one day I sprayed without noticing, through the thick vines, that the washing was out next door. The neighbor flew at me, said she would have to wash everything again; her husband could not sleep on a pillowcase that had been in the yard while my spray was in the atmosphere. This was not a question of the clothes being accidentally sprayed; we were much too far away for that. The asthma the man had was real; how many, if any, of his attacks were induced by the distant spray, I don't know.

The wife of one of my clients had trouble with her hands if she arranged roses cut a day or two after I had sprayed them. I myself have always been slightly allergic to smoke and dusts but I never had a spray bother me until I tried captan. If I used that all day in hot weather there would be small blisters over my arms. Yet this is supposedly a very safe spray.

You always have to worry about children and pets when spraying gardens; you can never leave anything poisonous around that they can get into while your back is turned. Dogs are fond of green apples and sometimes these fall into rose beds. I try to find them and get them out of the way before applying a spray that contains lead arsenate. Dogs will drink from any pail of liquid so we guard against that. We are exceedingly cautious in pouring out any left-over spray; it goes down a drain or into a gravel drive where it is soaked up instantly. We don't let it go on an impervious surface where puddles will tempt birds and dogs. Cats are usually too particular to drink or eat unknown material but kittens will try to catch the end of the spray rod and sometimes have to be shut up during spraying.

I have always been a stickler for not spilling anything that will make a permanent stain on a driveway or walk but I have been fussier than ever since we had to scrub off a blue copper spray inadvertently spilled on the road in front of a house. It is a little hard to enforce a non-spill policy when a tree concern pours out its remainder all over a driveway but I try.

CONSULTING

My reputation has been built on three words: "I don't know." There is nothing in the world that will build up confidence as fast as being willing to admit ignorance. I said I don't know so many times in early years people were more than ready to believe me when I knew the answer. Once a client called in, for advice on a problem, her county agent, her tree expert, a man from the U.S.D.A., and me. When she later gave her gardener instructions he asked, "Who told you to do that?" "Dr. Westcott." "All right, then, I'll do it; I don't trust those men."

I used to do quite a lot of consulting for a moderate fee, going around the garden with a client, taking copious notes, sometimes soil for a pH test, and then sending back a voluminous written report. I seldom do it now for there is no time to make set appointments in trying to service fifty gardens weekly, nor time to write out the reports. I can service up to fifteen gardens in the time it would take to complete a consultation but I'd hate to charge fifteen times the service fee for giving advice. I am convinced that giving advice is fairly useless if there is no one competent to carry it out. And for the do-it-yourself gardener I have given all the help I can in books.

One of my colleagues started a "Plant Doctoring Service" a few years ago but his service was advice and it didn't work out.

With consulting now mostly confined to answering inquiries by mail or telephone it is entirely in red ink and it does take a vast amount of time. A lot of mail comes from people who read the books and articles I write and if you take money for a book there is a definite obligation to answer questions arising from it. Also, the questions are helpful in providing more background to use in the next book.

Here is a recent sample, sent care of the publisher of my first book, *The Plant Doctor:*

"Dear Sir,

In school we had to take a hobby to learn about and experiment with. I chose plants which I am very much interested in. I would appreciate it very much if you would send me a pamphlet on plants.

Thank you,

Linda ——"

In the same mail was a letter from a man who knows all about plants, Dr. Edgar Anderson of the Missouri Botanical Garden. He wanted to know the safest chemicals to use on house plants. His inquiry was a lot easier to answer than Linda's.

Also in that mail was a request from the *American Rose Magazine* for me to do a monthly article on rose pests during 1957 to replace the "Keeping Roses Healthy" column Dr. Massey is relinquishing for reasons of health. Of course I said I'd do it, but it means more red-ink time.

Occasionally the letters are from scientists who want to know the source of some statement I have made in *The Gardener's Bug Book* or in the *Plant Disease Handbook*. To date, I have been able to find the answer but it has often taken a whole day of digging in the files. To my amazement, if not consternation, more than once the letter has been from a club planning to devote a whole program to Cynthia Westcott, and wanting everything there is in print about me.

Some years ago a poignant inquiry came from England, from a man who was celebrating his golden wedding anniversary. He wanted to know how to make the All-Purpose Hoe I had mentioned in an article. He wanted to give it to his wife. They were just now starting a new rose garden, having had to give up their old home.

I couldn't diagram a hoe so I sent one as an anniversary gift. I had to saw the handle in two to comply with postal regulations but I believe he was able to bolt it together again.

An insurance company in Indiana wanted to know why their hemlocks were peaked. I thought perhaps they might have smothered the roots by applying too much peat moss on the surface but who am I to say at long distance that a recommendation of a local tree concern might have been mistaken kindness? Another tree concern asked me about a dark effluent on liquidambar. I said it sounded like bleeding canker although I had not seen it reported on sweet gum. The next day I read an abstract of a new paper listing sweet gum as a host for this disease.

An expert rosarian wanted to know what to do about the black stuff, that he called "rust," on his rose leaves. It wasn't rust at all, merely a sooty mold growing in honeydew secreted by aphids. The tiny aphids were there on the sample sent, but too young for him to notice. There is a quick and very definite answer for such an inquiry but often the causes are obscure even if I am on the scene and impossible by mail. Often I know the answer merely because I am seeing the same thing in my own gardens. Years ago a man wrote to ask about his rose buds blasting. I thought it was Botrytis blight, influenced by my pathological work at Cornell. After I had worked in rose gardens a few years I knew the trouble had been due to thrips. A very common inquiry in late summer is, "Why are my rose leaves turning yellow?" I know, from years of observation, that some roses have occasional yellow leaves starting in late July or early August. It is not blackspot and it is not due to mites; it is the beginning of normal old age, perhaps a bit premature just as some of us get gray hair a little early.

TESTING

The most important bed in my own rose garden is the one that has not received any spray or dust for the last ten years. It lets me know that some of the things clients call spray injury in their gardens are merely weather reactions. Also, it is encouragement to those who say they have no time to care for roses. These neglected guinea pigs of mine are alive even if not as thriving as their sprayed neighbors.

Keeping up a garden of 500 roses is, of course, on the red-ink side of the ledger. Some of the spray materials I try out are sent free by the manufacturers but sometimes they expect a lot of report for a small amount of chemical. If the materials are already on the market it is cheaper to buy them and omit reports.

I used to test many types of combination dusts and for at least a couple of years before recommending them. Now the manufacturers change their combinations so fast one may no longer be on the market by the time I think it safe for an amateur to try. I still test some chemicals but the people who come to Rose Day are more interested in new varieties. Some of these are sent free for testing. Free? I've just filled out a whole stack of questionnaires on the 17 rose varieties sent for trial last summer.

LECTURING

This is pure fun. I enjoy talking to people. There is always someone in the front row who goes to sleep but there is always an eager gardener who seems to agree with everything said. Giving a lecture means a day off from day laboring, a chance to dress up and act partly like a lady (I never can get my hands clean enough to feel very ladylike). It usually means a good meal in pleasant company in contrast to a sandwich gobbled between sprays in a garden. Some lecturers are bored by entertainment. I lap it up. I am interested in seeing the ways the plant doctor does *not* live although I sometimes get restive at very formal service that removes one plate at a time when it is near time for me to be on the platform. I am fascinated by the competence of young matrons, brought up in luxury themselves but bringing up their own families without help, who put on a luncheon for eight or ten without turning a hair, then preside at the meeting. I have been nonplussed by mature matrons who get flustered with a simple salad lunch for four.

I have been too well fed. I have eaten lunch on the train before arrival, been taken to two teas and a cocktail party, then to an annual dinner before being called upon to speak, and I was so stuffed I did a rotten job. I have foregone lunch on the train and the expected entertainment has not materialized.

I don't know how many lectures I have given but I imagine nearly a thousand. Some years I have averaged a lecture a week, more often it is twenty-five or thirty a year plus a few more donated to the various organizations to which I belong. Theoretically this should be mostly black ink, an addition to the profit from doctoring. If the lectures could all be on rainy days, or on the days Henry takes off, or at the end of the growing season, it would be fine. In practice, it often means taking off a good spraying day and a $35 lecture fee does not quite equal the $50 I need to gross each nonrainy day to keep out of the red.

I have been berated for keeping my fee too low, yet even $35 is a lot more than many garden clubs can afford to pay. After all, pests don't have the drawing power of an arrangement lecture by Gregory Conway where people will pay almost anything to get in. When I make a winter trip by Ford I increase the fee slightly and do not charge expenses if the clubs are willing to have me en route. I work out an itinerary from the first clubs that ask me. Because I want time for writing in between and because I do not have time for the correspondence involved in getting engagements other than those that come to me unsolicited I seldom cover the entire expenses of a winter trip by talking. I am always operating on a slim margin but the Lord always provides. I am sure the *New York Times* is psychic. Whenever there is an unexpected expense with the Ford I receive a letter or wire asking for an article.

I have been lucky enough never to have to cancel a talk because of illness and I failed to show up on time just once, when something went wrong with the Ford's internal workings. At that, I was only a few minutes late. I had an engagement to speak in Wilkes-Barre, Pennsylvania, the day after hurricane "Hazel" swept through this region. I had to pull limbs off my driveway to start out before dawn and fallen trees cluttered up the roadsides. Requiring gasoline in the Poconos I was dismayed to learn that the gas stations were closed because there was no electricity for their pumps. Fortunately, I found a place with a manually operated pump before the gas tank was empty. I was paged as I was having lunch in the hotel dining room. Going to the telephone I remarked to the garden club chairman that she must have been afraid I could not get through. "Oh, no," she said, "we just wanted you to get to the lecture hall early to have your picture taken."

It is often easier to lecture in a distant city, taking a sleeper one night, back the next, than it is to talk nearer home and have a several-hour drive back after the talk or have to take time off the next morning to return. Some clubs want you only on their regular meeting day even if it means paying all your expenses, when they might have shared expenses had they been willing to take you while in the vicinity. I made a special trip to Lake Forest, a suburb of Chicago, soon after I had been in Chicago talking to other clubs. I made a special trip to Grosse Pointe, Michigan, less than a week before I had to start cross-country again to the West Coast.

When I do try to combine engagements and save clubs some travel expense the schedule turns out to be fairly hectic. Like the time I talked in Detroit one evening, took the train to Grand Rapids next morning, was given lunch there and driven to Holland for an afternoon talk. The Wilson Campbells, ardent rosarians, picked me up there and drove us hell-for-leather one hundred miles across country back to Lansing and to a buffet supper at their home. The evening lecture was at the University. I had been told 8 p.m. and insisted on arriving early to get out material. Coming in at 7:30, I faced a sea of faces; the talk was scheduled for then but they had not told me so I wouldn't get nervous. The meeting was exciting and we had a lot of round-table discussion. About 9:55 I asked the chairman if we shouldn't stop. It was high time for the room had to be cleared by 10 p.m. I threw my lecture stuff together and someone else drove me back to Grand Rapids, arriving well after midnight. I talked there the next morning.

Some clubs have a lot of faith in their lecturers. They say they will meet a certain train but you don't know who is coming or where the meeting is; you have no way of telephoning in case of emergency—if you miss the train or fail to find the person meeting you. Very, very few clubs send you the notice of the meeting that goes out to members but life would be a lot simpler if they would. You could discover beforehand that the title for your talk was not the one in your engagement book. Once I went to Massachusetts to talk to two clubs having a combined meeting. One club had announced to its members that my subject was "Anyone Can Grow Roses," the other that I was talking on "Garden Enemies." I combined as best I could. Also, you would know that they actually had called the meeting. One club forgot to send out notices until I telephoned a day or two ahead and said I had not been told where to go.

Life would be a lot easier if clubs would let you know if they decide not to have you. They write to ask if you are free on a certain date, what your fee is; then you hear nothing more and wonder how long you should hold that date, if at all. I usually wait about two weeks, then cancel. A couple of years ago a woman telephoned long distance to make a date for a year hence. She promised a confirming letter immediately and I had neither her full name nor her address. I heard nothing more and after some months crossed out the date. Luckily I had not filled the time when she telephoned the next year, a few days before the meeting, and said they expected a large crowd for neighboring clubs had been invited to hear me.

I could write a book on introductions. They should be short and simple, spoken, not read. Sometimes the program chairman trembles visibly beside me, dreading her part; sometimes she has a long,

long page of my activities, dug out of the *New Yorker* and else-where, which she proceeds to read, stumbling over unfamiliar words like phytopathology; sometimes she says just the right thing, in less than fifty words, and sits down. If I am asked, about one minute before starting time, what I want said about me I ask them to just say, "Here's the plant doctor" and let it go at that.

I never start a talk, "Madame President, members and guests." I never tell a funny story by way of introduction. I usually say, truth-fully, how glad I am to be there, and there is always some com-mendatory remark about local plantings, public or private. After that I feel free to scold the club members for their shortcomings in the line of garden health and I try to tell them how to improve without too much expenditure of time, effort, and money. Because I am continually doing these things myself in gardens I can be very practical. I never have to worry about what to say and the words flow out without apparent effort. The audience very definitely "makes" the lecture and usually, even with the harsh subject of bugs, a rapport can be established that makes it a joyous experience on both sides. People say I seem to be having a good time. I am, but afterwards, when I am driving home, I realize that I have given more of myself than I thought; I'm tired.

I am still partly the schoolteacher I expected to be when I went to college. Lecturing is a kind of teaching, a justification of the days spent day-laboring in gardens, but it is easy. All I have to do in advance is to shuffle in the right order some of Mrs. Shirrefs' wonder-ful paintings.

Teaching a short course laboratory fashion with specimens for each person to study is not exactly harder but it does take a lot more time in preparation, not only the day before but for all the months working in gardens and traveling through the country. I have collected and mounted material almost everywhere and, as I sort it over, the aphids on oleander recall a lovely week in Savannah. They were from the patio of the comfortable Hotel de Soto, head-quarters while I taught a short course, had a wonderful Sunday at

Wild Heron Plantation, saw Judge Solomon's camellias. The bag-worms came from dead evergreens put out for the trash man to collect on a sidewalk in Houston. The earwig is my memento of a beautiful garden in Seattle; the cottony-cushion scale is from a rose bush beside a lake in Winter Park; the rose rust means happy days in California. I've collected postcards, too. They pile up for-gotten, unseen. I like my specimens, for I've had so much fun getting them.

WRITING

Once or twice in recent years the amount received from writing, book royalties and articles, has exceeded total *net* income. It looks as if the writing were having to subsidize the doctoring and I'd be better off to give up the arduous days and wax fat in an armchair. That is not quite a true picture. In the first place, I'm no armchair writer. Unless I can be continually learning by doing and continually being reminded of what happens in gardens I have nothing to say. Then, too, I have accumulated so much reference material it over-flows this eight-room house, half of which is charged to the Plant Doctor business, half to me personally. If I did nothing but write, the Internal Revenue Service might consider it all a personal expense. Also charged to the business are several hundred dollars annually for professional dues and attendance at meetings, for books and periodicals.

I write in the vernacular, clichés and all. I consider myself a liaison agent between the university and the home gardener. I don't talk down to people, I don't patronize them, but I do try to translate what is happening in science into ordinary everyday language. And it is all filtered through my own experience both at home and across the country. I have visited gardens and talked to gardeners in nearly every state; the rest have been traversed by train.

Mr. Kinkead said I had an anthropomorphic approach in my writ-ings. I have. We have all had drilled into us in school that plants do not have feelings. We know it, but how much better to say, "Roses like it here" rather than, "It is apparent that this location provides optimum growth conditions for roses." I have had pitched battles with pedantic editors who think my simple and obvious approach will contaminate the public, make it doubt the textbooks.

I get books out because I have to. There are so many days between the end of spraying in the fall and the new start next spring. Dividing the expected length of the book by the number of days, I know how many words have to be produced every day. In the beginning it's fun, toward the end it's a chore, and the index is fiendish, but I like it.

In 1934, that cold winter when Irene and I were traveling back and forth to New Brunswick to keep ourselves alive, Irene was abstracting references for a professor doing a book on insect pests of ornamentals. I have been waiting for that book to come out ever since and so have many other people. We need it very much. I saw the professor last winter and asked when it would be done. "Well," he said, "you have to eat so you get books finished, but the University keeps paying my salary and there are always so many other things that seem more important."

My first book, *The Plant Doctor,* was dedicated to Margaret Clay Ferguson, the Wellesley professor who started me off on botanical lines. It did not occur to me until after he died that Professor Whetzel might have been slightly hurt that I did not dedicate it to him for he was the one who started me off as an actual plant doctor. The *Plant Disease Handbook* was in memory of Herbert Hice Whetzel, *"Beloved Prof who taught me how to learn from plants and sent me forth to doctor them."*

The rose book was in memory of John and this one is dedicated to John's father. My brother and I do not share many interests. He does not understand my devotion to pests, is not much interested in gardens. I don't understand how he can be so wrapped up in bridge that he has become the leading bridge player in New England nor how he has become so successful building bridges that he can order a new airplane to get around to his jobs with less hesitation than I order a new Ford to get around to mine. We do have love in common and I hope Frank will not mind seeing this personal history in print. He still lives in New England where it isn't quite seemly to tell other people too much about your affairs.

BELONGING

I belong to far too many organizations but they are all tied up with the different cycles of activities. Their literature provides information for the books and if I had time and money to get to all the national meetings I'd have a lot more useful material. Since I am trying to interpret the university to the gardener it behooves me to get around to congregations of scientists as well as of gardeners. I do go to many more meetings than I can afford, forgetting that an inactive old age is still unprovided for.

American Phytopathological Society? I am legitimately a plant pathologist and I need to renew contacts before redoing the *Plant Disease Handbook*, but I couldn't scare up the carfare for the meeting this year.

Entomological Society of America? They let me belong, but I sneaked in the back door without any training. I managed the meetings this year because they were close to home.

American Association for the Advancement of Science? Receiving *Science* weekly is worth the yearly dues.

Sigma Delta Epsilon? I belong now to the New York Chapter, make about one meeting a year, but I remember gratefully that the meeting I went to in 1943 helped me solve the azalea problem.

American Horticultural Council? I am vitally interested in this organization to coordinate horticultural interests; yet I could not stay on the Board because I could not afford a day off each month.

Brooklyn Botanic Garden? I feel much at home here because I taught a short course for several autumns, have given advice on their pests, have helped edit an issue of their Quarterly, but it has been over a year now since I have had a chance to get there.

New York Botanical Garden? I taught a course here one fall long ago, part of one recently, and I supervised the spraying one spring after Dr. Dodge retired, before Dr. Pirone took over. I turn to their marvelous Library and Elizabeth Hall when I have exhausted the possibilities in my own. I wish it were nearer.

Horticultural Society of New York? Formerly I had time to go to many more meetings and I always enjoyed them. Now I drop in at the Library when I am in the city on other business.

Garden Writers Association? The garden supply houses think we are all editors so I receive a lot of literature and photographs for which I have no outlet but sometimes a nugget of real information.

National Council of State Garden Clubs? They keep me on the Board of Directors as chairman of Garden Enemies even though I can so seldom afford the conventions. I do answer inquiries, have sent out loan exhibits.

Women's National Farm and Garden Association? When the New Jersey Division made me an honorary member I protested I could do little. The only meeting I managed was the one where I gave the talk until recently when, on Henry's day off, they had a United Nations tea for the Ambassador from Ceylon. "Ha," said the new president, "when I asked you to take over conservation you said you didn't have any free moments; now, since you are here, I know you have." Shall I ever dare show up at another meeting?

Garden Club of Montclair? Here I do pull my own weight, even more since they made me an honorary member. I may not get to many meetings but I spend hours in the Rose Garden, help with rose workshops and forums.

American Camellia Society? I may not grow camellias but I am certainly interested in their troubles. The Society Yearbooks and Quarterlies are excellent.

New England Gladiolus Society? I don't grow gladioli either but they have a lot of diseases I need to know about.

American Rose Society? I am a Director-at-Large and a Consulting Rosarian. The bulk of donated time is here and with our North Jersey Rose Society. By concentrating on giving in this field I have, I think, made some contribution to human happiness. The Garden Club of New Jersey gave me its horticulture award for 1956, a silver medal, for "promoting the rose and its culture all over the United States."

New Jersey Wellesley Club? My spirit is always present, sometimes my flesh.

Women's Club of Glen Ridge? I keep paying dues for the time when I retire and can enjoy the splendid daytime programs.

HOUSEKEEPING

Eugene Kinkead said in the Profile that I was, by my own admission, the world's worst housekeeper. That is true. I don't mind cleaning if I can concentrate on it but there are too many other things more important. Faced with a deadline I can ignore dirty windows, dusty window sills, but I can't ignore the deadline while I wash the windows.

The trouble with cleaning is that I can't clear out enough first. My office has four large filing cases, two 5-foot desks, a huge cabinet for chemicals, a lot of bookshelves. They're all full. Everything that has arrived in the mail for a month is sitting around on chairs, on the floor, on top of the desks. One rainy day I started to clean up. After four hours, and a few wastebaskets filled, I could almost see the top of one desk. But when I began on the other there wasn't any place to put that stuff except on the first desk. In the midst of the confusion my cold got worse and I went to bed. I resumed working on this manuscript upstairs, refusing to look at the mess in the office.

The upstairs telephone extension went dead, because I had not kept the wisteria vine pruned off the outside cord. Trying to replace the cord in the upstairs study the repair man had to move dozens of boxes I use as sectional bookcases. He asked about putting them back but I said to leave them, I would sort out their contents, figure which periodicals could be sent to the attic. So then I ignored the mess in the middle of the sleeping-room study and kept on writing in the guest bedroom.

Cooking is easy. I can get a reasonably good and well-balanced meal in about fifteen minutes at the end of a day's work; it often takes all evening to get energy enough to wash the dishes afterwards. I love to cook for company and I'd ask friends in far more often if I had time to get the mail off the hall table, the living room couch and other places where I drop it when the office desks are too full. For Rose Day and one or two other special occasions through the year I get things more or less off the surface (it is always hard to find them afterwards) and the place shiny clean. I don't own a vacuum (my money and storage space go for books) but Henry brings over his. I fill every nook and corner with roses, not arrangements but nice color combinations, and people don't see the peeling paint. They say, "How lovely your house is!"

I have been asked for recipes for the Rose Day punch and cookies so I am giving them to you in an Appendix. They are not original and some of the sources are forgotten. I also give a few recipes for other concoctions mentioned on these pages. My cooking is all the old-fashioned way. I don't own a mixer and my arms get too tired trying to beat the prepared cake mixes. Besides, I only do real cooking when I can do it on an assembly line for a crowd. For myself, I try to forget these calorie-rich viands.

SATISFACTIONS

Surveys are always being made to find out how much money college graduates make in different fields and I am always ashamed to put down my net income in dollars and cents because it would certainly pull down the average. But I get paid in other ways.

I have a car, even though it is used almost entirely for business.

I have a pleasant home, spacious for one person, even though it does overflow with work. I have a garden, even though it is a test plot. I have a Cabin in the woods, even though I reach it only three times a year.

I travel with expenses paid, visit the loveliest homes and gardens. My clients are appreciative friends. Each autumn as they send the last monthly check they tell me how much their roses have meant to them, how many are still blooming in their gardens. I have other garden friends that I have met while lecturing across the country, and apparently hundreds of gardeners that I have never met have faith in what I say. And I am my own boss, free to say what I think.

If I had my life to live over would I still choose the same vocation? Of course! For me, plant doctoring is FUN.

SLAPDASH COOKERY

C OOKING had little place in my bringing up. As I remember it, my culinary efforts were confined to doll cookies and English Monkey, a cheese dish taught by a Sunday-school teacher who instituted a cooking class to keep us out of mischief during the week. Father had two masterpieces—corn cakes on Sunday mornings in summer, fudge on Sunday afternoons in winter. I have tried and tried to duplicate his meltingly tender griddle cakes made by scraping fresh corn, adding milk, eggs, and a speck of flour, but I have never been able to match his efforts.

My aunts were the fancy cake bakers in mother's family—the Tourtellots. At home we had good wholesome Mother's Cake for birthdays and similar occasions. We had baked beans and brown bread every Saturday night but never the pie for Sunday breakfast said to be New England tradition. Sometimes during the week the big earthenware bean-pot was used for a delectable casserole of beef cubes. Fanny Farmer has a recipe for a bean-pot roast and it sounds like the one mother did but it doesn't taste as good when I try it. Our clam chowder was the Rhode Island kind made with

tomatoes; not the milk variety ascribed to New England. I didn't
know there was any controversy on the subject until I moved to
New York.

I learned my slapdash cooking in that state, in Ithaca, because I
had to, same as I learned typing. I learned over Cornell picnic fires,
over a Sterno in an attic bedroom, on an enormous stove in the
fraternity house, later on a two-burner gas plate in a one-room
apartment in New Brunswick, New Jersey, and finally here in Glen
Ridge in a big but horribly inconvenient kitchen. It has six doors
and two windows and no wall space left for shelves and cupboards,
no place to put things away.

Initiation into breadmaking came from a chemist, the same man
who insisted that I buy a typewriter if I hoped to pass his course
in physical chemistry. Dr Frank Wilcoxen went to Boyce Thompson
Institute from Cornell and one New Year's weekend after I moved to
Glen Ridge he and Freddie, his wife, came the forty miles from
Yonkers by bicycle. On New Year's morning they scoured the neighborhood to find a delicatessen that had a yeastcake and then Frank
taught me to make whole-wheat bread. He was the one who did it
at home, with Freddie at hand for the cleaning-up. Later I found
a recipe for oatmeal bread that I used more often; but I'll always be
grateful to a man for teaching me that breadmaking was easy and
fun.

I have a whole shelf of cookbooks, starting with Fanny Farmer
(the *Boston Cooking-School Cook Book*) in the 1923 edition. The
rest symbolize episodes in my life or travels. The *Merry Mixer Cook
Book* was a reward from Dan Walden of Stokes for doing *The
Plant Doctor*. Myra Waldo's *Round-The-World-Cookbook* and *The
Molly Goldberg Cookbook* came from Clara Claasen to lighten the
revision of *The Gardener's Bug Book* for Doubleday.

The Joy of Cooking, by Irma S. Rombauer and her daughter,
Marion Rombauer Becker, reminds me of the one-day short course
for gardeners that Mrs. Becker arranged in Cincinnati. It also reminds me of a luncheon prepared and served with such apparent

ease by a young garden club president. It was no trick at all, she said. She merely used one casserole from *The Joy of Cooking* for the main course, another for dessert.

New Orleans Recipes takes me back to happy days and good food in that city. I have used many times from that book a recipe called simply "Cake for Parties."

De Bonnes Choses a Manger reminds me of Houma, Louisiana, and a wild night ride along the bayous. Just before I talked in Houma that afternoon I had a telephone call from Morgan City saying they were collecting azalea growers to hear me that night. So I hastily packed, but it was dark before the first meeting was over. As I drove along the narrow road by the water, with no shoulders on the highway, no fence, I kept thinking of the newspaper item I had seen on arrival. A car had that week slid off the road into the bayou, upside down with only its taillight left to mark the spot.

There are church cookbooks, mementos of visits to McGehee, Arkansas; Marietta, Georgia; Elmira, New York, and one put out by my own Congregational Church in Glen Ridge. Cornell is represented by Mary Spahr's *Honor Among Cooks*. There's a *Wellesley Cook Book,* and *Cutting Corners in Cooking* by the Montclair Business and Professional Women's Club to remind me of the pleasant associations there before gardening groups took all my time.

The Williamsburg Art of Cookery signifies participation in the 1956 Garden Symposium. I never enjoyed three days more. It was not the luxurious surroundings for I had been entertained in style before; it was not the old houses for I had visited Williamsburg before; it was not just the old plantations we visited for I had already seen some of these; and it was not just the lectures for I have heard hundreds of excellent garden lectures. There was a spirit, a camaraderie that I have not felt elsewhere in a large group. We all liked each other and the speakers and the management and the old houses and the old taverns and the spring flowers and the candle-light concert. They said maybe they would ask me back to talk sometime. I hope they will! As an aftermath, after driving the 400 miles home the next day, I found a cold house, no heat, no lights, gas or water. The plumber had forgotten I was coming home that day from my winter tour and it was Saturday night. The reminder letter I had sent arrived ten days later. The plumber was with me for the next ten days—more old pipes had to be replaced, more floors torn up. But I ended up with cheerful new linoleum in the kitchen, ready for more cooking sprees.

I have two large drawers of cooking booklets from the makers of flour, and baking powder, shortening, molasses etc. etc. etc., and clippings from every sort of newspaper and magazine. When Rose Day approaches, or Christmas, or a buffet party, I paw through the drawers, leaf through the cookbooks, select two or three things I have not tried before and then get out the small box of 3 x 5 index cards. Here are the old reliables. The recipes I append in these pages are from that little box. Don't take the amounts of flour for raised bread and rolled cookies too literally. It varies with the batch, with the brand. You can always knead in more, so don't overdo it in the beginning.

Oatmeal Bread and Rolls

1 cup rolled oats
2½ cups boiling water } Pour boiling water over oatmeal and let stand 1 hour.

Then add
    ⅓ cup molasses
    2 tablespoons melted shortening
    1 teaspoon salt
    ½ yeastcake, or ½ package, softened in ⅓ cup lukewarm water
Stir in 4 to 5 cups flour, depending on brand.

Cover and let rise until double in bulk (2 to 3 hours, usually).

Then knead more flour into dough, about 1 cup, and shape into bread loaves. Let rise another hour and bake at 400° F. for about 1 hour.

For rolls, take out portions with a spoon before adding the extra flour and put into greased muffin pans. Let rise and bake for 20 to 30 minutes.

I found this recipe many years ago. I think it was in *This Week* Magazine, of the *New York Herald Tribune,* possibly in the *New York Times* Magazine. (I take them both on Sunday. I have early breakfast, answer letters until the papers come, then go back to bed with a second cup of coffee, read, and clip garden or cooking news.) I like a slightly lighter bread than the original so I use almost a whole yeastcake or package. This slices better the next day but who can wait? I cut it fresh with the serrated bread knife brought back from England. Oatmeal bread makes delicious toast.

Butterscotch Rolls

1 cup boiling water
¼ cup sugar
1½ teaspoons salt
1 tablespoon shortening

} Mix together; cool to lukewarm.

1 yeastcake, or 1 package, softened in ⅛ cup lukewarm water containing ½ teaspoon sugar.
Stir into first mixture and add 1 beaten egg.
Add 4 cups of flour, 2 cups at a time beating thoroughly after adding the first half.
Cover and let stand about ½ hour, then put in refrigerator for overnight or until needed.

When ready to make rolls, let dough stand in kitchen a few minutes, until it can be handled easily. Roll out half into a thin rectangle on a well-floured board, table, or waxed paper. Spread well with softened butter or margarine, then thickly with brown sugar, and cover with broken pecans or walnuts. Roll up like a jelly roll and cut into slices ½ to 1 inch wide. Place each in a well-buttered muffin pan.
An extra sprinkling of brown sugar and a whole nut may be put in the bottom of each pan but it is not necessary. Let rise until double in bulk (1½ to 2 hours). Bake 15 or 20 minutes at 425° F. Remove from pans immediately.

The basic recipe is perfectly good for plain rolls but my friends demand the butterscotch variation. I have been baking these ever since I moved to Glen Ridge and do not know the origin of the recipe.

Orange Bread

3 cups flour   1 egg, beaten
3 teaspoons baking powder   1 cup milk
¼ cup sugar   1 cup orange marmalade
½ teaspoon salt

Sift dry ingredients, add the rest, put in small greased bread pans and let
rise 10 minutes before baking in a moderate oven.

This came from the *Wellesley Cook Book* and I was sure they had
forgotten the shortening, so I made a duplicate and added some.
There was no difference in the two batches; hence this recipe is
good for anyone on a fat-free diet. The bread is marvelous toasted
for tea for two but it is also good for sandwiches for a big tea. Wait
until the second day to make real thin slices.

Mrs. Cullen's Sponge Cake

4 eggs separated, putting yolks into a large bowl.
Add ½ cup of hot water to yolks and beat until light.
Add 1 cup sugar and beat again.
Add 1 cup of sifted flour (preferably cake flour) and beat again.

Beat whites of the 4 eggs stiff, adding ½ teaspoon cream of tartar as they
begin to froth. Fold into first mixture and add 1 teaspoon vanilla.

Bake 1 hour in slow oven in ungreased tube pan. Invert on cake rack to
prevent falling after removal from oven.

I do all the beating with an egg beater, not a spoon, and I put
a small pan of water in the bottom of the oven. The only time I
ever had a failure with this cake was when I got to thinking about
pests and absent-mindedly put the cake pan inside the pan of water.
The recipe came from a really fine cook, my sister-in-law's mother, and
it is the nearest thing to a foolproof sponge cake I know—economical,
too, for it takes only four eggs. I made one for the Diggers when
they came for the rose picnic and Mrs. Perry took the recipe home
for her cook to try for the next birthday in the family.

For dieters I frost this with the biggest full-blown rose in the garden, the short stem stuck in a tiny vial of water in the center hole. For others, I sometimes use the magic, easy chocolate frosting from Mildred, my sister-in-law, which is as good for cupcakes made with a mix as for the sponge cake.

Easy Chocolate Icing

Melt 2 squares of chocolate with 1 tablespoon of butter or margarine. Cool slightly.
Stir in quickly 1 unbeaten raw egg.
Add immediately 1 cup confectioners sugar and 1 teaspoon vanilla.

Stir until of spreading consistency.

Mrs. White's Chocolate Cake

Beat yolk of 1 egg (or 1 whole egg) into ½ cup sour milk.
Stir 1 teaspoon soda into ½ cup sour milk.
Melt 2 squares of chocolate with 1 heaping tablespoon of butter or margarine, cool slightly.
Add 1 cup sugar and the sour milk mixtures to the chocolate.
Add 1½ cups sifted flour and 1 teaspoon vanilla.

Bake in a moderate oven.

White Frosting

1 unbeaten egg white
1 cup sugar
3 tablespoons cold water
Put in double boiler over heat and beat 7 minutes with egg beater.

I usually bake this cake in an oblong pan and leave it in the pan to carry to picnics, using a simple confectioner's sugar icing—a bit of butter added to the sugar and moistened with warm milk or cream until of spreading consistency. In this case I use the whole egg in the cake; when I have energy enough to beat 7 minutes I use only the yolk and save the white for frosting.

Weary Willie Cake

Mix together thoroughly
1 cup sugar
1 cup flour (all-purpose)   3 level teaspoons baking powder
                                   ½ teaspoon salt

Break 2 eggs into measuring cup, fill with milk.
Melt together and then cool
    2 squares chocolate
    ¼ cup butter or other shortening
Combine mixtures *in order given;* add 1 teaspoon vanilla.
Bake in a square pan in a fairly slow oven.

Icing

1½ cups confectioners sugar   1 tablespoon melted butter
    3 teaspoons cocoa   Moisten with hot, strong coffee

The consistency should be such that you can mark a fancy design on top of the cake with a fork and have it stay, not run together.

This is the cake mentioned in the Profile, the recipe from Mrs. Florence W. Speirs, executive secretary of the Women's Club of Glen Ridge. She, too, has to bake when she is weary at the end of a hard day. This cake is very easy, very good, keeps well.

Mildred's Brownies

2 squares of chocolate melted with ½ cup butter or margarine
Stir in 1 cup sugar, cool slightly.
Add 2 unbeaten eggs, 1 at a time, stirring well after each.
Add ½ cup sifted cake flour, resifted with ¼ teaspoon baking powder.
1 teaspoon vanilla
1 cup chopped walnuts

Bake in square pan at 375° for 40 minutes. Temperature and time are approximate. The trick is to take these out while just slightly underdone so they stay meltingly moist.

This rich recipe makes only 16 squares so I don't try it for the hordes at Rose Day; it will, however, bring people out to a Board Meeting.

Cake for Parties

½ cup butter or margarine   3 eggs
 1 cup sugar   2 cups sifted flour
½ cup corn syrup   1 cup chopped dates
½ cup milk   1 cup raisins
⅓ cup cocoa   1 cup chopped pecans or walnuts

Bake in slow oven in shallow greased pans. Cut into small squares and coat with powdered sugar by shaking together in a paper bag.

The book of *New Orleans Recipes* says that these are delicious with Creole coffee. They are equally good with Yankee coffee.

Date Pinwheels

Filling

1 pound pitted dates, cut up ⎫
½ cup water   ⎬ Cook together until thick, stirring constantly
½ cup sugar   ⎭
Add 1 cup nuts and cool

Dough

½ cup butter or margarine   2 cups sifted flour
½ cup brown sugar, firmly packed   ½ teaspoon baking soda
½ cup granulated sugar   ½ teaspoon salt
 1 egg, well beaten   ½ teaspoon vanilla

Cream butter, blend in sugars, add egg and vanilla; beat well; add flour sifted 3 times with soda and salt.

Work dough until smooth; chill thoroughly.

When dough is chilled remove half from bowl and roll into a rectangle on waxed paper. Spread with half of the date mixture and roll up like a jelly roll, using the paper to help handle the tender dough. Repeat with the second half.

Chill overnight, or several hours; cut in ¼ inch slices. Bake at 375°-400° F.

I have never quite fathomed the amount of dates given in the recipe but I don't use quite a whole pound of the packaged dates already pitted. I always double the recipe and use 3 of the small packages, which means 10 to 12 ounces of dates for a single batch.

These are the favorite Rose Day Cookies, judging by the howl that goes up if I don't provide them.

In regard to oven temperatures and baking times, I have learned that the baking sheet makes a lot of difference. I have some ancient cookie sheets that are very fast and require a slower oven than some of the new ones that seem to resist heat. I think you have to bake cookies by trial and error. Cooking is like growing roses. Different people use different methods with equally good results.

Highland Toffee

⅓ cup melted shortening (I use Crisco)
2 cups quick-cooking oatmeal
½ cup brown sugar
¼ cup light corn syrup
½ teaspoon salt
1 teaspoon vanilla

Stir shortening into oatmeal, add other ingredients, mix well, and press into well-greased 8-inch pan. Bake in hot oven 12 minutes. When cool, loosen edges and remove from pan.

Spread with 1 cup (1 package) semi-sweet chocolate bits melted over hot water (don't let the water boil). Sprinkle with chopped nuts, walnuts or pecans. It takes about ¼ cup.

The recipe says to cut into squares and then chill but I find that too gooey. I let the toffee harden for several hours, then cut into 36 small squares.

This came from my good neighbor, Mrs. E. L. Stohlberg, who likes to experiment with cookies even more than I do. I have made her toffee for years and it is highly popular at Rose Day. Just recently I have seen the directions in magazine advertisements under the name of Scotch Toffee.

Ginger Cookies

1 cup molasses, heated and poured over
½ cup shortening (I use Crisco)
3 cups sifted flour, resifted with
½ teaspoon salt
½ teaspoon soda
2 teaspoons ginger
1 teaspoon cinnamon

Chill dough a short time; roll thin and cut with a cookie cutter. Bake at 350° F. (I am usually in a hurry and increase the heat a little but that means careful watching.)

This was an A&P wartime recipe that has remained a favorite with me as well as with men and children. I start baking for Rose Day with these for they keep well and I have more time to roll out cookies a week or two ahead. For June I use a star cutter, for Christmas a tree cutter and sprinkle the cookies with green sugar, put silver balls at the branch tips. I have tried many recipes for ginger cookies that call for more ingredients, are more expensive, but I like these much the best.

Honey Chocolate Chip Cookies

⅓ cup shortening
½ cup honey
1 beaten egg
½ cup quick-cooking oatmeal
1 cup sifted flour

½ teaspoon salt
½ teaspoon soda
1 package chocolate chips
½ cup chopped nuts

Cream shortening, add honey and beat; add egg and beat again. Add oatmeal, flour sifted with soda and salt, nuts and chocolate bits. Drop by teaspoon on greased pan. Bake at 375° F. for about 10 minutes.

This is another war recipe I still use. The cookies are not as brittle as Toll House cookies and travel better by mail. They keep well.

The next two recipes I have not used much since World War II but they were much appreciated on the early rationed Rose Days.

Chocolate Drops

2 squares chocolate, melted ⎫ Cook in double boiler until thick, stirring
1 can condensed milk ⎭ constantly.
½ cup rolled oats
1 teaspoon vanilla
⅛ teaspoon salt

Mix the oats into the chocolate mixture, add the vanilla and salt, and drop by spoonfuls onto a cookie sheet. Place nut on each. Bake in moderate oven.

Chocolate-Cornflake Macaroons

2 squares melted chocolate
1 can condensed milk
Add 4 cups cornflakes, 1 teaspoon vanilla, and mix well.

Drop by spoonfuls on cookie sheet. Bake in moderate oven.

Tea Cookies

1 cup butter or margarine
⅔ cup sugar
1 beaten egg
2½ cups all-purpose flour

½ teaspoon baking powder
⅛ teaspoon salt
1 teaspoon almond extract
(or vanilla)

Cream butter and sugar, add egg and mix well. Add dry ingredients sifted together. Put through a cookie press using a disk that will make a star or flower. Put ¼ of a preserved cherry in center of each. Bake at 400° F.

This recipe and the next were on the bottom of the box with the cookie press I purchased more than twenty years ago. I have been given a modern press and new recipes but stick to the old. The dough has to be just right, at room temperature, not chilled, with the exact amount of flour determined by trial and error. It is hard to get preserved cherries in June but I want them for color on the cooky plates. I try to remember to buy extra jars at Christmas to save for rose time.

Chocolate Press Cookies

½ cup shortening
1 cup sugar
1 beaten egg
2 squares melted chocolate
2½ cups cake flour

½ teaspoon salt
½ teaspoon soda
½ teaspoon vanilla
4 tablespoons milk

Cream shortening and sugar, add egg and melted chocolate. Add sifted dry ingredients alternately with milk. Put through press and decorate each cookie with a blanched almond. Bake at 400° F.

Panocha Squares

¼ cup shortening, melted
1 cup brown sugar
1 beaten egg
1 cup flour

1 teaspoon baking powder
¼ teaspoon salt
½ teaspoon vanilla
¾ cup chopped nuts

Blend sugar into melted shortening, add egg, beat until fluffy. Sift in dry ingredients, add nuts and vanilla. Spread evenly in greased 8-inch pan. Bake in moderate oven about 30 minutes or until barely done. If baked too long they will be hard instead of chewy. Cool in pan; cut into squares.

Coconut-Orange Refrigerator Cookies

½ cup shortening
1 tablespoon grated orange peel
½ teaspoon lemon extract
2 tablespoons brown sugar
½ cup granulated sugar

1 beaten egg
1½ cups sifted flour
¼ teaspoon salt
1½ teaspoons baking powder
1 cup shredded coconut, chopped

Cream shortening with peel, extract and sugar. Add egg; beat. Add sifted dry ingredients, stir in coconut. Shape in rolls, wrap in waxed paper, and chill overnight. Bake.

I think, but am not sure, that this recipe and the next came from the pages of *Better Homes and Gardens*. Refrigerator cookies take no time at all. You can mix them up while watching the oven for rolled cookies and then bake them while getting breakfast.

Mincemeat Refrigerator Cookies

¾ cup shortening
1 cup sugar
½ teaspoon vanilla
1 teaspoon grated lemon peel
(orange will do)
1 beaten egg

2½ cups all-purpose flour
½ teaspoon salt
½ teaspoon soda
1 teaspoon cinnamon
½ cup mincemeat (prepared, not dry)
½ cup chopped walnuts or pecans

Thoroughly cream shortening and sugar. Add vanilla, lemon peel, egg, and mix well. Add sifted dry ingredients alternately with mincemeat. Stir in nuts. Shape in rolls, cover with waxed paper and chill overnight. Slice ¼ inch thick and bake on ungreased cooky sheet in moderate oven (375° F.) about 15 minutes.

Sugar Cookies

⅔ cup shortening (I use margarine)
⅔ cup granulated sugar
2 eggs, well beaten
1 teaspoon vanilla

2 cups sifted cake flour
½ teaspoon salt
1 teaspoon baking powder
(combination type)

Cream shortening, add sugar gradually. Add eggs, vanilla, and mix well. Add dry ingredients sifted together. Chill dough; roll out on lightly floured board; cut into desired shapes. Bake at 400° F. for about 10 minutes.

I keep trying recipes for sugar cookies and always come back to this one in my 1933 edition of the *Good Housekeeping Cook Book.* I think, however, more flour is called for. I try Swansdown Cake Flour and Gold Medal all-purpose flour and always have to work in a little more than the 2 cups when I am ready to roll out the dough.

For Rose Day I use a diamond cutter and decorate with chocolate shot or a nut in the center, but for Christmas I make Santa Clauses for the children, red sugar for his coat, multicolor decorettes for his pack, raisins for his eye and buttons. For the grown-ups I make wreaths (with a doughnut cutter) with a red cherry bow, citron leaves. The center circles, sprinkled with any color sugar, are fine for filling the chinks in mailing boxes.

Chocolate Raisin Nut Cookies

½ cup shortening
1 cup granulated sugar
2 eggs, well beaten
3 squares chocolate, melted
½ cup milk
½ teaspoon vanilla extract

¾ cup chopped nuts
¾ cup seedless raisins
1½ cups sifted cake flour
1 teaspoon baking powder
   (combination type)
½ teaspoon salt

Cream shortening, add sugar gradually, then beaten eggs, melted chocolate. Stir in milk, vanilla, nuts and raisins, then add dry ingredients sifted together. Drop by teaspoonfuls on greased pan. Bake at 400° F. for 15 minutes.

This also came from the *Good Housekeeping Cook Book.* I have given it last because the cookies are much better fresh; they are the very last kind I make before Rose Day.

Rose Day Punch

8 cups sugar
2 quarts water
2 quarts tea
1 quart pineapple juice
1 quart lemon juice

1 quart orange juice
1 quart grape juice or crushed fresh
   strawberries
2 gallons ice water or part ginger ale

Mix sugar and water in a saucepan, boil 5 minutes and cool.
Make strong tea by adding 2 quarts of boiling water to 3 tablespoons tea; steep 4 minutes, strain, add to syrup.

I have given the ingredients as printed in the *Merry Mixer Cook Book* but I don't like punch quite that sweet. I usually use a third less sugar or sometimes only half as much and then add syrup from canned peaches or pears or apricots for flavor. I use mostly the concentrated lemon and orange juice now, diluted as directed, but I prepare some fresh, then simmer the skins in water for an hour or two, then strain and use as part of the water given in the recipe. I think the oils in the rind give added flavor to the punch but one year I discovered the bottles of this in the refrigerator the day after Rose Day and the punch had seemed about the same as always.

In preparing for the hordes, I borrow Mrs. Powell's enormous aluminum preserving kettle and use also the biggest kettle I could buy for myself. I start with 5 times the punch recipe, which is supposed to serve 100, and add a couple of boxes of frozen strawberries as well as all the grape juice. Sometimes I add cranberry cocktail, apricot nectar, almost anything in the line of fruit juices. I always have extra tea and sugar syrup made, more cans of concentrated juices in the refrigerator. The ginger ale is added as we fill the punch bowl and keep refilling it. To prevent diluting the punch too much on hot days by melting ice I take out the partitions in the ice trays and freeze ice in large blocks.

Cynthia's Fudge

2 cups sugar
2 squares chocolate, cut up or grated a bit } Mix in a saucepan.
⅔ cup milk

When the mixture starts to boil add a piece of butter the size of a walnut. Cook until the syrup forms a soft ball when dropped into a cup of cold water. Then remove from stove and *without stirring,* set saucepan in larger pan of cold water for 5 to 10 minutes. Add 1 teaspoon vanilla, ¼ teaspoon salt.

Then beat and when nearly thick enough to pour into buttered pan add 1 small package (¼ pound) of marshmallows broken into pieces.

The secret of this creamy and not granular fudge is the cooling period before beating. Also, the marshmallows are not amalgamated in the fudge but retain their identity, softened just enough to be meltingly tender.

I never did care much for fudge, even in the days when I dared eat it, but I have made this marshmallow fudge for more Decembers than I can remember, with the directions never before written down. I wouldn't dare go home to New England for Christmas without bringing along several batches. Cynthia's fudge is tradition.

ODDS AND ENDS

I have a few other specialties that I am called upon to provide for gatherings but my methods are too slapdash to give exact directions. I bake beans by Fanny Farmer but I use less sugar and more molasses, added bit by bit during the long day of baking. I also use Fanny for waffles but add more milk.

My brand of cole slaw to go with beans has a little sugar, a little salt, a little vinegar, some cream, and some mayonnaise mixed with the shredded cabbage. Everyone asks for more but I can't give an exact recipe for preparing it.

Potato salad goes back to the way mother did it, olive oil and vinegar added to the cubed potatoes while they are still hot. I never know how much but enough oil to lightly coat the cubes and enough vinegar to nearly cover, but if the vinegar is very strong you have to dilute it with water. Salt and pepper are added to taste, and the merest trace of mild young onion. When the salad is cool I add chopped hard-boiled eggs and mayonnaise, sometimes a bit of celery. This salad should not get icy cold in the refrigerator. To serve, I line a shallow wooden bowl with lettuce, spread out the potato mixture, then embellish with quartered eggs, wedges of yellow tomatoes, wedges of cucumbers, bits of parsley.

I have learned that chicken salad is lots better, far quicker, no more expensive, if you stew up the tender frying chickens rather than a plump old fowl.

All my cooking is extremely incidental except for Rose Day. That is a bear by the tail; if I stop baking cookies I may be torn limb from limb.

If you want to taste any of the cookies listed here, and maybe some new experiments besides, just come to 96 Essex Avenue, Glen Ridge, New Jersey, the second Sunday of any June, any time from 2 in the afternoon until dark.

INDEX

Addoms, Ruth, 82
Alabama, 93, 143-163, 169, 176
　Garden Clubs, 150
Alampi, Phillip and Ruth, 228
Alpine, 178
Altadena, 115
American Association for Advancement
　of Science, 68, 180, 234, 252
American Camellia Society, 253
American Garden Guild, 174
American Home, 98, 127
American Horticultural Council, 186,
　225, 252
American Phytopathological Society, 252
American Rose Foundation, 40
American Rose Magazine, 243
American Rose Society, 128, 192, 216,
　219, 224, 227, 254
　Penn-Jersey District, 220, 228
Anderson, Dr. Edgar, 186, 243
Anderson, Maxwell, 139
Anyone Can Grow Roses, 215, 217, 233
Arizona, 113, 114, 178
Arkansas, 170, 180
Asheville, 175
Augusta, 207, 209
Austin, 200
Avon Park, 90
Azalea blight, 84, 141, 151, 160, 161,
　169, 210

Baird, Bessie, 208
Bamberger's clinic, 48
Baton Rouge, 149, 200
Bay St. Louis, 150
Beadle, Dr. G. W., 122
Beaumont, 177
Bechtel, Edwin deT., Mr. and Mrs., 228
Becker, Marion Rombauer, 258
Bellingrath Gardens, 93, 147, 152, 157,
　159, 161, 163, 169

Belsterling, Louise, 125, 224
Berkeley, 123, 179
Better Homes & Gardens, 132, 133
Biddle, Dorothy, 130, 171
Biloxi, 93, 94
Birmingham, 96, 176
Bitancourt, Dr. A. A., 57, 175
Blauvelt, Dr. William, 139
Blume System Tree Experts, 177
Bobbink & Atkins, 40, 54
Bodger, Elizabeth, 24, 29, 57, 115, 120,
　179
Bodger Seeds, 24, 116
Boerner, Eugene, 219
Booke, Stephen, 191
Bordeaux mixture, 41
Bournemouth, 39
Boyce Thompson Institute, 45
　Arboretum, 114
Bradenton, 176
Bradley, Camilla, 95, 149, 154, 159, 164,
　169
Brady, George, 123, 229
Bread, oatmeal, 260
　orange, 262
Brenchley, Dr. Winifred, 38
Brookgreen Gardens, 166
Brooklyn Botanic Garden, 130, 198, 252
Brother, 3, 21, 22, 47, 180, 251 (see also
　Frank)
Brownies, 264
Bulb Laboratory, 32, 34, 203
Bulbs, Dutch, 33
Butler, Dorothy Black, 118
Butterscotch rolls, 261

Cabin, 5, 75, 76, 78
Cake, Chocolate, 263, For Parties, 265,
　Sponge, 262, Weary Willie, 264
California, 29, 115-124, 179, 204, 205, 250
　University of, 118, 179

Camellia blight, 204, 206, 210
Campbell, Avis, 218
Campbell, Wilson, 247
Caniff, Milton, 139, 232
Carco-X, 198
Carleton, Milton, 216
Carlsbad Caverns, 111
Carnegie Desert Laboratory, 114
Cedar Rapids, 132
Chapel Hill, 82
Charleston, 83, 84, 85, 166, 184
Charleston (W. Va.), 185
Charlotte, 215
Chattanooga, 215
Chicago, 180, 247
Childs, Dr. J. F. L., 142, 144, 145
Chocolate cake, 263, 264
  cookies, 267, 268, 270
Chopmist Ridge, 5, 6
Church, Congregational, 52, Universal-
  ist, 8
Cincinnati, 258
Claasen, Clara, 185, 229, 258
Clarksburg, 170
Coconut cookies, 269
Cohen, Mrs. Halle, 167
Collins, Dean, 198
Columbia, 182
Columbus, 217
Conard-Pyle Company, 40
Coniothyrium wernsdorffiae, 41
Connecticut Experiment Station, 137, 151
Connors, Dr. C. H., 48
Cookies, 137, 158, 265-270
Coombs, Mrs. Sarah V., 97
Consulting, 242
Cookbooks, 258, 259
Cooking, 231, 252, 257
Cope, John, 166
Copenhagen, 36, 37
Cornell, 12, 13, 16, 18
Corpus Christi, 200
Corvallis, 199
Covington, 167
Craig, Nancy, 211
Cunningham, Mr. and Mrs. George, 201
Cypress Gardens, 163

Dallas, 125, 180, 224
Danville, 81
Date Pinwheels, 265
Daunoy, Harry, 149, 159, 168, 206
Davenport, 131
Davey Tree Expert Company, 188

Davis, Mildred F., 120, 121
De Funiak Springs, 182
Denmark, 36, 37
Detroit, 247
D'Evereux, 156, 169, 176
Diary, plant doctor, 58
Diggers, the, 100, 101, 128
Dithane, 157, 159, 163, 164
Dobroscky, Irene, 23, 45, 47, 55, 168
Doctoring, 236
Dodge, Dr. B. O., 42, 130
Doubleday, 185
Dresden, 35
Dublin, 184
Duke University, 82
Durham, 82
  Rose Society, 201

East Orange, 99, 222
El Monte, 115
El Paso, 112, 178
Emsweller, Dr. Samuel, 141, 150, 224
England, 30, 31, 38
English, Dr. L. L., 147, 153, 162
Ensenada, 179
Entomological Society of America, 187,
  252
Essig, Dr. E. O., 180
Europe, 30-39
Evans, Mrs. U. B., 170
Everglades, the, 89

Father, 3, 4, 5, 21, 22, 26
Ferguson, Dr. Margaret C., 11, 251
Ferriday, 170
Florida, 85-93, 103, 163, 167, 176, 182,
  250
  University of, 91
  State College for Women, 92
Florists Exchange, 68
Fort Lauderdale, 176
Fort Worth, 125, 180
France, 36
Frank (Westcott), 3, 4, 5, 7, 9, 13, 21,
  22, 39, 252
Freeborn, Elbridge, 166
Frotscher, Lydia, 167
Fudge, 271

Gainesville, 91, 182
Galveston, 104
Garden Club of America, 74, 106
Garden Encyclopedia, 68, 73, 75, 78, 87,
  130, 131, 230

Garden Enemies, 189
Garden Writers Association, 253
Gardener's Bug Book, 2, 171, 173, 184, 243
Gardening with the Experts, 133
Gardner, Mona, 131
Garner, Charles, 224
Georgia, 85, 184, 207, 209, 249
Germany, 35-37
Gibbons, Thomas M., 167
Gill, Dr. D. L., 142, 169
Gillespie, Norvell, 123, 124
Ginger Cookies, 266
Girl Scouts, 15
Glaes, Fred, 220, 228
Glen Ridge, 47, 50, 52, 208, 228
   Congregational Church, 52
   Harvest Show, 137
   Victory Gardens, 136
   Women's Club, 55, 129, 130, 254
Gould, Dr. C. J., 198
Grand Canyon, 29
Grand Rapids, 247, 248
Gregg, Cissy, 227
Gross Pointe, 247

Habitations, 19, 43, 46
Hale, "Aunt Emmy," 198
Hamilton, Dr. C. C., 48
Hammond, Judge Henry, 207, 208
Hansen, D. R. H. N., 204
Haphazard Plantation, 170, 177
Harpenden, 38, 186
Harper, Dr. O. M., 186
Harris, Cora, 215
Harrison, Dr. A. L., 178
Harvard, 13, 25
Hass, Victor P., 217
Hastie, C. Norwood, 166
Hayes, Helen, 138, 139
Heckscher Research Foundation, 26, 27, 39
Heidelberg, 36
Helt, Phila, 10, 122
Henry, 221, 231, 237, 255
Highland Toffee, 266
Hires, Clara, 53, 138
Holland, 32
Holland (Mich.), **247**
Holiday, 200
Holly-Bluff, 199
Home Garden, 140, 156, 165, 171, 172, 174, 181, 185
Home Gardening, 154, 164, 165, 167

Honey cookies, 267
Hopedale, 3, 5
Horsfall, Dr. James, 151, 153
Hortensia, 150
Horticultural Society of New York, 55, 132, 253
Houma, 259
House & Garden, 135
Household, 180
Housekeeping, 254
Houston, 105, 128, 177, 200, 213, 214, 250
Huger, Margaret, 72, 84, 145
Hull, Helen, 202, 230
Hume, Dr. H. H., 91
Huntington Library, 117

Illinois, 180, 247
Iowa, 45, 131, 132, 196
Isaacson, Mrs. Henry, 197

Jacksonville, 85, 167, 176
Jenkins, W. R., 40
Jensen, Charles and Janice, 232
Jersey Life, 97, 98, 103, 129
John (Westcott), 139, 212, 251
Johnson, Malcolm, 181
Juarez, 112

Katz, Mr. and Mrs. Sigmund, 168
Kentucky, 180, 227
Kew, 30, 38
Kinkead, Eugene, 193, 194, 250, 254
Knoxville, 215
Koch, Minna, 167

Lacelle, 155, 160, 161, 171, 172
Lafayette, 168
Laguna Beach, 115
Lake, Mrs. Will, 125
Lake Forest, 247
Lake Wales, 90
Laredo, 109
Laurel, 167
Lawrence, Elizabeth, 152, 215
Lecturing, 245
Lester, Francis, 122
Lexington, 180
Lippincott Co., 184, 212
Lisse, 32
Long Island, 5, 76, 175
   Horticultural Society, 132
Los Angeles Times, 124
Lyngby, 36

Louisiana, 95, 149, 159, 167, 170, 177, 184, 200, 206, 259
Louisville, 180, 227
Lyle, Dr. Eldon, 180

MacArthur, Mrs. Charles, 138
Macmillan Company, 133
Macon, 176
Mademoiselle, 131
Magnolia Gardens, 84, 166
Maine, 12
Marion, Va., 96
Martin, Ruth, 55, 68, 75, 79
Massachusetts, 3, 56
Massey, Dr. L. M., 17, 26, 41, 42, 57, 141, 153, 243
Mason, Mrs. William, 167
McClure, Eleanor, 186, 229
McFarland, Dr. J. H., 211
McGehee, 180
McKeon, Miss Gen, 144
  Miss Maisie, 144, 148, 152, 158
McNeill, Mrs. Robert E., 218, 220
McWhorter, Dr. Frank, 199
Meade, Julian, 81, 126
Medina, Judge Harold R., 77
Melady, Eva, 156, 171
Memphis, 126
Meridian, 94
Merriam, Betty, 229
Mexico, 31, 107, 108, 179
Miami, 88, 103
Michigan, 247, 248
Middleton Place, 84, 166
Millbrook, 74
Mincemeat cookies, 269
Mississippi, 93, 94, 150, 167, 169, 199
Missouri, 185
Mitchell, Sydney, 123
Mobile, 142, 162, 160, 169
Monroe, 184
Monterrey, 107
Montclair, 39, 50, 55, 99
  Garden Center, 218
  Garden Club, 74, 181, 218, 219, 253
Montgomery, 176
Montreal, 202
Morrah, Mrs. Bradley, 208
Mother, 5, 13, 14, 21
Mt. Dora, 86, 90, 91
Mouquin, Mme., 100
Mulligan, Brian, 197
Myers, Martha Robbins, 198
Myers, Mabel, 117, 179, 191

Natchez, 169, 176
National Council of State Garden Clubs, 83, 97, 201, 202, 208, 253
Newark Evening News, 47
New England Gladiolus Society, 253
New Jersey, 43
  Experiment Station, 40, 48, 53
  Wellesley Club, 254
New Mexico, 29, 111, 125
New Orleans, 28, 95, 149, 159, 169, 200, 206, 214
  Garden Study Club, 150
  Garden Society, 95
  Floral Trail Association, 159
New York, 9, 13, 74, 132
New York Botanical Garden, 42, 46, 130, 135, 138, 216, 253
New York Flower Show, 75, 129, 184
New York Herald Tribune, 78, 228
New York Times, 98, 127, 129, 135, 140, 212, 246
New Yorker, 193, 195, 199, 249
Noble, Eva, 167
  Mary, 167, 209, 228
Norman Rose Society, 201
North Attleboro, 3, 5, 8, 10, 21, 132
Northboro High School, 13-15
North Carolina, 82, 83, 165, 166, 175, 207, 215
North Jersey Rose Society, 188, 220, 222, 232
Norway, 38
Nyack, 77, 100, 134

Oatmeal bread, 260
Ohio, 217, 258
Oklahoma, 196, 199, 201
Orange, 168
Orange bread, 262
Oregon, 198, 199
Oregon Agricultural College, 199
Orton Plantation, 165, 166
Osgood, Dana, 166
Ovulinia azaleae, 145
Ozona, 111

Paducah, 180
Palm Beach, 88, 89
Palmer, Marguerite, 200
Panama City, 93, 182
Panocha squares, 268
Paris, 35
Pasadena, 117, 119, 120, 205
Pascagoula, 169

INDEX 279

Peck & Wadsworth Tree Company, 121
Pelican vine, 91
Pensacola, 176
Pettis, Marjorie, 132
Philadelphia, 196
Phoenix, 113, 178
Photography, 79, 153, 182
Phygon, 160, 163
Pierates Cruze, 166
Pine Bluff, 170
Pinehurst, 83
Plant Disease Handbook, 2, 184, 188, 243, 251, 252
Plant Doctor Diary, 58
Plant Pathology Department, 13, 16
Portland, 198
Potomac Rose Society, 215, 224
Pridham, Dr. A. M. S., 175
Profile, 193, 195, 254
Pulling, Dr. Howard, 11
Punch, Rose Day, 255, 270

Queen Juliana, 34, 227
Quarantines, 202, 204

Radio Garden Club, 53
Raleigh, 199
Ransome, Betty, 120
Ranson, Nancy Richey, 125
Reader's Digest, 2, 131
Reinelt, Frank, 122
Reiter, Victor, 123
Rhode Island, 3, 5
Rickett, Dr. H. W., 130
Riverside, 117
Roanoke Rose Society, 184
Robbins, Dr. W. J., 147
Rochester, 215
Rockwell, Fred, 130, 140, 147
Rohm & Haas, 151, 157, 164
Rolls, butterscotch, 261
    oatmeal, 260
Rose black spot, 40
    brand canker, 40
    midge, 139
Rose Day, 101, 195, 209, 228, 255
    cookies, 265
    punch, 271
Rose Manufacturing Company, 57
Rose Show, 222, 231
Roses, 54, 137, 211
Rothamsted Experiment Station, 38
Rowntree, Lester, 121, 130
Rutgers, 40, 43, 55

Sailer, Dr. Reece I, 187
St. Louis, 185
Salbach, Carl, 123
San Antonio, 109, 110, 177
San Diego, 179
San Francisco, 123
Santa Barbara, 118, 119, 179
Santa Fe, 29
Santa Maria Inn, 121
Santa Monica, 179
Saturday Evening Post, 26, 141
Savannah, 85, 249
Scarborough, Opal, 117, 120
Sclerotia, 28
Sclerotinia, 27, 84, 144
Sclerotinia camelliae, 204
Scituate, 5
Seattle, 196, 250
    Garden Club, 198
Seckman, Mary, 170
Seed Laboratory, 44
Seymour, E. L. D., 68, 73, 130, 165, 226, 229, 230
Shackford, Martha Hale, 12
Sherwood, Margaret, 12
Shirrefs, Meta, 69, 70, 249
Short Hills, 53, 222
Shreveport, 206
Sigma Delta Epsilon, 21, 25, 120, 147, 234, 252
Signiago, Kay, 223
Slavia, 68, 69, 75
Smith, Gertrude, 181
    Miss Myra, 169, 176
Solomon, 56, 70, 99
South Carolina, 83, 84, 85, 166, 182, 184
Southeast, the, 81
Southwest, the, 103
Spillers, Mrs. G. C., 201
Sponge cake, 262
Sprayer, Paragon, 160, 167
Spring Hill, 142, 144, 157, 169
    College, 152
Stark, Lutcher, 168
Stevens, Neil, 51, 52, 127
    Russell, 127, 128
Stokes Co., 78, 184
Sugar cookies, 269
Sunset Club, 197
Sun-Up, 177
Sweden, 38
Switzerland, 36

Tabor, Gladys, 12

Tallahassee, 92, 167, 182
Tampa, 176
Teaching, 13, 14
Tea cookies, 269
Tearoom, 75
Tennessee, 126, 215
Ten Thousand Garden Questions Answered, 140
Testing, 245
Texas, 105, 109, 112, 125, 128, 168, 177, 178, 180, 200, 213, 214, 224, 250
The Plant Doctor, 78, 80, 83, 97, 131, 184, 212, 251
The Plant Doctor, 47, 48, 52
This Week, 191, 192
Thomas, Dr. H. E., 123, 204
Thorne, Mrs. Oakleigh, 74, 105, 118, 127, 179
Tommy (Westcott), 192
Topsfield Garden Club, 56
Tournament of Roses, 115
Tri-ogen, 57, 85, 129, 239
Tucson, 114, 178
Tulsa, 201
2,4-D, 129, 175
Tyler, 125, 180, 214, 224

Universalist Sunday School, 8
U.S.D.A., 39, 40, 143, 188
U.S. Rubber Co., 151

Van Nostrand, 181, 184, 185, 213
Van Slogteren, Prof. E., 32, 33, 203, 224, 225, 226
Van Yahres, George, 134, 175
Victory Gardens, 135, 136
Virginia, 81, 96, 182, 184
    Peninsula Rose Society, 224

Waco, 180
Wakefield, Dr. Elsie, 38

Waksman, Dr. Selman, 46, 48
Walden, Dan, 78, 80, 97, 131
Walther, Eric, 123
Wapello, 132
Wartime, 134
Washington, 195, 196
    University of, 197
    Western Experiment Station, 198
Washington, D. C., 9, 187
Waugh, Dorothy, 219
Weary Willie Cake, 194, 264
Weiss, Dr. Freeman, 145
Wellesley, 10, 15, 26, 47, 56, 77, 119, 197, 217, 254
Westhampton, 77
West Virginia, 170, 185
Westcott, Stukely, 3
Whetzel, Prof. H. H., 17, 25, 26, 30, 46, 72, 146, 154, 251
White, Dr. R. P., 16, 48, 126
Wilcoxon, Frank, 258
Wilkesbarre, 247
Wilks, Maria, 120
Williams, Roger, 3
Williamsburg, 81
    Garden Symposium, 259
Wilmington, 165
Winston-Salem, 201
Winter Park, 86, 87, 176, 250
Witherspoon, R. S., 201
Women's National Farm and Garden Association, 253
Woman's Home Companion, 137
Wood, George, 176
    Marie, 176
Wormsloe Gardens, 85
Wright, Richardson, 102, 135
Writing, 250

Yellowstone Park, 45

Zineb, 165